WILLERT & CAVEY

AUTO FILLING STATION

GASOLENE

WILLERT & CAVEY.
Gem Store
Toronto Ia.

Fill 'er Up!

The Great
AMERICAN GAS STATION

TIM RUSSELL

FLOUR·FEED
PAINTS·OILS

CRESTLINE

This edition published in 2013 by
CRESTLINE
a division of BOOK SALES, INC.
276 Fifth Avenue Suite 206
New York, New York 10001
USA

This edition published by arrangement with Voyageur Press,
an imprint of MBI Publishing Company.

First published in 2007 by Voyageur Press, an imprint of MBI
Publishing Company, 400 First Avenue North, Suite 400,
Minneapolis, Minnesota, 55401

Library of Congress Cataloging-in-Publication Data

Russell, Tim, 1952-
  Fill 'er up! The great American gas station / by Tim Russell.
    p. cm.
  Includes index.
  ISBN : 978-0-7858-2986-7
  1. Service stations—United States—History. I. Title.
TL153.R76 2007
629.28'60973—dc22
                            2007019565

Editor: Amy Glaser
Designer: Cindy Samargia Laun

Printed in China

Reprinted 2013 twice

On the cover: The smiling gas station attendant was a common
sight for many decades. He would fill your gas tank, check your
oil, wash your windshield, and wish you a happy journey.

On the frontispiece: Richfield gave Shell a good run for its money
with the flamboyant use of its Eagle trademark and extravagant
canopies. Richfield was immensely proud of this design and persisted with it until the early 1950s.

On the title pages: The country store was the most common outlet
for gasoline in the early 1900s, as seen in this example from Porony,
Iowa.

On the back cover:
(*left*) Atlantic spent lavishly on its city beautiful gas stations, which
probably cost at least three times more to build than a conventional station. This example, located in Roxbury, Massachusetts, was
built between 1916 and the early 1920s and was similar to the
Temple of Vesta in Rome. It was a smaller version of an Atlantic
station opened in Philadelphia in 1915. These extravagant designs
forced Jenney, Socony, and Colonial Beacon in New England to
build ornate neocolonial or Palladian stations.

(*top, right*) BP was launched in America on April 29, 1969, in
Atlanta, Georgia, thanks to a Department of Justice decision that
forced Atlantic Richfield (ARCO) to dispose of 10,000 gas stations, as well as oil refineries, in exchange for acquiring Sinclair. A
subsequent alliance with Sohio, a joint producer of Alaskan oil,
helped BP become firmly established in the United States.

(*bottom, right*) Texaco consolidated its reputation for nationwide
reliability with a series of color advertisements during 1940 and
1941 promising twenty-four-hour, all-night service for families
traveling long distances in July 1940 or the hard-pressed businessman in August 1941.

Contents

1

Beginnings—
Shed to the Temple 1913-1919

GAS STATIONS HAVE EXISTED for almost one hundred years in the United States and over eighty years in the rest of the world. The gas station's primary role is the sale of gasoline, motor oil, and a limited range of accessories. Its layout enables quick and convenient offstreet refueling, often twenty-four hours a day, without causing traffic congestion.

The gas station's development in the United States was hastened by two key events: the launch of the Ford Model T and the breakup of the Standard Oil Company. The spectacularly successful Ford Model T automobile, introduced in 1908, literally transformed American society. The "Tin Lizzy" became progressively cheaper to buy and came within reach of clerical workers and skilled artisans. The automobile was no longer the rich man's toy but the working man's friend. The Model T came in all shapes and sizes, was simple and easy to repair, and was remarkably tough and versatile. Farmers often attached drive belts to the rear wheels to run threshing machines or circular saws. Between 1909 and 1913, the number of motor vehicles in the United States increased fourfold from 312,000 to 1,260,000. From 1913 to 1918, the number of motor vehicles increased almost fivefold to 6,160,000!

Unfortunately, the roads in the United States did not keep pace with the increase in traffic. They were notoriously bad, often impassable in winter or the spring thaw, and poorly marked with signposts. Carl G. Fisher, President Woodrow Wilson, and President Dwight Eisenhower played key roles in their long-term improvement. Fisher

set up the Lincoln Highway Association in 1913 and persuaded individual motorists and manufacturers to donate money into a special fund for signposting and highway construction. The route was indicated by a capital "L" or red, white, and blue stripes on telegraph poles and gas pumps. Small paved sections of the highway were built in strategic locations to encourage state and federal government departments to build better roads. The route stretched from New York City via Pittsburgh, through the Midwest to San Francisco, and was finally completed in the early 1930s.

Woodrow Wilson lobbied hard for the Federal Aid Road Act in 1916. This had little or no immediate impact as discovered by Dwight Eisenhower when, as a young army officer, he led a cross-country expedition in 1919 to test army vehicles and check on road conditions. He was appalled by what he experienced and wrote a scathing report. Later, as president, Eisenhower played a pivotal role in the development of the national Interstate Highway System in the mid-1950s.

Prior to 1910, one-gallon measuring jugs, five-gallon pails filled from barrels, or underground storage tanks were the most common means for refueling automobiles. It was a cumbersome, time-consuming process, and the motorist had to take on trust that he was being served the correct amount of fuel, let alone that it actually was gasoline rather than a counterfeit mixture with kerosene. The introduction of the curbside hand-operated gas pump in 1909–1910 was a major turning point. It considerably

The world's first purpose-built drive-in gas station was opened by Gulf Refining in Pittsburgh on December 1, 1913. The Gulf design was a revelation with its smooth concrete forecourt and excellent layout. The width of the ramps and the forecourt area allowed vehicles to arrive, depart, and be refueled two abreast without any inconvenience or delay. The sales office design blended in well with the surrounding neighborhood, and the canopy mimicked the two porches in the background.

The PIERCE-ARROW differs from other cars in three ways—in its engine, in its body and in the way the two are combined to make the most thoroughly artistic, comfortable, and dependable car ever built.—The Pierce-Arrow Motor Car Co., Buffalo

Prior to 1908, the automobile was the exclusive preserve of the rich. Pierce Arrow was America's most exclusive manufacturer with prices to match. This advertisement appeared in 1912. *Author collection*

sped up gasoline dispensing, guaranteed clean gasoline thanks to a built-in filter, and reassured the motorist he was getting full measure via a clock dial. Soon American towns experienced traffic congestion, partly due to automobiles waiting in line to fill up from curbside pumps. Some enterprising dealers provided offstreet refueling, but all too often these sites were little more than tin sheds on a vacant lot. Motorists appreciated the ease and convenience of these sites, while the neighbors condemned them for their shabby, nondescript appearance and for lowering the tone of the neighborhood, if not the value of their property.

The U.S. Supreme Court in 1911 ordered the Standard Oil Company of New Jersey (hereafter referred to as Exxon), the holding company, to dispose of all their subsidiaries, which enabled free and fair competition between oil companies.

Competition forced oil companies to come up with new ways of attracting customers. Up until then, the Standard Oil Trust, the predecessor of the Standard Oil Company of New Jersey, was set up by John D. Rockefeller in 1870 and virtually controlled the United States' oil industry from the wellhead to the curbside pump. The trust was a complex web of interlocking companies with names as diverse as Exxon, Atlantic Refining, Vacuum Oil (later Mobil), and Continental Oil. Standard Oil made it virtually impossible for any competitor to trade profitably by means of secret railroad rebates and cross-subsidised price wars. Prices would be raised in one part of the United States to subsidise low prices elsewhere in the country. Public and political opinion began to change in the early 1900s, thanks largely to the efforts of Ida Tarbell, a tenacious investigative journalist who wrote the book *The History of the Standard Oil Company* in 1904 and ran a vociferous press campaign highlighting these unfair practices. President Teddy Roosevelt campaigned tirelessly for the breakup of the Exxon and similar monopolies. At about the same time, the Gulf Refining Company was established in November 1901, largely through the efforts of the Mellon banking family. The Texas Company (Texaco) was established the following year in 1902. Both companies were set up to exploit the fabulous resources of the Spindletop oil gusher in Texas. Meanwhile, Royal Dutch-Shell, a Dutch-British enterprise, formed by the merger of Royal Dutch Petroleum and Shell Transport & Trading in 1905 (ratified in 1907), was making serious inroads into Standard Oil's dominance of European and Far Eastern kerosene and gasoline markets. In 1912, Shell set up a United States subsidiary in Seattle, initially as a gasoline importer, but it quickly diversified into American oil production, refining, and retailing. Gulf, Texaco, and Shell would subsequently play pivotal roles in gas station development.

The world's first purpose-built drive-in gas station was opened by Gulf Refining in Pittsburgh, Pennsylvania, at the corner of Baum Boulevard and St. Clair Street, on December 1, 1913. It was created by W. V. Hartmann, Gulf Refining's general sales manager. Baum Boulevard was on the Lincoln Highway, which may have been a deciding factor in its location. The Pittsburgh Gulf station design and layout marked a milestone in gasoline retailing. The driveways were made entirely of concrete and the service building was an octagonal pavilion made of brick and stucco. It supported a gently cantilevered octagonal roof that stretched out beyond the pavilion and covered part of the driveway. While the roof protected the pump attendant and automobile driver from the weather, the ceiling had electric lighting for night service. Two sections of the roof's lower extremities incorporated electric lamp bulb advertisements. The site was on a V-shaped piece of land between two roads, which not only provided ease of access and departure but

Before the introduction of curbside gas pumps, gasoline was dispensed from barrels via one-gallon measuring jugs or five-gallon pails through a chamois leather–lined funnel to trap impurities or moisture. The motorist had no guarantee about either the quality of the gasoline or that he was getting the full measure. Wise motorists often carried a spare two-gallon can with a potato on the spout to prevent dirt from getting into the can. *Author collection*

A typical garage, probably in New Jersey, from around 1910/1911 with two mobile fifty-gallon gas carts is shown here. The latter was a vast improvement on the barrel, pail, and funnel method. It saved time, was a better guarantee of quality, and the motorist could see from the clock dial how much gasoline he was getting. *Author collection*

doubled the number of potential customers from passing traffic. The company-owned site reassured customers that they were getting the genuine article as quickly and as conveniently as possible. The pleasant and functional design demonstrated corporate pride, inspired customer confidence, and showed respect for the neighbors' sensitivities. The Gulf station had antecedents dating as far back as 1907. These were, however, little more than tin sheds on cinder or gravel driveways. The Pittsburgh Gulf station created a precedent for all subsequent American gas station designs and layouts, which evolved very quickly from that date on.

Gas stations did not appear in Europe until the early 1920s with the introduction of gas pumps. Until then, European gasoline was sold exclusively in sealed, returnable containers through a variety of outlets.

American gas station design, layout, and construction were influenced by immediate surroundings, target market, community response, competition, and climate. Within the United States as a whole, three distinct patterns emerged during this period. Each was to have a far-reaching impact nationally and internationally in subsequent decades.

On the eastern seaboard and in Pennsylvania, both Gulf and Atlantic (a former Standard Oil Trust company) developed highly distinctive gas station designs that addressed two complementary requirements. Gulf opted for a functional, cost-effective design utilizing widely available brick, stucco, and wood. It could be built by any competent builder and adapted to any location. Key elements from the 1913 design were used by Gulf until the early 1930s.

Atlantic, by contrast, embraced the aspirational "city beautiful" style. This was an eclectic mix of the classical order and Beaux-Arts and was first introduced at the 1893 Chicago Columbian Exposition. It epitomized the United States' growing self-confidence and, on a local level, proclaimed civic pride. The city beautiful style was absolutely ideal for both town planning and administrative buildings. At this juncture, it is important to emphasize the direct and indirect influence expositions and world fairs would have on gas station design over the next sixty years, most significantly with art deco in the 1920s and 1930s. The Atlantic gas station designs were elaborate and expensive. They relied on custom-made terracotta blocks and highly skilled labor. The Atlantic designs probably cost at least three times more to build than the Gulf design. While laudable in intent, the Atlantic designs were clearly an overreaction to Gulf's expansion plans and were incongruous with their surroundings. This is amply demonstrated by Atlantic's response to the Gulf station in Pittsburgh and a subsequent Gulf station in Philadelphia. Atlantic built a highly elaborate station on Baum Boulevard within the immediate vicinity of the Pittsburgh Gulf station. Gulf then opened a gas station on North Broad Street in Philadelphia, which was virtually identical to the Pittsburgh station. Atlantic immediately

(Above and top right) Gulf achieved excellent brand recognition with consistent advertising visuals and messages in magazines and road maps for almost twenty years, from 1912 to the late 1920s. Both advertisements date from around 1916. *Author collection*

responded with an even more extravagant design diagonally opposite to the North Broad Street Gulf station.

Wadhams Oil in Milwaukee, Wisconsin, made a dramatically different, high-risk decision, which fortunately paid off. In 1917, it introduced its eye-catching Chinese pagoda gas stations, designed by Alexander Eschweiler, a prominent Wisconsin architect. They were held in such high affection by the local population that Mobil

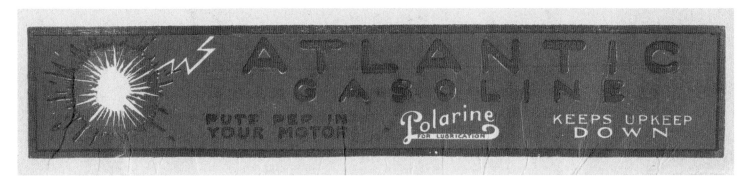

(Above and right) Atlantic opened its first elaborate city beautiful gas station in late 1914 down the road from the Gulf station in Pittsburgh. Gasoline was almost certainly dispensed via a pressurized hydraulic system. Atlantic built two almost identical stations elsewhere in Pennsylvania. Atlantic advertising had less flair and originality than that of Gulf. *Author collection*

Gilbert & Barker introduced the first gas pump with an electrically lit globe, the T-8, in 1912. The T-8 not only enabled night service but provided additional brand identity, amply demonstrated in this circa 1915 photo of a Socony pump near Springfield, Massachusetts. *Author collection*

(which acquired Wadhams Oil in 1930) did not replace them until the early 1950s.

In the Midwest and adjoining Rocky Mountain region, Standard Oil of Indiana and Conoco (another former Standard Oil Trust company) respectively developed distinctive gas station designs in 1917 that utilized cement render or brick that could be adapted to harmonize with the immediate surroundings, particularly residential neighborhoods. The Standard Oil of Indiana design, known as the "Joliet," was created by Allan Jackson, divisional manager of Joliet, Illinois. The Joliet design consisted of a brick building, bare or covered with cement render depending on the location, and a flat-roofed canopy over one of the driveways. The front elevation had a very high entablature that bore a close resemblance to the Lincoln Memorial, which opened in Washington, D.C., in the same year. The Joliet design was modified in 1921 with a pitched roof. Both the Standard Oil of Indiana Joliet and Conoco designs were developed in response to local community unrest over unsightly tin sheds and dirt track forecourts (refer to Chapter 6 for further reading). Texaco also developed a

In Philadelphia, Gulf opened a carbon copy of its Pittsburgh station around 1916, as shown here in 1922. Atlantic responded with an even more extravagant domed structure that can be seen in the left background. Gulf, unlike Atlantic, was as consistent in its station design as in its advertising and used key elements, such as the bricks and the color scheme, from its Pittsburgh station right up to the early 1930s. *Vintage Photos*

Every detail of the National Supply service station chain, acquired in 1914, from the prefabricated station design; the red, white, and blue color scheme; to the white uniforms with starched collars and caps was used until the early 1930s by Chevron. They had over 200 virtually identical company-owned stations when this photograph was taken in 1919, almost certainly in San Francisco. *Author collection*

Chevron's advertising underwent a subtle change after 1914. The emphasis was now on its expanding company-owned gas station network. Until then it had extolled the potency of its gasoline with discreet offers of bulk supply to private automobile owners. *Author collection*

domestic design that blended in with residential neighborhoods. Uniquely, Texaco built around one hundred virtually identical domestic gas stations nationwide, as far afield as Atlanta, Georgia, and Seattle, Washington, between 1918 and 1925.

On the West Coast, Standard Oil Company of California, hereafter referred to as Chevron, and Shell made widespread use of prefabricated units that were cheap, easy to assemble quickly, and provided excellent corporate identity with strong color schemes. California had the fastest human and motor vehicle population growth, which dictated speed and ease of construction rather than purely aesthetic considerations. Chevron acquired the National Supply Stations' Californian filling station network in 1914 and

retained both the design and bold color scheme of red, white, and blue. Shell created a highly distinctive design with an eye-catching red and yellow color scheme. The "Class A" station was known affectionately as the "crackerbox." It was originally developed as a temporary structure for the 1915 Panama–Pacific International Exposition in San Francisco and remained largely unchanged until the early 1930s.

Climate also played a key role in the choice of building materials. California has a fairly constant warm climate, which is compatible with uninsulated, prefabricated units. The Rocky Mountains, the Midwest, and to a lesser extent, the East Coast, have long, cold winters that require thick, durable insulation to retain heat. Clay bricks are ideal for this type of climate.

As previously mentioned, each of these patterns established a particular trend. Gulf, Chevron, and Shell placed a premium on functional, highly recognizable, and cost-effective designs, which in many respects anticipated the emergence of industrial design as a discipline in the late 1920s and Walter Dorwin Teague's classic streamlined modern design for Texaco in 1937. Shell and Chevron's extensive use of prefabricated units was widely copied by other oil companies throughout the United States and significantly in Germany by BV Aral and BP OLEX in the late 1920s.

Standard Oil of Indiana's adaptable design gave birth to the domestic style, which was widely imitated by competitors for residential neighborhoods. Some oil companies and independent dealers took this concept a stage further and developed the cottage design. This was either used as an attractive, harmonious feature or

Shell's ingenious 1915 crackerbox station design provided superb brand identity and could be assembled in ten days or less. It remained virtually unchanged until the early 1930s, as shown in this post card from the late 1920s. A Shell executive joked that the eye-catching red and yellow color scheme was so effective there was almost no need for advertising! *Author collection*

a blatant gimmick. The cottage design was widely adopted in Great Britain, France, and Germany from the mid-1920s on.

The Atlantic city beautiful and the Wadhams Chinese pagoda designs created precedents for fantastic, pastiche designs, such as Roman temples, Palladian pavilions, mosques, Spanish colonial haciendas, and Arabian palaces, particularly on the West Coast during the 1920s.

Most oil company gas station designs had a canopy or covered driveway. The canopy would remain an integral feature of most American and European gas station designs until the mid-1930s. In all instances, oil companies paid close attention to the landscaping of the gas station by ensuring there were clean and freshly painted boundaries (i.e., fences, curbs, or walls) and, where appropriate, neatly trimmed lawns and flower beds. There were some marked regional differences in gas station nomenclature, staff dress, and customer service. East of the Rocky Mountains, gas stations were known as filling stations or auto supply stations. Staff were not supplied with uniforms nor given any specific instructions on customer relations or forecourt service. West of the Rocky Moun-

tains, gas stations were known as service stations. Staff at oil-company-owned sites on the West Coast wore smart white uniforms with bow ties. They were under strict instructions to be as courteous and helpful as possible but prohibited from hand-cranking customers' automobiles (because many pump attendants' wrists were broken by the kickback of the starting handle). Staff training, uniforms, and forecourt service were introduced nationwide during the 1920s. Elaborate forecourt service was subsequently introduced in the 1930s to differentiate one brand from another (refer to Chapter 3 for further reading). American motorists were quick to appreciate the many benefits of oil-company-owned drive-in gas stations because of the ease of access and departure, absolute guarantee of product quality and accurate quantity, helpful staff, and fair pricing. Chevron and Standard Oil of Indiana both lost garage and store accounts when they introduced company-owned gas stations but took the calculated risk that increased retail sales would more than make up for the loss of wholesale business.

Customer repeat-purchase incentives were first introduced in 1914 by Gulf in the form of free road maps. These generated

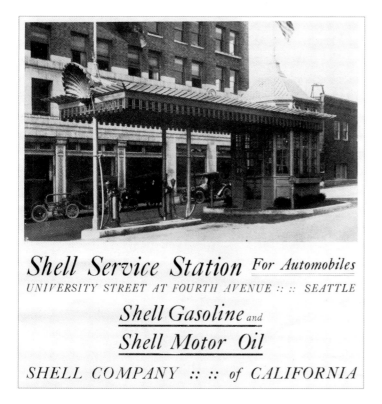

Shell Service Station For Automobiles

UNIVERSITY STREET AT FOURTH AVENUE :: :: SEATTLE

Shell Gasoline and

Shell Motor Oil

SHELL COMPANY :: :: of CALIFORNIA

Shell used elaborate, custom-made designs for prestige locations like this 1917 Fourth Avenue and University Street station in Seattle. Note both the Shell motif on the decorative canopy and the very ornate sales kiosk. *Author collection*

tremendous customer goodwill and repeat gasoline purchases for Gulf. Atlantic quickly introduced its own free maps. Virtually every oil company supplied free road maps by the early 1930s and would do so until the late 1970s (refer also to Chapter 4). Other oil companies, most notably Socony (Standard Oil Company of New York, later Mobil) and Exxon, hereafter referred to as Exxon, offered free gas tank dipsticks.

In the mid-1910s, marketing, branding, and advertising were inexact sciences. There were, however, two phenomenally successful product launches that crystallized the importance of an instantly recognizable trademark and packaging. Camel cigarettes were launched in 1913, and a camel was prominently featured on the front of the brightly colored pack. Anyone, irrespective of whether they were illiterate or could not speak English, could immediately ask for a pack of Camels or the one with the animal on it. Coca-Cola introduced its iconic contour bottle in 1916 to similar acclaim and even greater recognition. Advertising agencies in New York, Cincinnati, Detroit, Chicago, and San Francisco quickly became adept at isolating a brand's key attributes, developing an iconic trademark, and creating hard-hitting advertising campaigns. Fortuitously, Shell and Texaco already had instantly recognizable trademarks, a bright yellow scallop shell and a red star, respectively. Even an illiterate person could immediately recognize the brands. These

unique trademarks allied with shrewd marketing undoubtedly accounted for Shell and Texaco's later nationwide success in the 1920s and 1930s (refer to Chapter 2 for further discussion).

Chevron, Standard Oil of Ohio (Sohio), and Standard Oil of Indiana, in particular, made good use of the Red Crown brand name, which they inherited with the breakup of the Standard Oil Company in 1911. Unlike Shell or Texaco, none of them could use either the Standard name or the Red Crown brand name outside their assigned territory without the risk of prosecution for trademark infringement by another Standard Oil company. This would be a perpetual problem for the next sixty years. The only solution was a subsidiary brand name or, more radically, a corporate name change. Exxon changed its corporate name to Exxon in 1972 and for the first time was able to sell gasoline throughout the United States under one brand name: Exxon.

Only one grade of gasoline was sold, and this would remain the case until the introduction of premium grades in 1925 by Gulf and Exxon. One specialty brand, Amoco-gas, was introduced in Baltimore in 1915 and was to all intents and purposes a premium grade. Amoco-gas was a blend of gasoline and benzole, which virtually eliminated engine knock (preignition) and provided superior fuel economy. Benzole is a byproduct of coal gas manufacture and coke production for steel making. Amoco-gas was extremely popular and forced other local competitors to stock similar blends. It became widely available along the eastern seaboard in the 1920s and was copied by many oil companies nationwide. Gasoline-benzole blends also became very popular in Europe during the 1920s.

Gasoline continued to be sold in parallel, as a secondary item, by grocery, hardware, paint and bicycle stores, blacksmiths, machine shops, auto agencies, and garages. Many of these outlets supplied competing brands of gasoline in exactly the same way they sold competing brands of jam, soap, paint, or tires. These were known as split-island or multibrand sites. They would remain a common feature in the United States until the early 1940s and, similarly, in Germany and Great Britain up to the early 1950s.

The period between 1913 and 1919 is remarkable both for the number of precedents that remained intact for the next fifty years and the speed of development. The design precedents were both pragmatic in meeting the customers' requirements cost-effectively (Shell prefabricated units) and in being acutely sensitive to the neighbors' concerns (Standard Oil of Indiana). Key marketing and sales promotion techniques were developed in this period, including brands with strong trademarks, color schemes, and corporate identity; courteous, helpful uniformed attendants, and forecourt service; and repeat-purchase incentives (maps). The gas station's rapid development and impact between 1913 and 1919 are uncannily similar to those of the cell phone and the Internet over the past ten years.

Standard Oil of Indiana created custom-made designs for residential neighborhoods. The station's gabled roof and dormer window matched the frame houses on either side, while the window boxes, trellises, and pergola-style canopy added a bucolic touch. This was probably one of the earliest examples of a cottage style gas station. It was opened in April 1918 and photographed around June 1922. *Author collection*

Standard Oil of Indiana's Joliet design, introduced in 1917, was highly adaptable and blended in well with virtually any location. It created excellent community goodwill and quelled resistance to gas stations in residential areas. This particular station was opened in June 1918 and photographed in the early 1920s. The Joliet design was widely copied by competitors nationwide. *Author collection*

Conoco, like Standard Oil of Indiana, went to great lengths to appease community unrest over unsightly gas stations. This is a classic example of how an eyesore could be turned into a community asset in Denver, Colorado, in 1917. Conoco used this highly distinctive design throughout the 1920s.
Author collection

Magnolia Oil, later acquired by Mobil, introduced a highly distinctive gas station design in Texas during 1918. The key feature was the low lying banquettes on either side of the Gilbert & Barker long-necked T-35 pumps. The photograph was taken around 1925. *Author collection*

Drive-in gas stations quickly spread across Canada as well. This example was owned and operated by Imperial Oil, the Canadian subsidiary of Exxon. The site was located in Lethbridge, Alberta. The long-necked Gilbert & Barker T-235 pump indicates that the station was opened around 1918. *Author collection*

You Can Be Sure of Happy Motoring

"PUT A TIGER IN YOUR TANK," "Flying Horsepower," "Trust Your Car to the Man Who Wears the Texaco Star," and "You Can Be Sure of Shell" are just some of the slogans that made Exxon, Mobil, Texaco, and Shell, respectively, such highly successful brands in the United States and Europe.

Advertised brands with distinctive names and trademarks have always been guarantees of predictable dependability. Indeed, instantly recognizable trademarks like the Camel cigarette pack, the Coca-Cola bottle, the Shell scallop shell, the Mobil Pegasus, and Texaco's red star transcended language and could be immediately identified even by illiterate people. Motorists traveling long distances placed their trust in familiar brands they could rely on rather than risk engine trouble with an unfamiliar local brand. This was the cornerstone of Texaco's brilliant national marketing/advertising campaigns of the 1920s and 1930s.

The Texaco strategy was identical to that developed by other national household brands during the 1920s, namely Coca-Cola, Maxwell House coffee, and Camel cigarettes. These national brand advertising campaigns coincided with fairly large population shifts to the West Coast, in particular, and to Florida during the 1920s from the Northeast. In the midst of all the upheaval, newly relocated people were looking for the reassurance of a familiar, dependable brand. There were often perfectly good local brands, but none could match national brands' lavish full-color advertising campaigns.

In spite of highly successful national advertising campaigns by Texaco, Mobil, and Shell from the late 1930s on, the American gasoline market was and is a conglomeration of highly distinctive regional markets. Technically, this is even more so today with up to

sixteen different gasoline blends for cities or local climate conditions to minimize pollution. Apart from Texaco, Mobil, Shell, and Gulf, to a lesser extent, it was simply not cost-effective for other major United States oil companies to advertise in national magazines like *The Saturday Evening Post*, *National Geographic*, *Colliers*, *Life*, *Time*, or *Look*.

National advertising for former Standard Oil companies, namely Exxon, Standard Oil of Indiana, and Chevron was impossible because of trademark use restrictions outside their assigned territories. Exxon circumvented this in the early 1960s by buying expensive split runs or regional edition advertising space in national magazines for its Esso, Humble, and Enco brands, which entailed additional production costs for effectively three different advertising campaigns.

There were major changes in advertising from the mid-1960s on. Television had a fundamental impact on people's habits with a steep decline in cinema audiences and newspaper/magazine readership. *Look* magazine disappeared in the late 1960s, followed by *Life* magazine in 1972. Ironically, television advertising placed greater emphasis on local, tactical campaigns. A classic example was Flying A gasoline, which capitalized on the huge success of the *Bonnie and Clyde* gangster movie in early 1968 with a quickly produced gangster-style TV commercial that would have been impossible to do as a full-color magazine campaign in the time available. A declining readership, combined with inflexible six-week production lead times for full-color advertisements, made magazine advertising less and less cost-effective for major oil companies from the late 1960s on, apart from public service or corporate image campaigns.

Television commercials, initially with live spots as shown in this Philadelphia television station photograph for Atlantic, became an essential part of oil-company advertising in the late 1950s. By the early 1970s, television commercials supplanted national magazine advertising and spelled the demise of many iconic publications, most notably *Life* magazine. *Author collection*

Mobil's flying-horse trademark is the epitome of good marketing; it personifies the brand's strengths. Greater focus on the Pegasus trademark combined with extremely shrewd marketing gave Mobil superb international brand recognition and success during the 1950s and 1960s. This advertisement appeared in April 1950. *Author collection*

Simple hard-hitting advertisements were the cornerstone of Texaco's marketing success during the 1920s, amply demonstrated in this July 1923 example. The combination of dependable products and widespread availability provided vital reassurance to the long-distance motorist. By 1928, Texaco was sold in all forty-eight states. *Author collection*

Most American oil companies relied upon local newspapers, billboards, point-of-sale advertising, sponsored radio programs, or spot advertising and TV commercials for their advertising, particularly from the late 1960s on.

Europe, by contrast, has always been made up of compact national markets with national press/magazine advertising by all the major gasoline brands. Exxon's European marketing and advertising strategy was made far easier because of this, in spite of initially selling under nine local brands in a similar number of languages. Shell had the advantage of a unique, instantly recognizable trademark, the scallop shell, with an eye-catching yellow and red color scheme.

It would be fair to say that the two key gasoline advertisers and pace setters in the United States from the mid-1930s on were Texaco and, in particular, Mobil; whereas Shell and Exxon were the major arbiters in the European markets. The essential factors in a gasoline brand's success were technical reliability; a consistent logo; predictable service and facilities; empathy; and, where appropriate, humor in advertising.

Space does not permit a comprehensive survey of all the following oil companies' advertising campaigns. Instead the chapter will highlight the most striking campaigns that had a lasting impact. It should also be kept in mind that Chapters 3, 6, 9, and 10 contain a large number of advertisements, as well.

Texaco

By 1928, Texaco had the unique distinction of selling gasoline in every state of the union. Texaco's nationwide expansion during the 1920s is a casebook study of the perfect integration of efficient distribution and superb advertising. Texaco had a small presence in Europe, as well, which was rebranded Caltex after World War II, following Chevron's acquisition of 50 percent of Texaco's international operations outside North and South America in 1936. Texaco reappeared in Europe in 1968 after the European Caltex network disbanded.

Texaco's American branding was based upon four key elements: the instantly recognizable red star and green "T" logo, a bright red Wayne 276 gas pump, the distinctive green pump attendant's uniform, and the cream and pistachio green "Denver" gas station. Texaco's nationwide advertising exuded confidence, was concise, and promised predictable dependability. This worked perfectly with the nationwide introduction of high-pressure greasing during the late 1920s. The motorist could rely on Texaco's lubrication service as being as dependable as its gasoline and motor oil. Texaco's advertising during the 1920s set a precedent that was followed by all major oil companies over the next fifty years. Its advertising shrewdly used vicarious association by featuring young, affluent, Ivy League–educated couples to indicate it was a socially acceptable brand. This was probably the most social and widely traveled of all socio-economic groups, who drove long distances to Ivy League football games, polo and tennis matches, or to Florida for a winter vacation.

Texaco was at a slight disadvantage to Exxon and Standard Oil of Indiana during the late 1920s, in that it could not get a license to sell tetraethyl leaded gasoline until 1930. Texaco got around this by selling only a highly volatile "dry" gas, which was in effect a super regular grade.

With the introduction of Texaco Ethyl in 1930, Texaco advertising continued in the same preppy vein until the mid-1930s, when the combined effects of the Great Depression, Shell's development of elaborate forecourt service, and Gulf's promotion of its clean restrooms forced Texaco to fight back with more mainstream, hard-hitting advertising that deflected attention from an increasingly outdated gas station network. The late 1930s and early 1940s were probably the pinnacle for Texaco advertising with the highly memorable Circle Service, Registered Rest Rooms, and all-night service campaigns. These coincided with the introduction of Walter Dorwin Teague's trendsetting streamline moderne "EM" gas station design and the highly distinctive banjo pole sign. Texaco was the third largest marketer of gasoline in the nation with around 8 percent of the market in 1937. Even though Texaco was the only oil company to sell gasoline in all forty-eight states, it was not a dominant force in any particular region, unlike Socony-Vacuum (Mobil), the market leader, and Standard Oil of Indiana, the second largest marketer in the United States.

During the early 1950s, Texaco revived its Registered Rest Rooms campaign and ran it up until 1958. This was accompanied by a superb, updated version of the late 1930s Circle Service campaign that used stop-action photography in 1957. Texaco took this one stage further with a campaign in the late 1950s to promote its stations as one-stop service centers for prevacation and safety checks, as well as comprehensive servicing. This was, in part, dictated by the great success of the annual Mobilgas Economy Run and the adroit repositioning of the Mobilgas dealer as a car servicing specialist (see Chapter 3 for more details). This may also explain Texaco's excellent "Trust Your Car to the Man Who Wears the Texaco Star" slogan from the early 1960s, which maintained Texaco's sharp image but, just like thirty years previously, could barely disguise a rapidly aging gas station design. The "Matawan" station design, introduced in 1964, gave Texaco an improved

Texaco emphasized its gasoline's national consistency in exactly the same way that Maxwell House promised its coffee was "Good to the Last Drop" no matter where it was consumed. The crowded forecourt, combined with imposing archways, reassured the motorist that he was in good company, implying that Texaco was a socially acceptable brand. *Author collection*

image, but it was only viable for new stations built from the ground up. It was difficult to retrofit the changes onto existing structures and often made the service building look worse than before.

Texaco test marketed a new hexagonal logo in 1964 (it was rolled out nationally in 1966/1967) that owed much to Mobil's 1956 chevron logo and Sinclair's similar logo that was launched in 1959. Texaco's key asset, the red star with the green "T," was now just a footnote at the base of the red hexagon, just like the small red Pegasus in the 1956 Mobil chevron logo. Ironically, just as the new Texaco hexagonal logo was being rolled out, Mobil launched a new emphatic corporate logo that addressed all the drawbacks of the 1956 Mobil chevron logo and placed the Pegasus symbol at center

A better gasoline
has swept the country

The American motoring public has given an unprecedented country-wide endorsement of The Texas Company's latest motor product.

Daily, more and more of the *new* and *better* Texaco Gasoline is flowing into the tanks of motorists. Car owners and drivers are enthusiastic. Such a marked public expression of approval could only come from one thing—the appreciation of noticeably better results in the motor.

The results are immediate. The *new* Texaco forms *a dry gas*. It is this perfect vaporization to a dry gas that gives the easier start, quicker pick-up, greater power and increased mileage. You will notice, too, the new freedom from engine knock—attained without the addition of any chemicals or poisons. Try it—at any Texaco pump.

THE TEXAS COMPANY, U. S. A., *Texaco Petroleum Products*

A NEW *and* BETTER
TEXACO
GASOLINE

CLEAN-CLEAR-PURE

Servicing
the cars of a nation-

Since the days of the horseless carriage, Texaco has accepted the responsibility for keeping cars on the road—running smoothly, quietly, efficiently.

This very day, with Spring just around the corner, the cars of a nation are being serviced by 40,000 Texaco dealers. Differentials and transmissions are being lubricated with Texaco Thuban Compound. Crankcases are being drained and refilled with clean, clear, pure Texaco Golden Motor Oil. Car owners in each of our

48 States who have tested and compared, know that Texaco Golden Motor Oil meets their year-round driving needs. Those who try Texaco once use it consistently. For this golden motor oil has the body to withstand top engine temperatures — and the freedom from cold-sensitive impurities which assures thorough protection even at zero.

Today, stop under the Texaco Red Star with the Green T. Let a Texaco service man determine your lubrication requirements.

In 48 states motorists turn to TEXACO

THE TEXAS COMPANY
Refiners of a complete line of Texaco Petroleum Products including Gasoline, Motor Oil, Industrial Lubricants, Railroad and Marine Lubricants, Farm Lubricants, Road Asphalts and Asphalt Roofing.

TEXACO
GOLDEN MOTOR OIL

Texaco introduced a new "dry" gas in 1926 that provided complete vaporization and no dilution of the oil in the crankcase. It was an effective response to Esso super grade leaded gasoline and was quickly copied by Shell. Note the map of America dotted with red Texaco gas pumps apart from California. Texaco's subsequent acquisition of Calpet provided nationwide coverage. *Author collection*

This March 1930 Texaco advertisement is probably one of the first to place equal emphasis on service as well as on products. It reassured the long-distance motorist that every Texaco dealer from coast to coast provided a lubrication service every bit as dependable as Texaco products. Note the drop-in illustration of the highly distinctive green-roofed Denver gas station. *Author collection*

stage again. Many Texaco dealers persisted with the old-fashioned but highly distinctive round red star banjo pole signs right through the 1970s, which did nothing for brand consistency. To add insult to injury, the European Texaco hexagon logo did not contain the red star with the green "T."

Mobil

Mobil was created by the merger of Socony and Vacuum Oil in 1931 to form the Socony-Vacuum Oil Company. Socony and Vacuum Oil had each made rapid piecemeal acquisitions throughout the 1920s, and as a result, Socony-Vacuum was the largest gasoline retailer in America with a market share of around 10 percent by 1937. Neither oil company had previously run nationwide gasoline advertising campaigns, although Vacuum ran heavyweight advertising campaigns worldwide for Mobiloil.

Socony-Vacuum, without a single brand name or distinctive logo, was at a distinct disadvantage to Texaco and especially Shell, which had just invaded New England, its heartland. Fortuitously, Vacuum Oil had an ideal trademark, the Pegasus symbol, which had been used in South Africa for its gasoline brand, Pegasus motor spirit, from as far back as 1913. Socony-Vacuum introduced the Pegasus symbol in 1934 and the Mobilgas brand name across

TEXACO-ETHYL
THE "DRY" ETHYL GASOLINE
sweeping the nation

TEXACO-ETHYL
AT 40,000 DEALERS
AVAILABLE IN ALL OUR 48 STATES

TEXACO
the original
"DRY" GAS **+** ETHYL
nationally famous
ANTI-KNOCK COMPOUND **=** TEXACO-ETHYL
THE "DRY" ANTI-KNOCK
GASOLINE

Texaco finally obtained a tetraethyl lead license in 1930, which transformed its marketing. Motorists could now rely even more on Texaco for meeting all their motoring needs from coast to coast. With the exception of Shell, no other oil company could match this. Note again how prominently the Denver gas station was featured to make it as instantly recognizable as the Texaco logo. *Author collection*

America, apart from New York and New England where the Socony brand was retained, until 1939. The Pegasus symbol was launched during 1939 in France and Czechoslovakia on gas pump globes and enamel advertisements, but it was in conjunction with the CIP and Sphinx brands. The Mobilgas brand name was not introduced internationally until after World War II.

During the late 1930s, Mobilgas ran heavyweight nationwide magazine campaigns to promote its brand as America's favorite gasoline and promised friendly service. Apart from one market survey advertisement in May 1938, Mobilgas was rather coy in promoting its clean restrooms and relied more on inference than direct statement. This changed in the early 1950s with Mobilgas meeting Texaco head on in 1952–1953 with its Clean Rest Rooms three navy blue triangles logo campaign (see Chapter 3 for further discussion). Pegasus, in its own right, became a very potent advertising device throughout the 1940s, culminating in the highly effective "Flying Horsepower" slogan of the late 1940s and early 1950s.

After World War II, Mobilgas was at the forefront of developing consistent international corporate identity programs and advertising campaigns. It consolidated this with the introduction of the highly successful annual Mobilgas Economy Run in the United States during 1950 and subsequently in Australia and Europe, which was an international marketing triumph. It was probably at this point that Mobilgas overtook Texaco as the

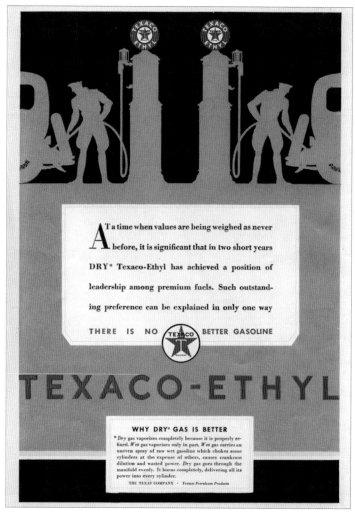

At a time when values are being weighed as never before, it is significant that in two short years DRY* Texaco-Ethyl has achieved a position of leadership among premium fuels. Such outstanding preference can be explained in only one way

THERE IS NO TEXACO BETTER GASOLINE

TEXACO-ETHYL

WHY DRY* GAS IS BETTER
* Dry gas vaporizes completely because it is properly refined. Wet gas vaporizes only in part. Wet gas carries an uneven spray of raw wet gasoline which chokes some cylinders at the expense of others, causes crankcase dilution and wasted power. Dry gas goes through the manifold evenly. It burns completely, delivering all its power into every cylinder.
THE TEXAS COMPANY · Texaco Petroleum Products

Texaco bravely used stylish art deco advertising during the early part of the Great Depression, as shown in this advertisement from March 1932. Campaigns like these did wonders for Texaco's brand image and compensated for its increasingly old-fashioned gas station network. The copy stressed Texaco Ethyl's value for money with complete vaporization and combustion. *Author collection*

marketing trendsetter in America. At the same time, the Mobilgas dealer was repositioned in the United States and overseas as an automobile service specialist who would ensure that your automobile ran as safely, reliably, and economically as possible. Mobilgas gained huge free publicity not only from press and newsreel coverage of the annual Mobilgas/Mobil Economy Runs, but also from automobile manufacturer advertising when its vehicles won either in the category or the event outright. Even automotive component manufacturers publicized the event when automobiles fitted with their parts won the Mobilgas Economy Run. The annual event ran in the United States for over ten years and was, ironically, phased out in Great Britain after the 1973 OPEC oil crisis when pressure was brought to bear to discourage unnecessary use of gasoline.

"Circle Service"

everything · your car needs—*done quickly*

QUICKER, MORE COMPLETE ATTENTION FOR YOUR CAR.

You want a sparkling clean windshield. You want your headlights cleaned for night driving. You want the assurance that your tires are in safe driving condition. You like to know as you drive that your oil has been recently checked. And the water.

So...we Dealers developed "CIRCLE SERVICE." It's a new systematic way to give your car these courtesy services...quickly...in one complete circling of your car. Thousands of Texaco Dealers have adopted it.

We're glad to render this thorough extra service and to deliver Fire-Chief gasoline to your engine.

Fire-Chief gasoline is the only gasoline made differently in the four seasons to meet the temperature conditions in 24 different U. S. climate zones. The result is quick starts (*in less than 10 turns of the engine*), freedom from cold weather engine stalling, and a saving up to 30% on gasoline on short trips.

For "CIRCLE SERVICE," we urge you to:

Try a Texaco Dealer next time...

TEXACO DEALERS

This message is published in behalf of more than 45,000 independent Texaco Dealers by The Texas Company. Sponsors of Eddie Cantor in "Texaco Town." (On the air every Wednesday Night—Columbia Network)... Makers of Fire-Chief Gasoline, New Texaco Motor Oil, Havoline and Marfak. Also more than 350 Industrial Lubricants... More tourists use Fire-Chief than any other gasoline.

"ZONED" FIRE-CHIEF. We studied 40 years of weather so that Texaco Fire-Chief could be made differently in each season to match the temperature variations of 24 different regions of the U. S. You get a livelier, quicker starting gasoline made for the exact locality in which you are driving.

WHO'S AFRAID OF THE COLD? Not your Texaco Dealer. He knows every cold snap wins new friends for Texaco Fire Chief gasoline. Because Fire-Chief is matched to the cold weather...the only gasoline made to suit your winter starting requirements...no matter where you do your driving.

★ Polishes left half of your windshield—doing a quick, thorough cleaning job.

★ Greets you cheerfully, then offers you your choice of either "FIRE-CHIEF OR ETHYL!"

★ Fills order for gasoline quickly and carefully, being sure not to overflow your tank.

★ Does a real cleaning job on the rear window and stop light.

★ As he circles your car he notes condition of the tires and remembers for your information.

★ Polishes right half of windshield and notes the condition of wiper blades and arms.

★ Cleans your headlight lenses. Checks the lights if you wish and replaces with new bulbs if needed.

★ Checks your radiator, adds water if needed, being careful to first check on your anti-freeze.

★ Checks your oil, using clean cloth or napkin . . . presenting the gauge for your inspection.

★ Reports on conditions observed and offers to service tires and batteries if you desire it.

Copyright 1937
The Texas Company

Texaco fought back with its highly effective "Circle Service" campaign during 1937 that promised every motorist thorough step-by-step forecourt service. This reinforced Texaco's reputation as a dependable, national brand and forced other major oil companies to respond, notably Mobilgas. *Author collection*

"We want the best ETHYL we can buy so we always stop at this pump"

"Why, what's the difference between one Ethyl gasoline and another—they're all the same, aren't they?"
"That's what we thought, too, until Fred told me it's the gasoline to which Ethyl is added that counts."

It's always the gasoline base you *start* with that determines how good the resulting gasoline is *after* the Ethyl fluid is added. In Texaco-Ethyl the base is Texaco *Fire-Chief*. Before *anything* is added, you've got fire-engine speed and power—plus an octane rating already outstanding. When Ethyl fluid is added to *that*—you've got just about the finest Ethyl gasoline that money can buy.

Try a tankful today at any Texaco Station. Find out for yourself what a big difference there is between Texaco-Ethyl and other premium gasolines.

Drive to the Century of Progress Exposition at Chicago. There are good roads—ample parking spaces—plenty of good hotels and tourist camps.

COPYRIGHT, 1933, THE TEXAS COMPANY

THE TEXAS COMPANY · Texaco Petroleum Products

TEXACO-ETHYL is *FIRE-CHIEF* + ETHYL

(Right) Texaco confirmed its national dependability with its "Registered Rest Rooms" campaign from 1938 on. This advertisement appeared in March 1939. Texaco shrewdly calculated that no woman driver, especially with children, would want to stop at any gas station unless she could be sure of the cleanliness of its restrooms. Unlike Gulf, Texaco could guarantee this in all forty-eight states. Texaco maintained high standards with its "White Patrol" team of inspectors. *Author collection*

(Left) Preppy women, along with their husbands, were the primary customers for Texaco Ethyl in this August 1933 advertisement. Intense competition from other major oil companies, notably Shell with their Seven Point forecourt service and Gulf with their Clean Rest Rooms, and cut-price operators later forced Texaco to develop advertising campaigns with broader social appeal and concentrate more on their regular grade Fire Chief that was introduced in 1932. *Author collection*

Our "*Powder Room*" on every road

"*You're lucky, Betty,*" says Mother. "I remember when it was hard to find clean attractive rest rooms like this.

"Now, we just look for the green-and-white Registered Rest Room signs at Texaco Dealers along the road. Then we can always be sure."

You, too, can always be SURE. Our Registered Rest Room signs are always a *promise* of clean fully-equipped rest rooms at our stations.

They are backed by our signed pledges . . . and by our famous fleet of "White Patrol" inspection cars on the road in all 48 States.

You'll find *Registered* Rest Rooms marked by the neat green-and-white curb sign at Texaco Dealers. Look for it on every road.

FIRE CHIEF sells for about half the price you paid in 1909 for the then regular gasoline, illustrating the continued success of the petroleum industry in providing the public with better products at lower prices.

Texaco "White Patrol" inspection cars guard Registered Rest Rooms. Many inspectors now have first-aid training and carry first-aid equipment.

TEXACO DEALERS

originators of REGISTERED REST ROOMS

Published in behalf of more than 45,000 independent Texaco Dealers by The Texas Company. Tune in The Texaco Star Theatre—Wednesday Nights—Columbia Network— 9:30 E.D.T., 7:30 E.S.T., 8:30 C.D.T., 7:30 C.S.T., 6:30 M.S.T., 5:30 P.S.T.

(Top) Gasoline octane ratings increased dramatically throughout the 1950s. Texaco was quick off the mark with its boxing glove device that simply but powerfully demonstrated the benefits of Sky Chief high-test gasoline in this 1951 advertisement. *Author collection*

(Above) Texaco consolidated its reputation for nationwide reliability with a series of color advertisements during 1940 and 1941 promising twenty-four-hour, all-night service for families traveling long distance in July 1940 or the hard-pressed businessman in August 1941. *Author collection*

(Left) The excellent "Trust Your Car to the Man Who Wears the Texaco Star" 1963 campaign sadly marked the end of Texaco's golden age in marketing and advertising. It placed equal emphasis on the Texaco dealer as an automotive expert and the efficacy of Sky Chief gasoline and Havoline motor oil. Texaco gas stations were not featured because their obsolescence would have undermined the message. Ironically, the new Texaco hexagonal logo rolled out nationally in 1966 made this catchy slogan redundant. *Author collection*

Texaco brilliantly updated their 1937 "Circle Service" campaign with this superb 1957 stop-action shot of a pump attendant performing eight steps in forecourt service. This is probably one of the best forecourt service advertisements ever produced and undoubtedly explains why Texaco was so successful.
Author collection

Texaco ran its "Safe-T Check-up" campaign during 1957 and 1958 in response to the repositioning of Mobilgas dealers as automotive service experts. Just as in the 1957 stop-action forecourt service advertisement, Texaco simply and clearly demonstrated the benefits of its safety inspections and lubrication services.
Author collection

Mobilgas was renamed Mobil in 1956 and received a new, sharper chevron logo that placed a greater emphasis on modernity at the expense of distinctiveness. The previous shield logo, a legacy of Socony, looked increasingly dated in comparison with Esso's simple oval and Shell's no-nonsense trademark. A number of company-owned gas stations in California, Australia, and Great Britain during 1954 and 1955 had special pole signs that featured the Pegasus symbol and Mobilgas brand name without the shield. For some inexplicable reason, Mobil's key asset, the iconic Pegasus symbol, was considerably reduced in size and demoted to the base of the new chevron logo. The old Mobilgas shield logo, however, was used in tandem with the new Mobil chevron logo until 1959. Mobilgas and Mobilgas Special were changed to Mobil regular and Mobil premium in the United States during 1962, but the Special label was retained in Europe.

There was growing American public and political unease during the early 1960s about the appearance of increasingly garish and unsightly gas stations, billboards, and other roadside architecture. In 1964, Mobil wisely decided to preempt any legislative action by commissioning Eliot Noyes to develop a new, highly distinctive gas station design that could be immediately recognized as a Mobil station with a minimum of branding and could harmonize with virtually any setting (see also Chapter 7). At the same time, Chermayeff & Geismar was hired to create a new emphatic logo that addressed all the drawbacks of the previous 1956 chevron

MOBILGAS AMERICA'S FAVORITE

TODAY
THE LARGEST SELLING BRAND OF GASOLINE IN THE UNITED STATES IS MOBILGAS

THANKS, AMERICA! We nominated a winning ticket. You elected it!

MOBILGAS...for President.
(It swept into first place with a landslide of votes. It's America's largest selling gasoline.)

MOBILOIL...for Vice-president.
(A real running-mate. Today it's the most popular motor oil in the world.)

TOGETHER, they've given your car a New Deal. If you want Power, Pick-up and Getaway

...try Mobilgas! It's sold from Coast to Coast ...wherever you see the Red Horse sign.
If you want a Cleaner, Tougher, Longer-lasting Lubricant...try Mobiloil!
It's absolutely the best oil made to withstand the terrific film-cracking heat in your car's crankcase.
The dealers who sell both Mobilgas and Mobiloil are dedicated to Public Service.
You'll receive a Friendly Welcome wherever Socony-Vacuum products are sold.

MOBILGAS AND MOBILOIL SOCONY-VACUUM OIL COMPANY, INC.

By July 1937, Mobilgas was America's leading brand, with around 10 percent of the national market when this advertisement appeared. The easy rapport between the attendant and the customer combined with Uncle Sam's folksy charm provided a winning formula for Mobilgas advertising. Note how the advertisement equated Mobilgas' popularity with the 1936 presidential election comparing a purchase of Mobilgas or Mobiloil with a vote! *Author collection*

logo. The combined efforts of Eliot Noyes and Chermayeff & Geismar created a design classic, the red "O" Mobil logo, the circular Pegasus symbol, and the "Pegasus" gas station design, which has stood the test of time aesthetically, if not ergonomically.

Shell

Shell has always had the unique advantage of an instantly recognizable trademark, the scallop shell with a highly distinctive yellow and red color scheme. The Royal Dutch-Shell Group (60 percent Dutch/40 percent British), formed in 1907, had British antecedents dating as far back as 1897. Shell was ruthless in imposing its scallop shell trademark and yellow and red color scheme immediately on any business or gas station it acquired. That being said, Shell has always prided itself on its ability to adapt to local market conditions with advertising campaigns to match. Because of this, the Shell logo used in North America from the late 1920s on differed from the logo used elsewhere.

Mobilgas made a virtue of market research by featuring a typical customer and demonstrating how it met her gasoline requirements, as seen in this May 1939 advertisement. By making the customer the heroine, Mobilgas showed a responsive, empathetic attitude that could not help but boost Mobilgas' image and build sales. Note the "Stop at the Sign of Friendly Service" slogan as well. *Author collection*

Like Texaco, Mobilgas featured older customers, a notoriously difficult group, to endorse the cleanliness of their restrooms in this July 1939 advertisement. Note the eye contact between the attendant and the customer. The Mobilgas advertising copy, however, was rather coy. There was no mention of restrooms, rather an implication in the photograph, which was perhaps a legacy of Yankee reticence. *Author collection*

From 1940 on, Pegasus, the flying red horse, took center stage as the potent symbol of acceleration and stamina, as shown in the May 1940 horse and colt advertisement. After World War II, Mobilgas reinforced its advertising with the powerful "Flying Horsepower" slogan in a 1946 winter service campaign. *Author collection*

In the spring of 1951, Mobilgas launched their "Mobil-Care" campaign that effectively repositioned their dealers as automotive service specialists rather than gasoline vendors. While spring oil changes were promoted by all major oil companies, Mobilgas was the first oil company to emphasize safety inspections of tires, batteries, windshield wipers, and lights as an integral part of a spring service. *Author collection*

Shell was well established in Great Britain, the Netherlands, Belgium, Italy, and Scandinavia during the early 1920s and entered Germany in the mid-1920s, followed by France in the late 1920s. Apart from Germany and Switzerland, Shell was the market leader across Europe up to 1939, thanks largely to its instantly recognizable trademark and color scheme.

Shell advertising in Great Britain relied largely on full-color lorry bills (truck posters) attached to the sides of tank trucks and other delivery vehicles. Shell and, subsequently, Shell-Mex and BP Ltd. (the British joint marketing operation set up in 1932) were renowned for commissioning a large number of artists to create eye-catching posters that ranged from the conventional to the

The 1950 Mobilgas Economy Run was so successful that it became an annual event. The tremendous free publicity generated by automobile manufacturers like Ford and General Motors, as well as Champion spark plugs, was unprecedented. It remained a crucial part of Mobilgas, known as Mobil after 1956, marketing until the late 1960s in the United States.
Author collection

During 1958, Mobil continued to focus on its dealers as automotive service experts who ensured that your automobile ran as safely and economically as possible. Note the emphasis placed on continuous training, particularly on braking systems and the use of state-of-the-art diagnostic equipment. Also note the pairing of the new Mobil chevron logo with the old Mobilgas shield and the old shield logo on the pumps.
Author collection

While gasoline continuously improved in quality during the early 1950s, it was subject to inflation, just like food. More than ever, people were looking for value. The celebrated Mobilgas Economy Run, launched in 1950, demonstrated how excellent fuel mileage could be achieved with careful driving and a well-maintained automobile. Mobilgas supplied all its customers with a helpful booklet entitled, "All the Gas Mileage Your Car Can Deliver." Both the Mobilgas Economy Run and Mobil-Care did wonders for dealers' business and Mobilgas' reputation. *Author collection*

The Mobil Economy Run was equally successful in Australia and Europe, particularly in France, because motorists worldwide welcomed any means of saving money! The advertisement appeared in October 1960. Mobil-Care dealer service was known as Mobil Economie-Service in France, but apart from the name change it was identical to its American counterpart. The annual Mobil Economy Run ran up to 1973 in Great Britain. *Author collection*

avant-garde for both BP and Shell gasoline brands. Their role as a patron of the arts appealed to the discerning, educated middle and upper classes, who were the key purchasers of gasoline in prewar Great Britain. Sir Kenneth Clark, the director of the National Gallery in London during the 1930s (later creator of the renowned BBC TV *Civilization* series) and a key arbiter of taste in art, praised Shell-Mex and BP's patronage. Jack Beddington, the brilliant head of publicity for Shell-Mex and BP, responded shrewdly and sensitively to vociferous campaigns led by the *London Daily Express* and the Council for the Protection of Rural England (CPRE) against billboards; garish, unsightly gas stations; and the deterioration of the countryside caused by hordes of automobiles

with a two-tier campaign. Shell-Mex and BP commissioned lorry bills throughout the 1930s that featured places of natural beauty and historic interest under the slogan "Wherever You Go . . . You Can Be Sure of Shell," which subliminally encouraged motorists to take a sensitive and responsible attitude toward the places they visited. This was reinforced by the classic Shell Guide series during the same period. Branding and advertising, apart from the title, were nonexistent. Each guide was devoted to a particular British county with places of interest to visit and illustrated with photographs or commissioned illustrations by leading young British artists Rex Whistler, John Piper, Paul Nash, E. McKnight Kauffer (American by birth), and Graham Sutherland, among others. The

Mobil went one better than the "Trust Your Car to the Man Who Wears the Texaco Star" campaign with its superb "See Your Mobil Dealer First" series in 1964 and 1965 that featured actual customers with their local Mobil dealers. The easy rapport between the customer and the dealer spoke volumes for the latter's reliability and helpfulness. It confirmed the levelheadedness of the "Mobil-Care" campaign launched in the spring of 1951. *Author collection*

Want to see America best? See your Mobil dealer first

A family restaurant or a thrill-filled rodeo. The trained Mobil dealer can help you find either — and aid you in dozens of other ways, too. He's trained to take the guesswork out of travel.

Getting killed is easy. Staying alive is work.

New Mobil: It actually cleans your engine while you drive.

Throughout 1967, Mobil ran a public service campaign urging customers to behave more responsibly: to avoid driving when upset, to ensure that their vehicles were in a safe condition, to concentrate on the road, not to drive when exhausted, or not to overtake where prohibited. This campaign owed much, subconsciously, to Shell's prewar "Share the Road" campaign. Like Shell almost thirty years previously, this campaign boosted both Mobil's sales and its image as a responsible organization. *Author collection*

Mobil promoted its new detergent gasoline in April 1968 in exactly the same style as its 1967 public service campaign. Mobil demonstrated that continual use of this gasoline would clean the engine, ensure efficient operation of pollution controls, and help protect the environment. After this campaign, Mobil relied more on television advertising. *Author collection*

editor was John Betjemin, the poet who also wrote the text for the guides for some counties. All these factors undoubtedly contributed to Shell-Mex and BP's market leadership.

Shell advertising became a national institution in Great Britain from 1930 on with the "That's Shell . . . That Was" campaign by John Reynolds with the two-headed road repairman looking left and right in amazement. This campaign captured the British public's imagination, irrespective of whether they owned automobiles or not, and became a national catch phrase and launched a series of even funnier campaigns, culminating in the famous 1933 Knockless monster poster, which was a topical reflection of people's fixation with the Scottish Loch Ness monster. A similar campaign with a two-headed policeman was used in the United States during the mid-1930s, either in press advertising or promotional material. The two-headed advertising motif was successfully revived in Great Britain during the early 1950s with the "Fill up with Shell and Feel the Difference" slogan. Humor, relying on puns and word play, became inextricably linked with all of Shell's British press advertising throughout the 1930s, which had a particular appeal to the educated middle and upper classes, who were the key owners of automobiles.

In France and Germany, Shell's advertising was less creative and relied more on spelling out Shell gasoline and motor oil's technical superiority, especially in Germany where special Shell racing fuels enabled the high-tech Auto Union race cars to dominate the European Grand Prix race circuits. The British Shell motor oil slogan "Every Drop Tells" was adapted in France as "Chaque Goutte Compte" (Every drop counts). French Shell advertising during the early 1930s placed strong emphasis on Shell's almost universal availability, from the midst of the Sahara Desert to the French West Indies.

In the United States, Shell had been present on the West Coast from as far back as 1912, was introduced in the Midwest in 1923 (although it had been producing and refining there from as early as 1917), and finally reached the East Coast in 1929. Shell probably had a national market share of 5 to 6 percent in the late 1930s, roughly equal to that of Gulf. Shell was, to all intents and purposes, a national marketer like Texaco, but until the mid-1930s, it effectively operated in America as three separate companies: Shell Oil Company (west of the Rockies), Shell Petroleum Corporation (central and southern states), and Shell Eastern Petroleum Products, Inc., (eastern seaboard). Each of these operations ran regional press and billboard campaigns. Shell united these operations with a national super service station design developed during 1934 and 1935 and nationwide magazine campaigns from the late 1930s on. The latter were almost certainly in response to the Texaco and Mobilgas full-color national magazine campaigns. Shell's national magazine

campaigns were largely devoted to Super Shell (regular grade) gasoline formulated for stop-and-go traffic conditions with two distinct campaigns: a humorous series illustrated by the celebrated cartoonist William Steig and "The City of Tomorrow" series featuring the renowned industrial designer Norman Bel

Shell's tank trucks were as eye-catching as its gas stations, as shown in this Canadian example from the early 1920s, and were ideal advertisements for the Shell brand. One American Shell executive claimed that there was almost no need for advertising with such an attention-grabbing color combination. *Author collection*

The British public took the "That's Shell . . . That Was" campaign to their hearts during the early 1930s, and it became a widely used catch phrase. The series, designed by John Reynolds, cleverly included a topical reference to the public fixation with the Loch Ness monster, which had been sighted in 1932. The sheer impact of "That's Shell . . . That Was" anticipated the mid-1960s Exxon "Put a Tiger in Your Tank" campaign. *Author collection*

fill up with SHELL

and feel the difference

SHELL

Shell revived the two-headed device in Great Britain during February 1953 with the reintroduction of branded, high-octane fuel after a fourteen-year absence and subsequently in July 1956 with the launch of 100-octane Super Shell. *Author collection*

This Shell advertisement probably appeared in California during December 1928. The J. Walter Thompson advertising agency was hired by the Shell Company of California in 1928 to create press/magazine advertising campaigns for the West Coast. Shell had run virtually no mainstream advertising in the United States before this date. Previously, Shell relied on its eye-catching red and yellow color scheme and point-of-sale promotions. *Author collection*

Shell cleverly promoted Super Shell during 1937 with Norman Bel Geddes' visionary designs for the cities of tomorrow which emphasized traffic flow. Super Shell's equally efficient formulation minimized waste in stop-and-go traffic. It was no coincidence that General Motors subsequently commissioned Norman Bel Geddes to design its Futurama pavilion at the 1939 New York World's Fair. *Author collection*

The long-running "Share the Road" campaign during 1939 and 1940 demonstrated how good lane discipline could reduce stop-and-go driving conditions by 25 percent and save fuel. The campaign was endorsed by seven leading experts. It appealed to the driver's better nature and showed that good fuel mileage would be a net result. This advertisement appeared in August 1939 and may have provided the inspiration for both the postwar Mobil Economy Run and its subsequent 1967 public service campaign. *Author collection*

Geddes, followed by "Share the Road," a long-running public service campaign that encouraged drivers to stay in traffic lanes and show consideration for others. The latter may have been inspired by the British "Wherever You Go . . . You Can Be Sure of Shell" countryside campaign that presented Shell as a caring and responsible brand that subliminally encouraged its customers to behave in the same way. They were a tad patronizing, but both campaigns seem to have paid off. Shell capped this with a research campaign throughout 1941 that demonstrated Shell's research cross-fertilization skills from manufacturing better gasolines to developing petrochemicals vital for products as diverse as anesthetics, lipstick, nylon stockings, and artillery shells.

During the early 1950s, most of Shell's advertising in America and Europe was devoted to promoting the TCP additive (known as ICA outside North America) as the engine deposit neutralizer and X-100 detergent motor oil. Shell used regional magazines in the United States to advertise its new grade names, Super Shell (solid white pump) and Shell regular (solid yellow

pump), between late 1956 and 1958. The sheer size of the American market may have forced Shell to roll out the rebranding on a region by region basis.

Shell was probably the first oil company in America to introduce a gas station design, the "Ranch," that integrated perfectly with postwar single-story housing developments. The one-off design created in the late 1950s to meet the zoning requirements of a local California planning board proved to be a big hit and was built nationwide throughout the 1960s. It was quickly copied by other oil companies, notably Exxon and Texaco. By the late 1960s, Shell realized that the ranch gas station design was a major public relations asset and used it in national full-color magazine campaigns to show its caring and responsible attitude (see Chapter 6). Shell even ran one advertisement that showed the demolition of a class A box station, emphasizing its commitment to build more harmonious designs. This campaign was virtually a repeat of the same strategy used by Shell thirty years earlier with its public service "Share the Road" campaign of 1938–1940.

Television advertising was used by Shell in Great Britain throughout the 1960s, and the most memorable featured Bing Crosby and Sammy Davis Jr., singing "Keep Going Well . . . Go Shell." France had a long running "C'est Shell que J'aime" (I like Shell) press campaign that sometimes featured a woman's red lipstick kiss on a Shell gas pump!

There was a marked divergence between Shell's American and European marketing strategies from the late 1960s on. While the European units experimented with new retailing methods, most notably self-service, and created an advanced gas station design, MAYA (most advanced, yet acceptable), the American operation preferred to maintain the status quo. The

(Far left) Shell continued its public service theme in April through August 1941 by demonstrating how the same research skills that created even better Shell gasoline were also developing rayon, 100-octane aviation gasoline, vitamin E, fertilizers, anesthetics, and TNT from petroleum byproducts. Petrochemicals played a vital role in the Allied victory of World War II and became a critical part of the postwar economy. *Author collection*

(Left) Between late 1956 and March 1958, Shell rolled out its new grade and pump identities: Super Shell in a solid white pump and Shell regular in a solid yellow pump. These remained in place for the next twenty years. The rollout may have been dictated by the sheer size of the United States' market and changes in key refining processes. The TCP additive was introduced in July 1953. *Author collection*

Shell's responsiveness to community concerns about incompatible structures enhanced both its reputation and sales throughout the late 1960s and early 1970s. The ranch-style gas station was a major public relations asset for Shell in the United States during the 1960s, and it was featured in advertising from August 1968 on. More examples can be found in Chapter 6. *Author collection*

Empathy was the key reason for Exxon's market leadership in prewar Germany. The smiling pump attendant was used in all of Exxon's German advertising and publicity material up to the mid-1950s. This simple but highly effective execution may well have inspired Exxon's United States strategy as well. *Author collection*

Pecten was created by Raymond Loewy and rolled out across Europe in 1972 and 1973.

Exxon

Exxon did little to promote its Standard brand in America until the mid- to late 1920s, due to concerns about possible intervention by the Federal Trade Commission (FTC) over local market domination. Aggressive marketing by Texaco and Gulf changed this, especially after the introduction of Gulf's No-Nox premium fuel in 1925. Exxon fought back in 1926 with the reintroduction of Esso leaded super grade fuel that was backed by a billboard campaign. The fuel couldn't be advertised in national full-color magazines, such as *Colliers*, *National Geographic*, and *The Saturday Evening Post*, because of trademark restrictions outside its assigned territory. There were, however, no such constraints in Europe. Exxon quickly expanded across Europe during the 1920s, most notably in Germany, France, and Italy in the face of fierce competition from Shell. While Great Britain was Europe's largest gasoline market,

Exxon had lost control of its British operation, the Anglo-American Oil Company, in the 1911 breakup of Standard Oil and finally reacquired it in 1930. It is, therefore, impossible to consider Anglo-American's 1920s marketing and advertising in the same context as Exxon's European campaigns.

Exxon was the market leader in Germany right up to 1939. The advertising featured friendly, helpful pump attendants, happy customers, and the contented neighbors almost to the exclusion of the brand's technical benefits. People felt a strong empathy with the brand. Exxon's German strategy during the 1920s and 1930s was very similar to that of Texaco in the United States. Exxon's French campaigns were fairly impersonal by comparison and placed a greater emphasis on reliability, technical superiority, national availability, and endorsement by prestigious automobile manufacturers.

Apart from Germany, Exxon was at a marked disadvantage to Shell with at least nine different local brands and logos across Europe. Exxon addressed this gradually with the introduction of a new solid red circle and five-star horizontal blue bar logo that

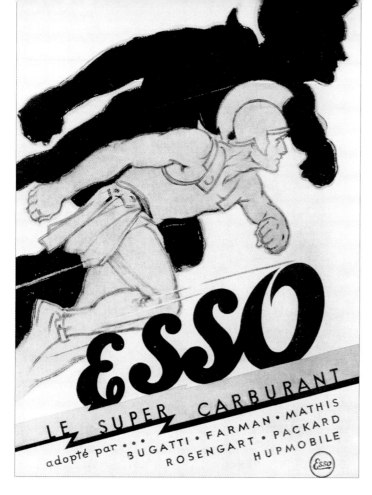

Esso super grade fuel was introduced in France, Germany, and Italy during 1929. This superb Roman centurion symbol was used in all three countries, personifying flexibility, pulling power, and responsiveness. It was a remarkably versatile device and worked equally well in no matter what context. Above all, the Roman centurion provided Exxon with an instantly recognizable symbol on par with the scallop Shell trademark. It is hard to understand why this excellent symbol was dropped two years later. *Author collection*

incorporated the local brand names during 1925 and 1926 across Europe. Shortly afterwards, Standard Motor Oil was introduced across Europe using the identical American red circle and horizontal bar logo. Esso super grade gasoline was launched in Germany, France, and Italy during 1929 with the same graphics and silver pump color as its American counterpart but with a unique European branding device, the Roman centurion, which symbolized dependability and effortless power. It was a brilliant branding device, and graphically it was remarkably versatile. It was a belated response to the instantly recognizable Shell trademark and inexplicably was dropped after less than two years. Standard was finally launched as Exxon's European brand, apart from Great Britain, during 1931 and did not finally disappear until just before World War II.

Intense competition from Texaco, Shell, Gulf, and Socony-Vacuum (Mobil) in America forced Exxon to relaunch itself as Esso with a new oval logo in June 1933. Essolene was the regular grade and had a new striking white and red pump color scheme and Esso super grade sported a white and blue combination. This marked a turning point for Exxon with a more aggressive marketing/advertising strategy in America that relied on highly imaginative billboard campaigns that often used humor. The "Happy Motoring" slogan was introduced in the mid-1930s by Exxon in the United States and was widely used on its maps. After World War II, the Happy Motoring slogan appeared on all American Esso gas station fascias.

The new Esso oval logo was gradually phased in across Europe, starting in Great Britain in April 1935. In Europe, during the mid- to late 1930s, there was better coordination of Exxon's

The Esso oval logo and Essolene regular grade gasoline were launched in the United States on June 3, 1933, with two prior advertisements on May 31 and June 2 of that year. In conjunction with the rebranding, Exxon introduced an elaborate forecourt service that was similar to that of Shell. Preparation for the rebranding commenced in March and April 1933, which was indicated by the leafless trees and the warm clothes worn by the motorists in the instruction booklet. *Author collection*

European advertising campaigns. There was a greater similarity between German and British campaigns with an emphasis on happy, young couples, while French and Italian campaigns used highly sophisticated, almost surreal designs that would have been at home in an art gallery.

During the late 1940s, Exxon concentrated on developing a systematic international corporate identity and highly distinctive gas station design, which eventually became as instantly recognizable as the Shell trademark. This was followed by the international adoption of the oil-drop figure, nicknamed Happy, which was first introduced in Denmark during World War II to encourage gasoline conservation. The oil-drop figure was especially popular in France and was a central part of French marketing until the late 1960s. Esso Extra was launched as the premium grade across Europe as "The Gasoline with Six Extras" during 1953 when the tiger made its first appearance in Great Britain, albeit in a highly naturalistic, aggressive form. The "Happy Motoring" slogan was also used in Europe as "La Route Heureuse" (Happy Trip) in France. "The Esso Sign Means Happy Motoring" was sung to a calypso tune on British TV commercials during the late 1950s and early 1960s. Esso introduced the Enco (ENergy COmpany) brand in the United States during 1960 for all territories where Esso could not be used. Apart from the phenomenally successful "Put a Tiger in Your Tank" campaign worldwide in the mid-1960s, Exxon launched "The New Europeans" campaign across Europe in 1969, which was aimed at affluent yuppies who could drive across Europe safe in the knowledge they could get Esso gasoline anywhere, often with a snack, car servicing, Esso tires and batteries,

From around 1935 on, Exxon coordinated its European advertising campaigns largely through the McCann Erickson advertising agency network. In Great Britain and Germany, there was emphasis on happy, carefree young people and weekend trips with Esso maps. Gasoline in both countries was relatively inexpensive. *Author collection*

The "Happy Motoring" slogan became an essential part of Exxon's advertising in the United States during the late 1930s and would remain so until the early 1970s, as shown on this 1937 map cover. Exxon, similar to Texaco and Mobilgas, heavily promoted its clean restrooms and myriad free services that the traveler took as an automatic right. *Author collection*

Esso was launched in Great Britain in April 1935 and was subsequently launched across Europe. The new oval Esso logo provided the European network with a strong corporate identity, which after World War II, rivaled that of Shell. This advertisement appeared in October 1935. *Author collection*

EVERY SECOND HUMBLE PROVIDES THE ENERGY OF 29 LIGHTNING BOLTS!

Man's progress is marked by his ability to harness and use energy. As America's Leading Energy Company, Humble supplies each second in gasoline alone, the energy-equivalent of over 2 dozen lightning bolts! Through research, Humble works wonders with oil—harnessing energy to run your car, heat your home, and help to make your life more pleasant. Look for the name HUMBLE—stop for world-famous Esso Extra gasoline. You'll see why "Happy Motoring" starts at the Esso Sign—the World's First Choice!

HUMBLE
OIL & REFINING COMPANY
America's Leading **E**nergy Company

Esso

In 1960, Humble Oil became the holding company for Exxon's United States operations with Esso and Enco as the key brands. At the same time, Exxon initiated split-run campaigns. The Energy corporate campaign of 1961 and 1962 and subsequent product campaigns considerably improved the image of both brands in the face of tough competition. The sheer complexity and expense of these split-run campaigns hastened the need for a single, noncontentious brand. Exxon was introduced in the fall of 1972. *Author collection*

The Italian Esso campaign was more impersonal and abstract because gasoline was considerably more expensive, owing to high taxes. This advertisement from 1935 announced blanket availability.
Author collection

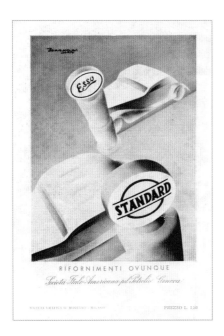

and stay the night at one of the many Esso motels that had been introduced across Europe during the mid- to late 1960s.

In America, Exxon pragmatically adopted the noncontentious Exxon brand nationwide in the fall of 1972, and with the help of the tiger, was quickly accepted by American motorists. The launch of the Exxon brand sharpened and galvanized Exxon's marketing in exactly the same way the launch of the Esso brand did in June 1933.

PUT A TIGER IN YOUR TANK

The Exxon "Put a Tiger in Your Tank" advertising campaign was launched in America during spring 1964 and across Europe in spring 1965, which coincided with the introduction of the new Esso logo. The tiger campaign probably ranks as one of the most successful and memorable advertising campaigns ever. Its success was even more remarkable when seen in the context of American and European markets during the mid-1960s, which were increasingly driven by price discounting and trading stamp offers that

LA BICYCLETTE ESSO

Une manière originale de résoudre un problème qui n'est pas nouveau, mais toujours d'actualité.

Les voitures sont un peu comme les hommes. Elles ne peuvent pas marcher indéfiniment. De temps à autre elles ont besoin d'un «examen», de quelques «remèdes» et d'un peu de «repos».

Si vous percevez un bruit de mauvais augure dans votre moteur à Elseneur au Danemark (ou bien dans quelque 100 autres endroits autour de Copenhague), vous avez de la chance.

En effet, bien que privé de votre voiture pendant le temps de la révision ou de la réparation, vous ne serez pas pour autant démuni de moyen de locomotion.

Dès l'immobilisation de votre véhicule vous pourrez nous emprunter une bicyclette et en disposer gratuitement aussi longtemps qu'il s'avérera nécessaire.

C'est simple, c'est efficace. Voilà un exemple bien typique des nouveaux services Esso dont peuvent bénéficier au Danemark les Nouveaux Européens.

Les Nouveaux Européens sont des voyageurs difficiles à satisfaire, toujours sensibles aux innovations les plus originales comme les plus pratiques.

Pour eux Esso signifie «Route Heureuse» une boisson fraîche et un sandwich pris rapidement au bord de «l'autobahn»; le prêt d'une bicyclette au Danemark le temps d'une réparation de voiture; un large éventail d'articles, depuis l'excellente batterie Esso jusqu'aux foulards de soie, et, bien sûr, un tigre dans le moteur.

En Europe, sous l'emblème Esso, vous trouverez ces produits et ces services de plus en plus souvent. Pourquoi ne pas rejoindre dès maintenant les Nouveaux Européens a l'une des 37 800 stations Esso réparties dans 15 pays européens ?

Les Nouveaux Européens n'ont pas de patience. L'il qu'un balai d'essui-glace se révèle inefficace, ils sirent le changer tout de suite. Ils peuvent désormais se le procurer ainsi que bien d'autres accessoires produits dans les stations ESSO SHOP sans cesse plus nombreuses en Europe.

Avant de prendre la route pour Rome, une boisson rafraîchissante pour les Nouveaux Européens; les snack-bars et les restaurants Esso de Suède et d'Italie offrent la possibilité de vous restaurer légèrement et vite ou l'agrément d'un bon repas pris sans précipitation.

Il n'est pas nécessaire d'être majeur pour devenir Nouvel Européen. Ils sont de tous âges. Regardant le monde avec des yeux neufs et toujours à la recherche du mieux dans l'Art de Vivre.

Tout pour rendre la route heureuse aux Nouveaux Européens (Esso)

For the New Europeans

Europe's largest wayside inn

Setting the pace in a new and international style of living, the New Europeans are the world's most demanding motorists. On holiday. On business. Or seeking the sheer pleasure of driving.

The New Europeans visit us at 35,000 Esso stations in fifteen countries, and they expect to find more than just the usual. They want a whole new world of products and services, and that's what we're giving them.

Esso today is auto clinics and diagnostic centers. New Esso tires and batteries. The latest in every kind of accessory. Plus snack bars, restaurants and Esso Motor Hotels.

In many parts of Europe, we're all these things right now. Where we're not, we're moving fast. For you and all the other New Europeans.

More than 50 Esso Motor Hotels in Europe offer the hospitality and convenience of a wayside inn. In 1970, they played host to over a million businessmen and holiday makers, providing a place to wine and dine, to hold meetings and conferences, and to spend a very good night's sleep.

Each one reflects the style of the region. For instance, in Hanover you can enjoy a drink while watching the deer in

the Tiergarten. At many of the Swedish Hotels saunas soothe away the troubles of traveling. And at Maidenhead, near Windsor Castle, you can dine in a Tudor-style manor house.

Wherever you stay you'll enjoy a private bath or shower, and a bedroom designed to make you comfortable. Visit an Esso 'wayside inn'. You'll understand why Esso have over a million guests a year.

New ideas for the New Europeans (Esso)

Exxon launched the New Europeans campaign across Europe in late 1969, which ran up to 1972. This aspirational campaign was aimed at baby boomers who liked to take off and travel where the spirit took them. In addition to gas and servicing, Exxon provided an increasing number of snack bars and a network of motels (some even had saunas!) across Europe. *Author collection*

43

undermined brand loyalty and turned gasoline into a price-sensitive commodity. Another worry for service station operators at that time was the decline in the highly profitable lubrication business. The introduction of multigrade oils with a comprehensive range of additives enabled automobile manufacturers not only to dispense with seasonal oil changes, but actually extend the periods between oil changes. Furthermore, greasing had virtually been eliminated with extensive use of sealed bearings or nylon bushes. Service station dealers desperately needed something that could bring customers onto the forecourt and hopefully sell them a tune-up, car wash, new tires, or a battery while filling the gas tank.

In retrospect, it is very easy to see why the Exxon tiger was such a success. The key factors were a sense of fun and empathy, which Exxon had used so successfully in its prewar German

"Put a Tiger in Your Tank" ranks as one of the most effective advertising campaigns ever created. Launched in the United States in spring 1964 and subsequently in Europe during spring 1965, it turned a routine transaction into a fun event, as shown on this Salt Lake City forecourt in August 1964. In the United States, the tiger character provided a common identity for Esso and Enco, which was so effective it was used in subsequent corporate campaigns. Like Charlie Chaplin, the Exxon tiger communicated brilliantly in any language. *Author collection*

advertising campaigns. The cartoon tiger is an immensely likeable, cheeky character much like a pet dog or cat, always ready with a warm welcome, occasionally a bit naughty, but intensely loyal. These factors transcend language in exactly the same way that Charlie Chaplin silent movies could be understood all over the world.

Exxon went the extra mile with its tiger campaign and dressed up the Esso or Enco Extra gas pumps as tigers, complete with the hose disguised as a tiger tail. Outsize cut-out cartoon tigers were placed on the pole signs, tiger bunting and posters festooned the forecourts and sales offices, and "Put a Tiger in Your Tank" stickers and tiger tails were given away. No one could resist these displays, especially children. The Exxon tiger brought back a badly needed sense of fun to an otherwise boring but necessary transaction. It also increased customer traffic even at full price for hard-pressed Exxon dealers. More significantly, the tiger transcended the Esso and Enco brands and for the first time gave them a single identity. The tiger has been an essential part of Exxon's marketing ever since and played a pivotal role in the introduction of Exxon in 1972 (see Chapter 10).

Exxon's British subsidiary made the first sustained use of the tiger as a promotional device from February 1953 on, when Esso Extra was launched with an aggressive, leaping tiger to represent instant response with sustained power. This potent symbol was a key part of Exxon's British marketing until around 1962. It undoubtedly provided the framework for the subsequent iconic campaign.

Exxon's association with tigers and other felines dates as far back as the 1920s. Exxon's Norwegian subsidiary sold gasoline under the Tiger bensin (gasoline) brand name during the 1920s, which was subsequently dropped in favor of the transitional Standard brand and, ultimately, Esso.

Anglo-American, Exxon's recently acquired British subsidiary, adapted an American Ethyl press campaign for its Pratt's Ethyl brand in 1932. The advertisement featured a circus lion tamer cracking a whip at a lion to emphasize how tetraethyl lead tamed and controlled fuel combustion. La Société Economique, Exxon's French subsidiary, used jaguars among other animals to promote Esso super grade fuel during the mid-1930s.

Tigers and other felines were not exclusive to Exxon. Standard Oil of Indiana ran an "I've Got Live Power" campaign during 1933 at the Chicago Centenary Exposition that featured lion and tiger circus acts together with promotional automobiles with full-size tiger and other animal models on their roofs. Gilmore (later acquired by Mobil) used a leaping lion trademark throughout the 1930s with the "Roar with Gilmore" slogan and Texaco featured a tiger in its Havoline motor oil campaign during 1949.

The Exxon tiger first appeared in Great Britain during February 1953, albeit in a highly natural, aggressive form. The tiger was so effective that it was used for almost ten years in Great Britain. *Author collection*

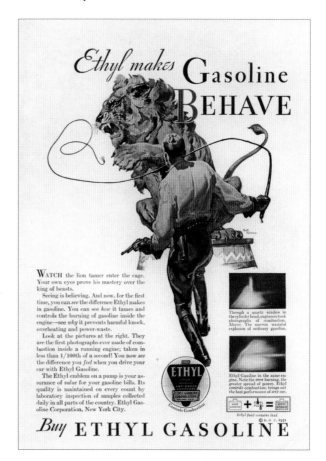

Lions, panthers, and jaguars were featured in British and French Exxon advertising from as far back as the 1930s. Pratt's Ethyl became Esso Ethyl in April 1935. Much of the inspiration seems to have been provided by a 1932 American Ethyl lion tamer advertisement. Exxon owned 50 percent of the Ethyl Corporation. The advertising reflected people's enjoyment of circus acts and the call of the untamed jungle. *Author collection*

Service with a Smile

TODAY WE GO TO A GAS STATION, serve ourselves, maybe buy a quart of milk, and count ourselves lucky if we get any change out of $30. Nobody under the age of thirty can even comprehend the fact that somebody actually served you gasoline, let alone wiped your windshield or checked under the hood. The idea that you could get your automobile serviced at a gas station is similar to recently being asked "What's a butcher?" by my niece. It's hard to believe now that any oil company would make clean restrooms a key reason for buying its gasoline, but it is exactly what happened during the 1930s and 1950s. Let's step back in time and capture a glimpse of the services provided to make the customer feel happy and return for more.

Unsung Hero

From the outset, pump attendants worked very long hours, often in ten- or twelve-hour shifts day or night, only had one rest day every two weeks, and were low paid and dependent on commissions from sales of motor oil or accessories.

Pump attendants were expected to have a good knowledge of automobiles' gas tank locations (with very early automobiles, gas tanks could be under the driver's seat, in the engine compartment, or at the rear), capacities, typical oil levels, tire pressures, and, above all, to be courteous, helpful, and capable of giving directions to lost motorists. Most oil companies forbade their pump attendants from crank-starting customers' automobiles simply because too many had suffered broken wrists or thumbs from the kickback of the crank. The pump attendant was expected to be resourceful and, if possible, capable of improvising a repair to get the motorist home or to a repair shop. This became less problematic with the introduction of super service stations in the early 1930s, especially with oil companies' preventative maintenance programs. In the United States, the vast majority of pump attendants were men, mainly because it was assumed that men had a better mechanical aptitude and also because of security. Gas station holdups were frequent during the Great Depression. Women gas pump attendants were a common sight during World War II because the men were fighting in the war. There were enterprising women who successfully ran gas stations across America. Mary Hudson ran a large chain of Hudson Oil cut-rate gas stations in the Midwest and along the eastern seaboard from the mid-1930s until the company filed for bankruptcy in 1984. In Europe, by contrast, women pump attendants were a common sight from the outset. By the early 1950s, they had specially tailored outfits rather than white dust coats.

National Supply Stations, a Los Angeles chain acquired by Chevron in 1914, was the first company to have uniformed staff in white outfits with black bow ties. Shell and most other West Coast retailers quickly introduced white uniforms, too. In the late 1930s, Shell introduced khaki uniforms. Pump attendant uniforms did not become common in the rest of the United States until the mid-1920s.

This changed with Texaco and Gulf's aggressive expansion and both oil companies' use of distinctive pump attendant uniforms as part of their respective corporate identities. Texaco's olive green uniform was as familiar as its red star logo and Denver-design gas stations. Gulf opted for a light brown outfit. Initially, the Texaco and Gulf uniforms consisted of dispatch rider breeches with boots and were widely copied by other oil companies, notably Atlantic Refining. The breeches and boots were later replaced in the

Chevron was the first oil company to introduce pump attendant uniforms with the acquisition of the National Supply Station chain in 1914. Apart from the addition of a flat cap with blue, white, and red diagonal stripes in the early 1930s, the white uniform remained unchanged for over fifty years. These pump attendants were photographed in San Marino, California, in March 1960. *Author collection*

mid-1930s with more practical trousers and shoes. Standard Oil of Indiana and Exxon used Casey Jones–style railroad blue and white striped overalls instead of the breeches and boots route. Exxon used these overalls worldwide up to 1966. Mobil used dark blue overalls with bright red lapels and collars throughout the 1930s. After World War II, Mobil followed Shell's example and moved over to khaki. Gas pump attendant uniforms were introduced across Europe after World War II, but dress code was never as rigidly enforced as in America, except at prestige company-owned sites. Most European pump attendants preferred to wear overalls or dust coats over their own clothes. AGIP, the Italian oil company, was the

exception. All AGIP pump attendants wore very striking light blue outfits that consisted of a baseball hat, light jacket, trousers, and a bright yellow shirt.

Oil companies were too well aware that the pump attendant was the key point of contact and could make or break an oil company's hard-earned reputation. During the early 1930s, American oil companies created on-the-job and correspondence course training schemes for customer forecourt service and lubrication bay servicing. These were later replaced by intensive three to five day residential courses that were initially held at bulk depots with mockup gas stations, but later they were held at special company-owned gas stations with classrooms attached. These courses could turn a semiskilled worker into a highly competent lubrication bay technician. All of these training schemes were put to very good use throughout Europe after World War II.

Gulf, Mobil, and Texaco ran full-color national advertising campaigns in the United States throughout the mid-1950s to the late 1960s to promoting their friendly, helpful, and resourceful pump attendants. Exxon, Mobil, Total (in France), and AGIP (in Italy) ran very similar campaigns during the early to mid-1960s. The widespread introduction of self-service across Europe during the early 1970s made pump attendants and forecourt service redundant (see Chapter 8). Inevitably, the same fate befell American gas stations within a decade, which was hastened by the aftershock of the 1973 and 1979 OPEC Oil Crises.

Check the Oil

On the West Coast, by 1917, it was an implicit part of a fill-up to have your windshield wiped and the oil and water levels and tire

The Texaco pump attendant's olive green uniform, featured in this 1929 advertisement, was a virtual trademark, guarantee of absolute consistency, and a welcome sight the length and breadth of the United States. The breeches and boots were later replaced by trousers and shoes. The pump attendant became a central feature of Texaco advertising in 1956 with the "Mr. Service" campaign, further emphasized by the 1960s advertising strapline, "Trust Your Car to the Man Who Wears the Texaco Star." *Author collection*

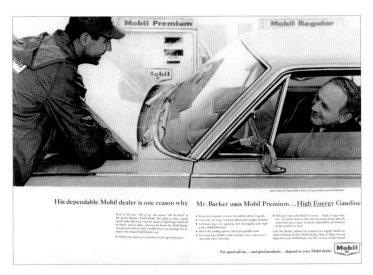

In 1964 and 1965, Mobil took the original and novel strategy of featuring actual, named customers with their Mobil dealers. The genuine rapport between the Mobil dealer and the customer confirmed that the Mobil dealer was as dependable as the advertising claimed. *Author collection*

pressures checked. This quickly caught on nationwide and was standard practice by the mid-1920s. There was, however, no standard or systematic procedure, and it depended entirely on who was performing the task.

By the early to mid-1930s, it was becoming increasingly difficult for motorists in America to differentiate between competing brands of gasoline due to more uniform refining methods, a blanket use of lead as an octane booster, and identical octane numbers. The same situation applied to motor oil with standardized Society of Automotive Engineers (SAE) viscosity ratings. American oil companies had to come up with new ways of creating brand loyalty and encouraging motorists to keep coming back.

Elaborate forecourt service became the new way for American oil companies to differentiate their brands from another. Shell was probably the first oil company to introduce Seven-Point Service, an elaborate step-by-step forecourt service procedure, in 1932. The seven steps are as follows.

1. *At the pump, greet your customer as he or she drives in.*
2. *Proceed with customer's gasoline order.*
3. *After wiping the rear window, stop light, and license plate, check stop light and rear tires.*
4. *Wipe right half of windshield and right side light.*
5. *Wipe headlights, inspect front tires, fill radiator, and wipe radiator cap and nickel on radiator.*
6. *Check oil and call customer's attention to visible mechanical defects.*
7. *Wipe left side of windshield and left side light; solicit chassis service; advise customer if tires need air; offer other courtesy services, such as battery water, etc; collect money; thank customer and invite him to call again; and offer customer Shell literature.*

Gulf advertised a similar procedure in its maps by 1933. Neither procedure would have been feasible without the electric gas pump. The widespread introduction of the electric gas pump, especially with a cash computer, in the United States during the early 1930s revolutionized forecourt sales. Customers began to purchase by value rather than volume and were more prepared to round up to the nearest dollar, which increased sales. The electric gas pump provided faster fill-ups, which gave the pump attendant more time to wipe the windshield, check the oil and radiator as well as the tire pressures. Texaco followed Shell and Gulf's initiative with a Texaco Service press campaign in 1934.

A key piece of state tax legislation very nearly put paid to oil companies' promotion of elaborate forecourt service. During the

The Mobilgas uniform was an eye-catching set of navy blue overalls with a bright red collar and lapels. Mobilgas adopted Shell's light khaki uniform after World War II, but returned to a navy blue outfit in the 1960s. *Author collection*

STOP! . . . Where you see the "ORANGE DISC," you will find courteous attendants and friendly, helpful service.

The GULF man knows the roads... and the city streets... He will gladly give you whatever information about them you require.

When you approach a city "in a hurry," and you want to know the shortest route through it . . . *Ask the Gulf Man!*

If you are tired and want to know the names and locations of the hotels or private homes where you can find tourist accommodations . . . *Ask the Gulf Man!*

If you seek entertainment or recreation . . . if you care to hunt, to fish, to swim, or to play golf . . . *Ask the Gulf Man!*

He may not have the answers to ALL your questions, but he will gladly give you the benefit of his own knowledge and experience. He is trustworthy, competent, and offers you the best of service. Don't hesitate to ask for directions and recommendations . . . *Ask the Gulf Man!*

Gulf was probably the first oil company to use maps to promote its pump attendants as courteous, helpful, and reliable sources of local tourist information, as seen here in this 1933 map. *Author collection*

Filled to the brim and change from a dollar. Pump attendants often wore coin dispensers on their belts to speed up transactions. Note the concentration on both men's faces as the tank was carefully filled to the brim. This was photographed in Missouri during the early 1940s. *Author collection*

BP, similar to most European oil companies, introduced specially tailored outfits for their French male and female pump attendants in the early 1950s. BP's version of Christian Dior's "New Look" was especially popular with women staff. *Author collection*

mid-1930s, many Midwest states introduced anti-chain-store taxes. These were designed to protect local independent businesses from the predatory pricing tactics of large national retailers, such as Woolworths, A&P supermarkets, and Rexall drugstores. Oil company gas stations were subject to this tax, as well. Standard Oil of Indiana responded in 1935 with the Iowa Plan. All Standard Oil of Indiana station managers became lessees and thus avoided the tax. Most oil companies in the Rocky Mountain region, the Midwest, and the eastern seaboard quickly copied Standard Oil of Indiana's leasing scheme, irrespective of whether anti-chain-store taxes prevailed in their territories or not. The exception was the West Coast, which was unaffected by chain-store taxes, and oil companies maintained direct control of their outlets. This may explain why Los Angeles was such a hothouse for new gas station designs. Elsewhere there was considerable variation in service, pricing, housekeeping, and presentation. Texaco and Mobil ran huge national double-page-spread two- and four-color press campaigns in the late 1930s that sold elaborate forecourt service and clean restrooms as explicit brand benefits. These campaigns shrewdly placed the burden on gas station lessees to improve their forecourt service and customer restrooms. Texaco's "Circle of Service" double-page-spread press campaign in 1937 promoted its forecourt service as an explicit brand benefit. Mobil responded swiftly with its "I like . . . " double-page-spread press

(Below) Esso pump attendants wore blue and white striped overalls, which were introduced in around 1930 and used worldwide until the mid-1960s. Esso obviously meant "Happy Motoring" judging by the smile on this dealer's face! The photograph was taken in North Carolina around 1940. *Author collection*

(Above) Women pump attendants were less common in the United States than in Europe, perhaps because of misplaced assumptions about their mechanical aptitude and concerns about safety. Holdups were common during the Great Depression. This photograph was taken during the late 1920s in New England. *Author collection*

(Right) Women pump attendants like Rosie the Riveter were a common sight during World War II. Chevron widely recruited women to replace men called up for military service, as seen here in California circa 1942. *Author collection*

campaign that sold both elaborate forecourt service and clean restrooms as key factors in brand loyalty and repeat business.

The pump attendant's life was made considerably easier with the introduction of the automatic shutoff-latch gas pump nozzle in the late 1940s. This enabled the pump attendant to wipe the windshield and check the fluid levels and tire pressures while the car was being filled with gasoline. A pressure sensor in the nozzle automatically shut off the flow of gasoline as soon as it detected blowback from the automobile's gas tank. Ironically, this same device paved the way for the large-scale development of self-service and the demise of the pump attendant.

Elaborate forecourt service was successfully introduced across Europe once electric gas pumps had come into widespread use in the mid-1950s, by which time it had also become virtually impossible for the European motorist to distinguish between international brands of gasoline due to uniform refining methods and blanket use of lead as an octane booster, just like in the United States during the mid-1930s.

"Mr. Service" in all 48 states

HE WILL HAVE TEXACO TOURING SERVICE SEND YOU FREE ROAD MAPS WITH ROUTES INDICATED AND THE LATEST HIGH-WAY INFORMATION

MIGHTY HANDY...CON-SERVES CASH—TEXACO IS THE ONLY CREDIT CARD HONORED UNDER ONE SIGN IN ALL 48 STATES—AND IN CANADA, TOO

CONVENIENCE YOU AND YOUR FAMILY WILL AP-PRECIATE. STOP WHERE YOU SEE THIS FAMILIAR GREEN AND WHITE SIGN—CLEAN ACROSS AMERICA!

FOR THE FINEST PETRO-LEUM PRODUCTS, TIRES, BATTERIES AND ACCESSO-RIES, COURTESY, AND THE BEST OF CARE FOR YOUR CAR—SEE "MR. SERVICE"

TEXACO DEALERS IN ALL 48 STATES
Texaco Products are also distributed in Canada and Latin America

Tour with Texaco

Gulf cares

about the little things that are important to *you*. And that goes for the things you *don't* see, too. Like the way Gulfpride Select motor oil guards your engine against wear. No other oil is so clear, so high in clean-working protection. And it won't break down even under the most severe driving conditions.

CLEARLY...THE WORLD'S FINEST MOTOR OIL.

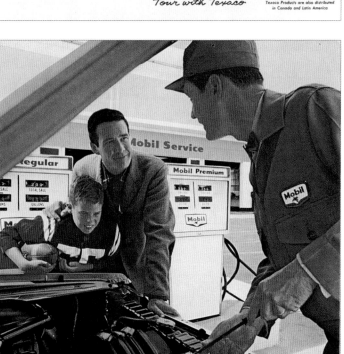

Mr. Kenneth H. McKinley gets a loose hose clamp tightened by the man who spotted it—his Mobil dealer in New Hyde Park, N.Y.

...and all he drove in for was a tankful of Mobil's High Energy Gasoline.

Mr. McKinley didn't know a loose hose clamp caused that "hissing sound." But his Mobil dealer did...and fixed it. Millions of motorists depend on Mobil dealers to spot little troubles which could otherwise lead to expensive repairs.

Mobil service is the kind *every* motorist should have this winter. The trained Mobil dealer can make vital checks of the fan belt, antifreeze level, and hose connections...watch your battery to maintain full operating power...check tire pressure and condition...put in easy starting Mobiloil Special...protect the chassis with high-grade Mobil lubricants...give you quick starts with Mobil's High Energy Gasoline...and recommend the extra convenience of a Mobil Credit Card.

For good advice... and good products ...depend on your Mobil dealer

Low Energy   High Energy

What is High Energy Gasoline? Mobil takes straight-run gasoline—the basic product all refiners start with—and further refines it so that light, low-energy atom groups are replaced by huskier, high-energy atom groups. Result: more power...more power for hills, for passing, and the economy of long mileage.

(Top left) In 1956, Texaco made a subtle shift in its advertising by making pump attendants and dealers the focal point. The emphasis was now placed on the pump attendant as a warm, caring, helpful individual. This set a trend for the next ten years, which was widely copied by other United States and European oil companies. *Author collection*

(Above) Gulf quickly responded with its slick, superbly presented "Gulf Cares" campaign. The chief drawback of this campaign was presentation over substance. Everything was too perfect. The people were too good-looking and the color-coordinated clothes and automobiles were beyond belief. It simply did not relate to reality. *Author collection*

(Left) Mobil took a dramatically different approach with a brilliant national advertising campaign in 1964 and 1965 that featured actual customers at their local Mobil gas stations. Every reader could relate to the natural human warmth that underlined the Mobil dealer's dependability. *Author collection*

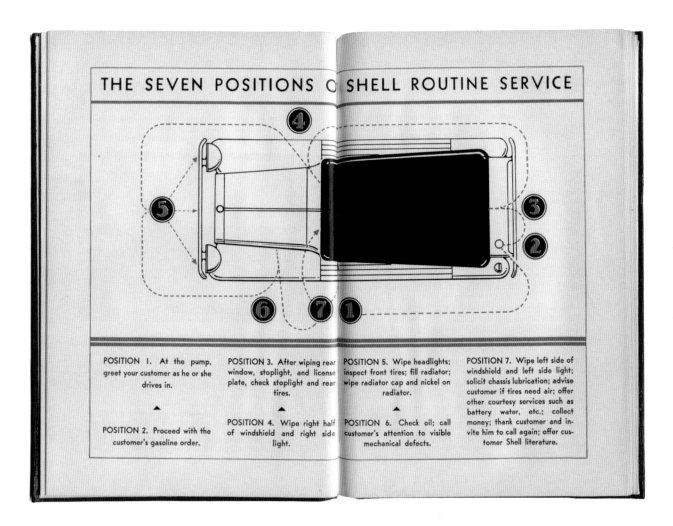

THE SEVEN POSITIONS OF SHELL ROUTINE SERVICE

POSITION 1. At the pump, greet your customer as he or she drives in.

POSITION 2. Proceed with the customer's gasoline order.

POSITION 3. After wiping rear window, stoplight, and license plate, check stoplight and rear tires.

POSITION 4. Wipe right half of windshield and right side light.

POSITION 5. Wipe headlights; inspect front tires; fill radiator; wipe radiator cap and nickel on radiator.

POSITION 6. Check oil; call customer's attention to visible mechanical defects.

POSITION 7. Wipe left side of windshield and left side light; solicit chassis lubrication; advise customer if tires need air; offer other courtesy services such as battery water, etc.; collect money; thank customer and invite him to call again; offer customer Shell literature.

Shell's salesmanship manual introduced the first systematic, step-by-step forecourt service procedure in 1932, which quickly became known as Seven-Point Service. This was made possible by the widespread introduction of the electric gas pump, which sped up refueling and gave the pump attendant more time. Prior to this, forecourt service was haphazard and entirely dependent on the individual concerned. *Author collection*

Freshly Greased and Laundered

By the early 1920s, most American gas stations offered a crankcase or oil-change service using either outside oil drain pits or wooden ramps. Oil changes provided lucrative, repeat business for gas stations since 1920s automobiles required oil changes every 500 miles, as well as in spring for a thicker summer grade of oil and in late fall for a thinner winter grade. Greasing was a hit or miss affair with the motorist turning the automobile grease cups a couple of turns every week or so in the hope the bearings would last. In the mid-1920s, high-pressure greasing was introduced, which guaranteed complete and lasting lubrication. At the same time, the hydraulic hoist was launched. It was a safer and more practical alternative to the outside drain pit and enabled more thorough grease penetration with the automobile wheels and springs slackened off. There were a number of specialist lubritorium, lubriservatory, or lubritory businesses in the Midwest that offered high-pressure greasing and oil changes in purpose-built

structures that consisted of either a series of bays with hoists or a drive-through assembly line.

Sinclair is credited as the first major oil company to introduce super service stations with enclosed lubrication bays, known as "greasing palaces," with gasoline forecourts in the late 1920s in the Midwest. The reasons for this can only be surmised, but the Midwest gasoline market was extremely competitive in the late 1920s. Standard Oil of Indiana had the exclusive Midwest franchise for the new high-octane ethyl gasoline additive, which put it at an immediate advantage over two highly aggressive newcomers, Shell and Texaco, who were going for growth almost at the expense of profit. Sinclair's lateral move into high-profit, value-added greasing was both shrewd and prescient. Standard Oil of Indiana, Diamond, Texaco, Sohio, and White Star immediately followed Sinclair's example and introduced super service stations in the Midwest. Super service stations were subsequently introduced nationwide during the early 1930s. Major oil companies were quick to realize that the initial high-capital investment could be quickly repaid with value-added services, such as greasing, oil changes, washing, and tire/battery sales, and could compensate for any losses on gasoline sales during the Great Depression. Exxon, in particular, invested very heavily in a chain of Servicenters along the eastern seaboard, especially in Baltimore, Philadelphia, Pittsburgh, New Jersey, and New York during the early 1930s to maintain its market leadership and earn some badly needed profits.

In 1929, the Atlas Supply Company, a jointly owned organization, was established to source and supply tires, accessories, and, in 1931, batteries for Chevron, Standard Oil of Indiana, Standard Oil of Nebraska (an affiliate of Standard Oil of Indiana), Standard Oil of Kentucky (later acquired by Chevron), Sohio, Exxon, and Colonial Beacon (just acquired by Exxon). Colonial Beacon had noted the growth in tire sales by mail-order houses, such as Sears

Roebuck and J.C. Penney, and successfully introduced tire sales at some of its gas stations. Texaco, Shell, Gulf, and Mobil quickly followed suit but sold Goodyear, Firestone, Goodrich, or similar-brand tires. The gas station had now become a convenient "one-stop shop" with lubrication/wash bays and tire and battery sales. The Sinclair greasing palace design set the pattern for American and, especially after World War II, international gas station design for the next forty years.

Most oil-company-owned gas stations in France and Germany during the 1930s provided oil changes and high-pressure greasing. These services were provided outdoors on hydraulic hoists, mainly because an automobile on top of a raised hoist was such an eye-catching advert. Moons, one London chain of gas stations, always placed its hydraulic hoists in the most prominent position on the forecourt. Exxon was the exception in France with a chain of company-owned gas stations that contained semienclosed greasing bays (similar in style to the Sinclair castle design) parallel with the refueling islands (see Chapter

Texaco ran this low-key campaign in the May 1934 issue of *National Geographic* magazine. To all intents and purposes, it was a direct copy of Gulf's 1933 map advertisement. Unlike Gulf, Texaco could guarantee quality service and products from coast to coast. *Author collection*

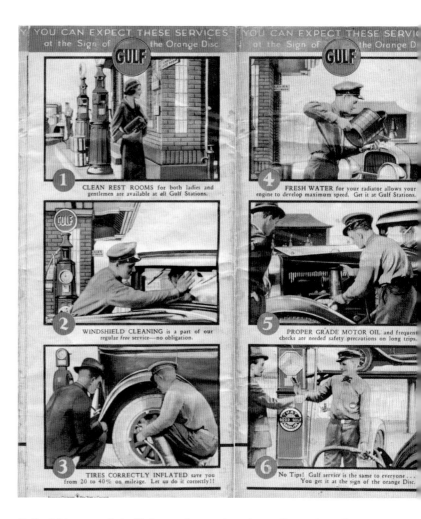

Gulf quickly responded with its own forecourt service routine and was the first oil company to promote clean restrooms as a customer benefit, as shown in this 1933 map. Gulf pump attendants always had an excellent word-of-mouth reputation for courtesy and service, but this was the first time they were promoted as brand benefits. *Author collection*

7). The French design bore no relation to Exxon's American designs of the same period and was far less practical.

Texaco heavily advertised its Certified Lubrication service in the United States during the early 1930s (changed to "Marfak" in the late 1930s), and Shell responded on the West Coast with its sophisticated Shellubrication preventative maintenance program in 1935. Shell demonstrated that regular, systematic lubrication with comprehensive inspections and adjustments could actually extend the life of key components, such as the battery, and the automobile as a whole. Shell effectively poached highly profitable automobile servicing business from franchised automobile dealers and set a trend that would prevail until the late 1960s.

The American super service station model was introduced across Europe in the early 1950s by Exxon and very quickly copied by all the major oil companies. Except in Germany and

(Above) Texaco raised the forecourt service stakes with this emphatic advertisement in November 1937, which set the standard for the next thirty-five years. The motorist knew exactly what to expect each time he or she visited a Texaco gas station. It was a clever means of forcing Texaco lessees and dealer/operators to raise their standards. *Author collection*

(Below) Mobilgas responded in May 1938 with its " I Like . . . " campaign, which featured a typical customer and spelling out what he or she liked about Mobilgas service. As with Texaco, Mobilgas placed the burden on dealer/operators or lessees to improve its service. *Author collection*

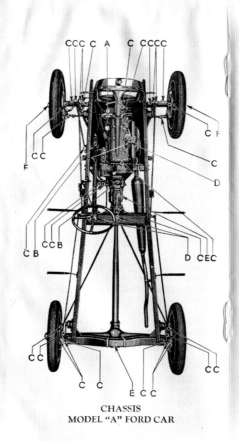

MODEL "A" CHASSIS LUBRICATION CHART

A. Sinclair OPALINE Motor Oil in accordance with Recommendation Index

B. Sinclair OPALINE Pressure System Grease every 2000 miles (pressure gun)

C. Sinclair OPALINE Pressure System Grease every 500 miles (pressure gun)

D. Sinclair OPALINE Motor Oil every 500 miles

E. Sinclair OPALINE Gear Lubricant every 5000 miles

F. Sinclair OPALINE Pressure System Grease. Pack every 5000 miles

CHASSIS
MODEL "A" FORD CAR

SINCLAIR RECOMMENDATION INDEX

FOR MODEL "A" FORD CARS

	After 1,000 to 2,000 Miles	After (*) 10,000 to 12,000 Miles
New Engine		
Opaline Medium Heavy	Heavy	Ex. Heavy

FOR MODEL "AA" FORD TRUCKS

	After 500 to 1,000 Miles	After (*) 7,000 to 9,000 Miles
New Engine		
Opaline Medium Heavy	Heavy	Ex. Heavy

*Unless new pistons are installed or rings refitted

Sinclair was the first major oil company to introduce service buildings with integral greasing or lubrication bays (depicted in this Midwest photograph from about 1928) and set the pattern for the next forty-five years. Greasing and ancillary services like car washes and tire and battery sales were highly profitable and compensated for minimal gasoline profits or losses during the Great Depression. *Author collection*

Socony General, the western division of Mobil, introduced its own certified lubrication service in 1932. Most oil companies invested heavily in education programs that could turn a semiskilled worker into a competent lubrication bay technician with three to five days of intensive training. *Author collection*

Scandinavia, the canopy disappeared (see Chapter 10) from European stations.

In 1950, Mobil took Shell's sophisticated Shellubrication preventative maintenance program one stage further and introduced the highly successful Mobilgas Grand Canyon Run, which was an adaptation of the Gilmore Economy Run that had been a yearly event on the West Coast between 1936 and 1941 (Gilmore was acquired by Mobil in 1945). The Mobilgas Economy Run, as it was subsequently known, demonstrated how excellent fuel economy could be achieved with careful, alert driving, and, most importantly, a well-maintained automobile. A free booklet showed how poorly adjusted brakes, dirty spark plugs, and low tire pressures could increase fuel consumption, while a good service and tune-up at your Mobilgas dealer would deliver better fuel economy. Strangely, there was little emphasis in the booklet on Mobilgas/Mobilgas Special gasolines' technical benefits. Effectively, the Mobilgas dealer was repositioned more as a car maintenance specialist and less as a gasoline vendor. The Mobilgas Economy Run became an annual event in the United States and Europe and gained tremendous third-party publicity from automobile manufacturers, particularly Ford, who had won the annual event or came first in its class. Texaco responded in the mid-1950s with national full-color press campaigns that promoted its comprehensive preventative program (see Chapter 2).

By the mid-1960s, oil companies had become the victims of their own success. The widespread use of multigrade oil with a

Forecourt service was adopted throughout Europe after World War II. In this 1963 Italian AGIP advertisement, the copy reads as follows: "AGIP Service: four operations in two minutes. Check the oil and water levels, check the tire pressures, clean the windows, and fill up with Supercortemaggiore, the powerful Italian gasoline." *Author collection*

Texaco unveiled its "Certified Lubrication" service in 1932, complete with an annotated certificate, to provide the customer with an absolute assurance that every lubrication requirement had been fulfilled. This reinforced Texaco's reputation as a dependable brand. *Author collection*

Shell outflanked Texaco in 1935 with its comprehensive Shellubrication program of checks and adjustments that extended the life of key components, such as the battery and the automobile itself. Shell effectively poached highly profitable automobile servicing from franchise dealers and created a precedent quickly followed by other oil companies. *Author collection*

The Mobilgas Economy Run was an instant hit with its emphasis on good vehicle maintenance and careful driving. It was a key part of Mobil's marketing for over fifteen years. *Author collection*

This 1951 Mobilgas booklet placed greater emphasis on the Mobilgas dealer as an automobile maintenance expert rather than as a vendor of high quality gasoline. *Author collection*

comprehensive additive package reduced oil consumption, extended the period between oil changes, and did away with seasonal oil changes. Greasing had virtually been eliminated by permanently sealed bearings or nylon bushes. Overnight, the lubrication bay had lost its reason for existence.

Another nail in the coffin for gas station automobile maintenance was the 1966–1967 U.S. federal government automobile pollution control/enhanced safety legislation that became progressively tougher between 1970 and 1975. This forced automobile manufacturers to issue stringent automobile warranties that were rendered invalid if the automobile was serviced by an unauthorized/nonfranchise repair shop. This reduced the amount of profitable automobile servicing business for gas stations.

The widespread introduction of self-service in Europe during the early 1970s required larger forecourts for more efficient refueling and greater through traffic. Service bays had to be torn down

With the largest gas station network in Europe, Esso had more technical experience with servicing European automobiles than any other United States oil company. Most European automobile manufacturers recommended Esso lubricants. This advertisement appeared in September 1959. *Author collection*

Texaco responded by presenting its dealers as skilled troubleshooters, well-trained mechanics, and above all, preventative maintenance experts. This campaign ran from November 1957 through June 1958. The Mobilgas and Texaco 1950s marketing campaigns were direct continuations of the 1935 Shellubrication campaign and confirmed the gas station's transition from a product vendor to a service provider. *Author collection*

YOU CAN EXPECT THESE SERVICES at the Sign of GULF the Orange Disc

1

CLEAN REST ROOMS for both ladies and gentlemen are available at *all* Gulf Stations.

A map advertisement from 1933 confirmed that Gulf was the first oil company in 1933 to promote its clean restrooms as an explicit brand benefit. The Great Depression forced oil companies to use every means possible to attract new customers and retain them. *Author collection*

Every Motoring Family will applaud: "REGISTERED" REST ROOMS

Pledged neat and clean from coast-to-coast by the men who supply "Fire-Chief" for your car

TEXACO DEALERS

Texaco followed Gulf's example and launched its Registered Rest Rooms in April 1938 with a massive full-color magazine campaign aimed at mothers with children. Customers had the reassurance of regular inspections by the Texaco White Patrol confirmed by certificates and availability in all forty-eight states. *Author collection*

to make the maximum use of available space. Inevitably, American service bays disappeared in the late 1970s and early 1980s, with the nationwide conversion to self-service.

Flushed with Pride

Customer restrooms have always been an implicit part of a gas station's service and layout. Weary long-distance travelers look to the gas station for refreshment and relief. Texaco was probably the first oil company to incorporate restrooms in its gas station design of 1918 (refer to the Atlanta, Georgia photograph in Chapter 1). One entire side of the station complex, facing the pumps and the sales office, contained men's and women's restrooms: a very extravagant use of space. It quickly became standard practice to place the women's restroom at the side of the sales building cordoned off by a lattice screen, while the men's restroom was entered via the sales office. On the West Coast, it was more common to have a separate restroom complex on the far side of the forecourt.

It was one thing to provide a facility, and it was quite another to ensure it was clean and fully equipped with toilet paper, paper towels, and soap. American and British trade publications during the 1920s constantly told gas station dealers their restrooms were a very poor reflection on their reputations. Oil companies were increasingly aware that women, while not always in the driving seat, often decided where to stop. Texaco was probably the first oil company to exploit this. By 1928, Texaco was the first oil company to sell gasoline in all forty-eight states and therefore guarantee consistent, predictable quality nationwide. It ran full-color nationwide campaigns in general interest and women's magazines that featured young, successful, preppy couples. While the husband needed a reliable gasoline for his Packard, his wife wanted predictably clean restrooms. "We know what to expect at Texaco. Why go anywhere else?" McDonalds, the hamburger chain, has pursued exactly same philosophy over the past thirty-five years with phenomenal success.

Oil companies became less reticent about advertising clean restrooms in the early 1930s, not in the least because they desperately needed to find new ways of getting and retaining customers during the Great Depression. Gulf promoted clean restrooms under the banner headline: "You Can Expect These Services at the Sign of the Orange Disc" in its 1933 maps, which took up a third of one section of the map cover. By 1935, this became even more explicit with the whole back cover of the Gulf map: "En Route, Clean Restrooms Can Be Identified . . . by This Sign." Meanwhile, in 1933, Exxon emphasized the importance of clean restrooms, especially for women, as a means of building repeat business in their training booklets. Texaco used a photograph of a mother and daughter walking towards a restroom as part of a Texaco Service advertising campaign in 1934.

(Right) Texaco advertised its Registered Rest Rooms heavily between 1938 and 1941, mainly with two-color advertisements. It refreshed its campaign in 1941 with this stylish four-color advertisement. *Author collection*

(Far right) Texaco revived its highly successful pre–World War II "Registered Rest Rooms" campaign in July 1952 with this equally stylish advertisement, naturally featuring the key target market: women with children. Texaco continued to advertise its Registered Rest Rooms in various formats up to 1958. *Author collection*

Shell responded quickly in June 1938 with its "White Cross of Cleanliness" campaign with an endorsement by a prominent women's club public health activist, Mrs. Marjorie B. Illig. Mobilgas had already responded in May 1938 with its "I Like . . ." campaign. Phillips 66 quickly got in on the act, too, with women inspectors dressed up as nurses. *Author collection*

Mobilgas launched its restroom campaign featuring a mother and daughter in 1952. Mobilgas introduced a triple-blue-square clean restrooms logo that was advertised throughout 1953 in small two-color bookend advertisements in 1952. *Author collection*

Clean restrooms began to be heavily promoted to women as an explicit brand benefit in 1937, particularly by Texaco, which reached a crescendo in 1938 with its "Registered Rest Room" full-color, double-page-spread national campaign. Mobil responded immediately but with a more discreet "I Like . . ." campaign. Shell replied with a White Cross of Cleanliness clean restroom campaign, complete with an endorsement by Mrs. Marjorie B. Illig, chairman of the Division of Public Health of the General Federation of Women's Clubs from 1935 to 1938. All the advertising featured women as the key beneficiaries. Texaco continued to heavily promote its Registered Rest Rooms until early 1941. Texaco and Mobil both reintroduced heavy national full-color press campaigns for restrooms in America during the early 1950s, again featuring mothers and daughters. Texaco persisted with its "Registered Rest Rooms" campaign up to 1958. From then on, clean restrooms were an integral but discreet part of all oil company service campaigns, apart from a 1962 Union 76 "Sparkle Corps" campaign that featured women restroom inspectors dressed like air hostesses, and a similar 1968 Gulf campaign that featured a woman inspector in an air hostess uniform. Restrooms were provided by all European gas stations from the 1920s on, but were never used as the key part of a marketing campaign. Sadly, by the late 1960s, American gas station restrooms were taken for granted and abused, particularly in urban areas, by drug dealers, drug addicts, or thieves. Women were particularly vulnerable at night. Gas stations began to keep the restroom doors locked and supplied the keys only to bonafide customers. This was finally resolved by moving customer restrooms inside and putting them next to the sales office, so a member of the staff could keep an eye out for undesirable patrons.

Tour with Confidence

Free road maps have always been treated as an implicit part of the service provided by a gas station. What casually started out with pump attendants giving directions to lost motorists quickly grew into an essential part of an oil company's range of services. Oil company and tire manufacturers' guides and maps date back just over one hundred years and first originated in Europe. The celebrated Guide Michelin, published by the French tire manufacturer, is now best known as a superb restaurant and hotel guide. It actually started life in 1900 as a guide to stockists of canned gasoline across France. Within four to five years, similar guides were issued in Germany by Dapolin (Exxon) and Pratt's (later Exxon) in Great Britain. Between 1904 and 1909, Mex (later merged with Shell) and Pratt's issued A5-size map books that illustrated main routes in Great Britain. The maps were fairly rudimentary but more practical than the very large, extremely detailed British Government Ordnance Survey maps. The books had a lot of space for gasoline and related product advertising that Pratt's used to full advantage.

The first American oil company road maps were issued free of charge by Gulf in 1914 and Atlantic Refining in 1916. These were pretty basic and, particularly in the case of Atlantic, were designed more as a means of locating a gasoline outlet than a travel guide per se. As previously mentioned, American roads at this time were notoriously bad and often impassable in winter or during the spring thaw. Oil company maps were only as good as the routes they outlined and did not become the intricate detailed items that we know today until the 1930s when American roads considerably improved. Gulf maps went through a subtle change from

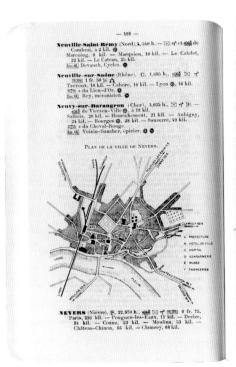
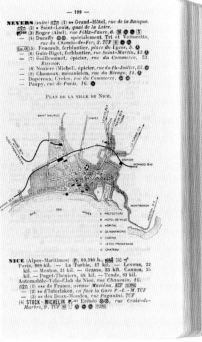

(Left two images) The Guide Michelin was created in 1900 as a free guide to those who stocked canned gasoline across France. Michelin, the French tire manufacturer, later transformed its guide into the now celebrated gastronomic authority. Michelin maps were renowned for their accuracy so much that facsimile copies were issued to the U.S. Army for the D-Day invasion of France in June 1944. *Author collection*

1917 on and became travel brochures with photographs or illustrations showing a region's key tourist or sport attractions.

Most oil companies began to issue free road maps in the mid- to late 1920s, particularly after the U.S. government came up with a system of routes in 1926 denoted by number rather than by name, and the odd-numbered roads went north and south and even-numbered roads traveled east and west. In addition to supplying free road maps, Exxon and Socony (Mobil) issued free tourist guides from 1925 on. Exxon issued a series of booklets entitled "Know Your Own State" that were full of state history, places of interest to visit, and good maps. Socony published a lavish four-color booklet entitled "Historic Tours in Soconyland" for New York and New England. This was more a romantic evocation of an illustrious past than a practical guide. Both sets of booklets contained detailed lubrication guides and product information. Exxon, known as Esso from June 1933 on, gained an enviable word-of-mouth reputation for its highly accurate maps, tourism/route planning service, and regular travel updates provided free of charge. This reinforced Esso's image as a dependable brand and undoubtedly increased gasoline sales. Shell-Mex & BP in Great Britain took note of Socony and Esso's efforts and introduced the iconic Shell Guides in the mid-1930s. The Shell Guides were edited by the poet John Betjemin, among others, and contained illustrations by renowned British artists, such as Rex Whistler, John Piper, Graham Sutherland, and Paul Nash. The Shell Guides had no product advertising but were a constant reminder to the discerning motorist which gasoline he or she should buy. It was perhaps not by coincidence that Shell had the largest share of the British gasoline market.

Gulf was probably the first oil company to use its maps to promote its courteous and helpful pump attendants, elaborate forecourt service, and clean restrooms. Other oil companies quickly followed Gulf's example and promoted their lubrication service, range of tires, and credit cards in their maps. By the early to mid-1930s, American oil company road map covers became artwork in their own right, much like celebrated rock music album record covers from the late 1960s and early 1970s. Sinclair, Exxon, Chevron, Associated/Flying A, and Richfield, among others, produced some wonderful two- and four-color designs that are now highly prized by collectors.

Texaco promoted its maps as an integral part of its comprehensive service in the mid-1950s. Gulf and American/Amoco pursued similar campaigns in the mid- to late 1960s. Throughout the 1960s, Mobil advertised its travel guide, which provided an impartial and comprehensive list of good hotels and motels in the United States. The Mobil travel guide had an excellent reputation among motorists and did wonders for Mobil's image.

Folded oil company maps were equally popular in Europe from the early 1930s on and replaced A5-size booklets or post-card-size sets of maps, but the motorist had to buy them at the gas station. After World War II, Exxon set up a European tourist advice center in Paris, France, which handled all of Exxon's European itinerary requests, which curiously were supplied free of charge. Applicants received a set of maps, with Exxon's suggested routes highlighted with an orange felt-tip pen, and an appropriate phrase book. This high level of service and attention to detail allied with an absolutely consistent brand image/gas station design made Exxon the market leader in Europe during the 1950s.

The 1973 OPEC Oil Crisis forced international oil companies to examine the cost-effectiveness of all their activities. Exxon's European tourist service was the first victim, and by the early 1980s, the free road map had become a thing of the past in the United States.

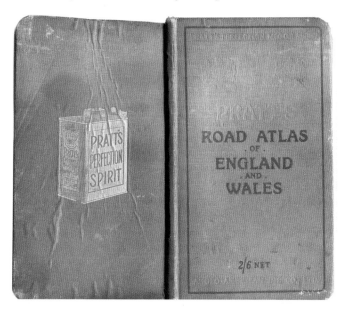

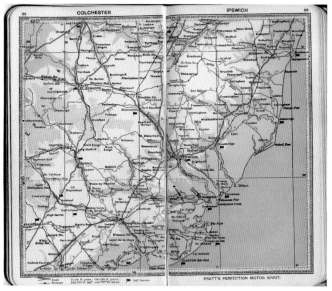

Pratt's, the British affiliate of Exxon, first issued road atlases in 1904 and 1905. This is an updated edition from 1915 and cost two shillings and six-pence, roughly equivalent to $1.50 at today's prices. The maps were fairly basic, 6 miles to the inch, but more convenient than the highly detailed British Government Ordnance Survey maps. *Author collection*

Gulf was the first United States oil company to issue free road maps in 1914, as shown in this 1934 Gulf corporate advertisement. Free maps created customer goodwill and repeat purchase. They were quickly copied by other oil companies, notably Atlantic Refining, and set a pattern for the next sixty years. Early examples of Gulf maps are extremely rare and highly sought after and often sell for well in excess of $75. *Author collection*

STANDARD

KNOW YOUR OWN STATE

VIRGINIA

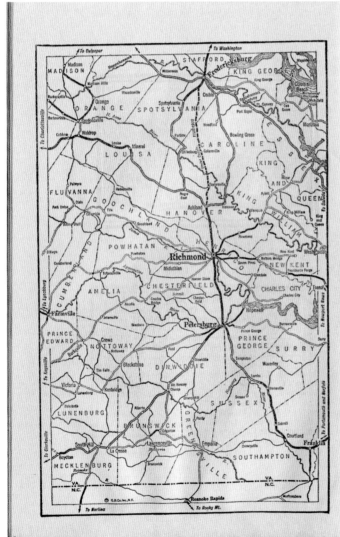

were defeated by the Governor, and "Bacon's Rebellion," a forerunner of the Revolution, was over.

Our next stop is Petersburg, the "Cockade City" around which centered much fighting during the Civil War. Even in Revolutionary days Petersburg was battle scarred, for the British captured it in 1781 but were driven out when Lafayette shelled the town.

Near Petersburg the Blandford Church, founded in 1734, should be visited. It is now a Confederate Memorial. Here too are the graves of some thirty thousand Confederate soldiers who fell in the Petersburg campaign. There are also national cemeteries at City Point and at Poplar Grove.

At Petersburg you can still see the scene of one of the bloodiest episodes of the Civil War—the "crater" which was formed when a Confederate fortification was mined. This operation still stands as one of the greatest pieces of military mining even though the attacking Federal troops who poured into the crater were cut down by thousands.

"Violet Bank," near Petersburg, General Lee's first headquarters

19

In 1925, Standard Oil of New Jersey (Exxon), issued a series of "Know Your Own State" booklets throughout its marketing territory. Each booklet contained the state's history, places to visit, good maps, practical tips for trouble-free touring, and product information. Exxon later developed a comprehensive tourist advice and route planning service. The maps had an excellent word-of-mouth reputation for accuracy. *Author collection*

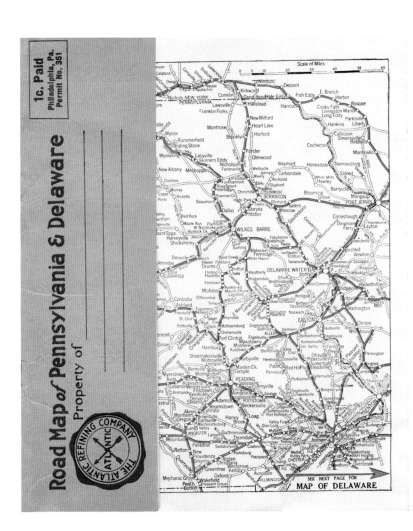

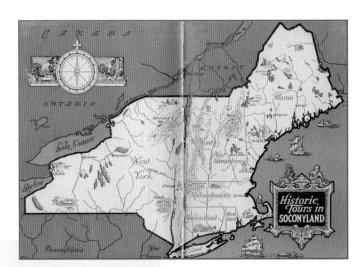

Atlantic Refining quickly followed Gulf's example and issued its own free maps in 1916. This example was for Pennsylvania and Delaware, which also listed all the Atlantic stations in the area. It was pretty rudimentary with a scale of just over 20 miles to 1 inch. Roads in the United States at this time were notoriously bad, often impassable in winter or spring, and poorly signposted. This map was published by the Automobile Blue Book Publishing Company, the leading road map publisher of the time. *Author collection*

Buried Treasure

Long Island

FROM New London, a ferry for automobiles connects with Greenport, Long Island. Just off Greenport lies Gardiner's Island, seat of the manorial home of Lyon Gardiner, the first sturdy Englishman to begin that westward encroachment into the territory of the Dutch Colony of New Netherlands. The Gardiner of Captain Kidd's day was a friend of the buccaneer; and of all the tales of the lost treasure of Captain Kidd, the most likely is that which tells of its burial on Gardiner's Island by the consent of the Manor Lord.

This was probably the first English settlement within the present boundaries of New York State.

Nestling behind Shelter Island, which is most appropriately so named, and on an offshoot of Gardiner's Bay lies Sag Harbor, one of the few New York towns which divided with their New England sisters at least a part of the glory of the old whaling days. A number of little stone houses bear silent though eloquent testimony to the fact that their former owners shared the

Along Long Island

Socony (Mobil) issued its "Historic Tours of Soconyland" booklet that covered New York and New England in the same year as Standard Oil of New Jersey issued its own booklet. Socony's booklet was very lavish with full-color illustrations but far less informative or practical than the "Know Your Own State" booklet. *Author collection*

To see America best, see your Mobil dealer first

Need special accommodations? Weekly rates? A kitchenette? Your Mobil dealer can help you find them. He's trained to take the guesswork out of travel.

From the best restaurant to the best route... whatever your need, thousands of Mobil dealers are trained to help. Here's what they can do for you:

Your one-man Travel Center. With the new 1965 Mobil Travel Guide, your Mobil dealer can give you frank quality ratings on over 20,000 hotels, motels, and restaurants. Facts on service, values and prices...to help budget your trip. Help with information about baby sitters, coin-laundries, sight-seeing, even spe-

cial facilities for children and pets.

Help with routes. He can provide you with reliable, easy-to-road Mobil maps. Or, by ordering special maps showing the best fast or scenic route to your destination.

Provide local information. The Mobil dealer knows his area...it's part of his training. He knows landmarks, places of worship, recreation areas...even emergency information.

Let you "Charge It." A Mobil Credit Card lets you charge many high-quality Mobil

products and services including tires, lubricants, batteries, and Mobil Premium... High Energy Gasoline. It's good at any Mobil station. Let Mobil be your Travel Guide.

For good advice...and good products ...depend on your Mobil dealer

Mobil

NEW JERSEY-NEW YORK EDITION

Esso ROAD NEWS and DETOUR MAP

Compliments of Your Esso Dealer ➡

JUNE, 1951 — Published by Esso Standard Oil Company

CORNING GLASS DEDICATES MUSEUM; STOKES STATE FOREST PLACE TO PLAY

$3,000,000 Display Center Now Open

A top-flight attraction on the New York State touring scene is the brand-new $3,000,000 Corning Glass Center and Museum at Corning, N. Y., just opened in observance of the Corning Glass Works' first hundred years of glassmaking.

Behind this new museum's glistening glass walls visitors for the first time can watch the intricate processes by which Corning's famous Steuben glass products are made. And, in addition, the new center combines the world's largest glass reference library and a museum with a matchless display.

From comfortable lounge chairs in the visitors' galleries, you can

Vast Vacation Area Nicely Developed

A modest, frame building off Route S-31 some 5 miles west of Branchville, N.J., is the open sesame to the vast recreational area of Stokes State Forest in northwest Sussex County. It houses forest headquarters where you can get the lowdown on what to do in its 12,429 acres astride the Kittatinny Range.

Lake Ocquittunk is as good a place as any to start your explorations. On a small peninsula along its southern shore is a sandy bathing beach, bathhouse and picnic area.

Around its shores are vacation cabins—very much in demand but available to those who can make

FUTURE MOTORIST REDUCES ON THE B

Which suggests that you too, Mr. Motorist, would from a trip to the seashore, the lakes or the mou

---

(Above) Mobil promoted its highly regarded travel guide in 1965 as an ancillary part of the excellent "Depend on Your Mobil Dealer" campaign featuring actual customers. *Author collection*

1930 "STANDARD" ROAD MAP OF PENNSYLVANIA

Published by STANDARD OIL COMPANY OF PENNSYLVANIA

Your Route to Happy Motoring

Whether you are looking forward to a leisurely ramble through a pleasant countryside, sightseeing tour through many states, or a quick trip to your destination over the shortest possible route, Happy Motoring means carefree driving.

YOUR ROUTE
Esso Touring Service is glad to send these maps marked with the best route for the enjoyment of your individual trip. This selection is based on mileage, road conditions, and general attractiveness. These symbols were used in marking your maps:

◯ Starting point, destination, or desired stop en route.

✗ Construction avoided in selecting your route.

‖ Construction on your route; see paragraph following.

CONSTRUCTION
The condition of construction work varies from day to day, but the time when such work always meant a rough and muddy detour is past. Construction is now carried on with constant thought for the motorist and every effort is made to maintain traffic under the best possible conditions. Any work you encounter when following this marked route will not cause you serious delay or inconvenience.

MILEAGES
A key to distances between towns, numbers, and much other helpful

...is on each of your Esso maps. Mileages in larger cities can be easily special mileage charts.

MMODATIONS
symbols shown on the maps lations of cities and towns (1940 Census) 000 to 25,000 ⊕ 2,500 to 5,000 ⊙ 500 to 1,000 000 to 10,000 ⊙ 1,000 to 2,500 ⊙ Under 500

glance the approximate size of any n is helpful in planning stops for meals dging.

Esso Touring Service makes no ons, but the enclosed pamphlet plus local help you select accommodations in each ch will be best suited sonal taste.

"OF INTEREST"
motorists get increased pleasure in touring by food specialties of local fame and various types ommodations. Change and novelty are often the things that live longest in our memories of a motor trip. ded enjoyment also comes from visiting places of interest along the way. The locations of many f these are shown on Esso maps and illustrated in Esso pictorial guides.

Esso TOURING SERVICE *Happy Motoring!*
PLEASE MAIL ME **FREE** ROAD MAPS SPECIALLY MARKED WITH BEST ROUTE
FROM_____ TO_____
I EXPECT TO START _____
I WANT DIRECT ROUTE ☐ OR SCENIC ROUTE FOR PLEASURE ☐
ADDRESS_____
CITY_____ STATE_____

(Upper right and above two images) Exxon had a superb reputation for its comprehensive travel service that ranged from road maps, regularly updated bulletins with detours, and individually tailored travel itineraries. *Author collection*

By the 1950s, oil company maps were virtually identical in format and content. Gulf's maps were made by Rand McNally. *Author collection*

Throughout the 1960s and early 1970s, oil company map formats remained unchanged. The only external changes were for new logos or brand imaging. Sunoco maps were published by H. M. Gousha. *Author collection*

Gulf maps rapidly improved in detail, thanks to better road designations by number rather than name, which was introduced by the U.S. government in 1926. Other influences were major road improvements implemented by the Roosevelt administration in the 1930s and, most significantly, tough competition from Shell and Exxon. *Author collection*

(Far left two images) Shell's highly detailed four-color maps put Gulf's maps to shame, even more so with its 1939 New York World's Fair map and a Tour Tips Guide. Shell switched to a yellow front cover in 1940 and 1941, and after World War II, adopted the service station color scheme of cream with red wainscoting and a yellow pinstripe for its maps. Shell's map application forms provided potential credit card customers and leads for dealers. *Author collection*

4

Come Back Soon

EVERYONE IS FAMILIAR WITH CLIPPING COUPONS for the week's special offer at Wal-Mart, Rite Aid, Walgreens, Sears, or A&P. Manufacturers and retailers alike provide these special offers to guarantee more frequent repeat purchases.

Gas stations and oil companies have used similar inducements over the past eighty years to encourage customer loyalty and more frequent purchases. In the early 1900s, grocers and garages allowed local customers to purchase gasoline on credit and settle their credit accounts monthly by check. Credit sales guaranteed repeat customers and greater sales. Oil companies later followed exactly the same principle and introduced credit cards in the mid-1930s. Cash customers were always best but were less frequent than credit customers.

Courtesy and helpfulness created goodwill, but practical incentives for repeat purchase had to be created, as well. Gulf and Atlantic introduced free road maps in 1914 and 1916. American roads, at this time, were notoriously bad, poorly posted, and were often impassable in winter. The American motorist was more than grateful for anything that helped him reach his destination, or in the case of Atlantic, find the exact location of a gasoline outlet (see Chapter 3).

The gasoline gauge was not a standard feature until the late 1920s. Prior to this, the motorist had to check the gas tank level with a stick. Miscalculate and you could run out of gas miles from the nearest gas station. Socony (later Mobil) and other oil companies quickly introduced free calibrated dipsticks appropriate for each automobile model. These enabled the motorist to make accurate level checks with a constant reminder of an oil company.

The introduction of standardized SAE viscosity ratings for motor oil in the late 1920s, followed by octane numbers for gasoline in the early 1930s, made it virtually impossible for the motorist to detect any difference between major brands and potentially undermined brand loyalty. This was compounded by the Great Depression when large surpluses of gasoline were sold at ridiculously low prices by price cutters, some of which adulterated the gasoline with kerosene or naphtha. Major oil companies fought back with their brands as guarantees of quality and quickly introduced elaborate forecourt service and clean restrooms to restore brand loyalty and repeat purchase. Dealers and oil companies alike recognized that women, while not always in the driving seat, frequently decided where to stop. Clean restrooms were absolutely essential. Mobilgas and Texaco ran nationwide advertising campaigns in the late 1930s and early 1950s, promoting their clean restrooms (see Chapter 3). Mobilgas and Texaco epitomized dependability for both the car and the customer's well-being.

Enterprising dealers often supplied free hand-held paper fans to keep their customers cool in the summer or cardboard radiator covers to keep the car's radiator warm in winter. During the Great Depression, remaindered and unsold books were purchased wholesale by oil companies and given away to customers. These books were known as pulp fiction. Some oil companies, most notably Pan-Am, commissioned comics and illustrated books to keep the customers coming back. At the same time, some American cut-rate dealers supplied coupons that could be saved up and redeemed for crockery and glasses. Innumerable kitchens in the Deep South were furnished entirely with these items! Europe later adopted the same repeat-purchase incentives. At one point in the early 1970s, it was estimated that more glasses were being given away by gas stations in Great Britain than were actually sold elsewhere!

The save and redeem mechanic was taken one stage further with the trading stamp. Sperry and Hutchinson, a Chicago, Illinois, company had offered trading stamps, known as S&H Green stamps, that could be saved up and redeemed for catalog items from as far back as the 1890s. American gas stations introduced

During the early 1950s, Exxon gave away thousands of these photo albums to all their customers in the United States. The albums provided happy memories of vacations and a constant reminder of where to get good service. *Author collection*

We hope this photo album will soon be filled with snapshots to remind you of a wonderful vacation.

It's easy to avoid motoring worries...

just come to

ELLIOTT'S ESSO SERVICE
131 W. Main St.
Clarion, Pa.

for a thorough Pre-Trip Check-Up!

Have fun... be safe... on your vacation trip. Don't let motoring setbacks spoil things for you. Drive in to see us <u>before</u> you start.

we'll check your

✔ **OIL**   ✔ **BATTERY**

✔ **TIRES**   ✔ **ACCESSORIES**

✔ **BRAKES**   ✔ **CHASSIS LUBRICATION**

✔ **COOLING SYSTEM**

And we'll supply you with Flit, Atlas Champion Spark Plugs, Sun Glasses, Flashlights, and other vacation specials... You want your trip to be completely carefree. And so do we!

we hope you have a **Swell Time!**

Happy Motoring!

ESSO

trading stamps in the late 1940s, while Europe adopted them in the early 1960s. Trading stamps boosted gasoline sales but diminished brand loyalty.

Exxon and Shell fought back with two highly successful international campaigns in 1964 through 1966. Exxon introduced a sense of fun with its iconic "Put a Tiger in Your Tank" campaign. The company used eye-catching, colorful displays of gas pumps dressed up as comic tigers and hung banners and bunting. Free tiger tails and stickers generated huge amounts of publicity and goodwill (see Chapter 2). Shell appealed to the driver's greed with the British "Make Money" campaign. Drivers received one half of a coupon to be matched with an extremely rare winning half for a substantial cash prize. Both oil companies' sales increased enormously at the expense of other oil companies, especially cut-rate operators. Both the Exxon and Shell campaigns showed that motorists were prepared to repeatedly pay full price in exchange for either a bit of fun or a chance of winning a lot of money.

Exxon and Shell discovered that drivers were equally interested in commemorative coin and stamp sets. Some drivers went to extraordinary lengths to find the coin or stamp that would complete a set. There were more frequent visits, which was exactly what the campaign intended.

Oil companies in France found that the most effective repeat purchase campaigns were those aimed at children. French drivers welcomed anything that kept their children quiet. Woe betide any parent who drove past an Esso station offering Tintin collectibles! Shell operated one of the most clever international repeat-purchase schemes yet devised during the early 1960s. The European Shell tourist service provided detailed route plans with special

Anyone can take a trip like this. All you need is a Gulf Travel Card and a little money.

Coast to coast, there are over 800 Holiday Inns of America. The Gulf Travel Card is good at every one of them. So that takes care of sleeping and eating.

There are Gulf stations along the way in every state. (33,000 coast to coast.) So that takes care of gasoline, oil and whatnot.

The $24 covers bridge tolls, highway tolls and about 47 cups of coffee.

The point is, you won't need much cash for vacation driving if you have our piece of plastic.

Your Gulf dealer or Holiday Innkeeper has an application.

Gulf Oil Corporation

Gulf travel card advert "New York to California on $24 and a piece of plastic." Gasoline credit cards were the single most effective means of maintaining brand loyalty and repeat purchase. Introduced during the mid-1930s, gasoline credit cards came into their own in the 1960s with the boom in travel stimulated by the interstate highway network. This Gulf advertisement appeared in May 1967. *Author collection*

Clean, well-stocked restrooms were crucial for repeat purchase. By the end of the 1930s, motorists regarded them as their birthright. Dealers who neglected their restrooms automatically lost customers and any chance of them coming back. *Author collection*

In the days before air conditioning, handheld fans were essential for keeping automobile passengers cool in the summer heat. Shell, like all their competitors, supplied free fans for their customers, which were much appreciated. *Author collection*

The Exxon "Put a Tiger in Your Tank" 1964 to 1966 campaign was probably one of the most successful repeat purchase campaigns ever devised. It brought a sense of fun to an otherwise boring but necessary visit and built repeat purchase even at full price. *Author collection*

Free road maps generated customer goodwill and encouraged repeat purchase. Furthermore, by 1929, when this map was issued, Texaco was the only oil company selling gasoline in all forty-eight states, which underscored its dependability and guaranteed repeat purchase. *Author collection*

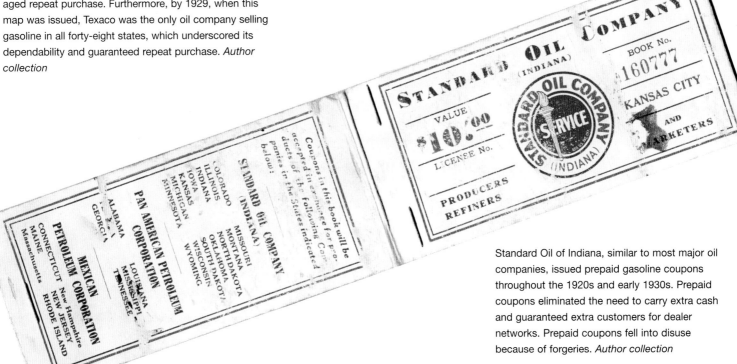

Standard Oil of Indiana, similar to most major oil companies, issued prepaid gasoline coupons throughout the 1920s and early 1930s. Prepaid coupons eliminated the need to carry extra cash and guaranteed extra customers for dealer networks. Prepaid coupons fell into disuse because of forgeries. *Author collection*

Shell "passports" for each child traveling with their parents. The Shell passport had to be stamped by Shell dealers on the planned route across Europe and was exchanged for a gift pack on return.

Buy Now, Pay Later

Oil companies introduced prepaid scrip or coupon books in America and Europe during the 1920s, which enabled the motorist to travel without additional cash and guaranteed incremental sales for the oil companies and gas stations alike. The chief drawback of this scheme was the difference between the face value of the prepaid coupon and the actual pump price, which was often lower because of an oil glut created by the Signal Hill oil field gusher in California during the mid- to late 1920s. The motorist found it virtually impossible to get the dealer to refund the difference. There were also quite a number of expert forgeries that made dealers reluctant to accept any coupons for fear of oil companies refusing to redeem them.

During the late 1930s, all major United States oil companies set up reciprocal arrangements with other oil companies where they had no coverage to provide nationwide acceptance of one particular card. This eliminated the need for carrying different cards and guaranteed increased gas sales for all participants. *Author collection*

By 1955, the sheer convenience of the gasoline credit card, first introduced in the mid-1930s, was absolutely indispensible for the United States long-distance traveler. He or she had up to twenty-eight days to settle the actual price charged at the pumps, a lubrication job, or a new set of tires. The recently introduced metal template sped up transactions and reduced fraud. *Author collection*

Gulf ran an enormously successful reciprocal deal with Holiday Inn during the 1960s and 1970s. This boosted the popularity of the Gulf credit card and was quickly copied by all major competitors, notably Exxon, which had reciprocal deals with Master Hosts, Howard Johnson's, Ramada Inn, and Marriot, as shown in this July 1969 advertisement. *Author collection*

The gasoline credit card, which became widely available during the mid-1930s in America, provided the answer to all the pitfalls of the coupon method. Oil companies carried out extensive credit worthiness checks on potential customers before supplying the cards and would only allow them to be used at carefully selected stations. The key benefit for the motorist was that he or she was charged the actual price at the pump and had twenty-eight days to settle the payment without the inconvenience of carrying additional cash. The credit card guaranteed repeat purchase and incremental volume for both gas stations and oil companies. According to a Shell trade advert from May 1939, a Shell credit card user on average purchased 200 gallons of gasoline more than a cash customer per year.

The reciprocal arrangement between Gulf and Holiday Inn was so successful that a number of Gulf station and Holiday Inn complexes were built near interstate highway exits across the Deep South during the mid- to late 1960s. *Author collection*

The credit card quickly provided oil companies with a comprehensive understanding of individuals' purchasing and travel habits, which helped them target their marketing, advertising, and gas station design to be more effective. A Shell credit card customer survey played a vital role in developing its post–World War II gas station design.

By the late 1930s, major oil companies set up national reciprocal agreements with other oil companies where they had no coverage so that a customer could use one credit card nationwide rather than several. The credit card's coverage was also extended for lubrication service and tire and battery sales.

Gulf probably had the most renowned reciprocal agreement with Holiday Inn and Avis car rental during the 1960s and 1970s. The Gulf credit card was accepted by both companies for rooms, meals, and car rental, which considerably boosted its popularity. The reciprocal deal with Holiday Inn was so successful that a number of Gulf gas station/Holiday Inn complexes were built near interstate highway exits across the Deep South during the mid- to late 1960s. There was talk of building similar complexes in the Netherlands and Belgium during the early 1970s, but the 1973 OPEC Oil Crisis put an end to that. By the early 1970s, all the major American oil companies

During the 1960s trading stamps boosted brand loyalty and repeat purchase for all major oil companies, who faced stiff competition from aggressive price cutters. Trading stamps were pasted into booklets, saved, and redeemed for items listed in catalogs. *Author collection*

followed Gulf's example and set up similar agreements with competing motel chains. Gasoline credit cards, apart from truck diesel cards and commercial accounts, did not exist in Europe. Comparatively large capital requirements (to cover very high European gasoline taxes), foreign exchange controls, and relatively small markets made the gasoline credit card impractical in Europe.

Lick and Save

Grocery and hardware stores offered trading stamps from as far back as the late nineteenth century to encourage repeat purchase. Customers were given a set number of stamps based on the cash value of their purchase, and the stamps were pasted into booklets that, once complete, could be saved up and redeemed for household goods listed in a mail-order catalog. Sperry and Hutchinson S&H Green stamps were the most popular brand, closely followed by Blue Chip, Double D, King Korn, Eagle, and Liberty.

While quite a few gas stations had supplied trading stamps in the 1940s to increase repeat purchase, it was not until the late 1950s and early 1960s that trading stamps became a vital part of gas retailing in America and, in particular, Great Britain. The increasing gasoline surplusses generated by new oil refineries globally created a substrata of very aggressive, price-cutting chains. Blue-collar workers, in particular, were keen to find a good value and forego elaborate forecourt service if they could save a nickel or more a gallon.

Both dealer-owned and oil-company-owned sites quickly realized that trading stamps offered the best means of repeat purchases. The customers still received their branded gasoline with elaborate forecourt service, but with the added bonus of stamps, they could save up for a toaster. The more frequent the visits, the faster they were likely to get the toaster! The additional attraction of trading stamps was that a person driving a company-owned automobile or truck could keep the trading stamps for his or her own benefit rather than pass on the cash savings to the company. This worked astonishingly well in Great Britain during the early 1970s with the introduction of self-service. Exxon, BP, and Shell offered triple or even quadruple Green Shield trading stamps (a British brand entirely separate from the American Sperry and Hutchinson operation) rather than outright price cuts to encourage repeat customers. One particular self-service station in Birmingham, Great Britain, offered quintuple Green Shield trading stamps, and sales representatives in company automobiles would make lengthy detours to get an even better deal.

The chief drawback of trading stamps for oil companies was that the same brand of trading stamps were offered by competing oil

Trading stamps were also an integral part of British gasoline retailing throughout the 1960s and early 1970s. Green Shield stamps were the most popular brand and were entirely separate from the American Sperry and Hutchinson company. Richard Tompkins, Green Shield stamps founder, cleverly appropriated Sperry and Hutchinson's green color scheme and forced them to use pink for the British market. *Author collection*

companies. Customers were more likely to go to a gas station that offered the best local deal on S&H Green or Blue Chip stamps rather than because it was an Exxon or Shell station. The 1973 OPEC Oil Crisis and subsequent high inflation marked the end of trading stamps as repeat-purchase incentives for gasoline sales. Trading stamp catalogs were often out of date as soon as they were published, which meant that people had to save even more stamps than they had originally planned. Consumers were also more anxious to save money rather than receive benefits in kind.

Steak and Wine

Spur was one of the first oil companies to offer coupons that could be saved up and redeemed for crockery displayed on the gas station forecourt during the 1930s. Other price cutters quickly offered similar repeat-purchase incentives.

Major oil companies introduced similar schemes in the 1960s. Initially Fire King glass coffee mugs were offered, followed by steak knives and highball, tumbler, and wine glasses. In every instance, the motorist was issued a coupon that could be saved up and redeemed for either one mug, a glass, or a set of six steak

IT'S FREE! The most valuable stam catalog ever! See 132 pages of valuable name-brand gift See new ideas for your home and family. Prove to yourse that you earn the best gift values with S&H Green Stamp

THE SPERRY AND HUTCHINSON COMPANY
IDEABOOK OF DISTINGUISHED MERCHANDISE
SINCE 1896 S&H GREEN STAMPS

She's smart! She's thrifty! She saves America's Most Valuable Stamps.... *S&H* Green Stamps

Announcing the New *S&H* Ideabook!

SINCE 1896 S&H GREEN STAMPS

GET YOUR FREE COPY TODAY ✦✦✦ JOIN THE 27,000,000 SMART, THRIFTY WOMEN WHO EARN THE BEST VALUES WITH *S&H* GREEN STAMPS

Just as with clean restrooms, the United States' housewife's choice of gas was determined by the station giving the best trading stamp deal. This S&H green stamps advertisement, which appeared in May 1961, cleverly played on the housewife's role as holder of the purse strings and frugal purchaser. *Author collection*

Shell ran a highly successful steak knives promotion in the United States and Great Britain during the 1960s. The items shown were part of the United States' promotion. Each time a motorist filled up, he or she was given a coupon. The knives could be redeemed for three coupons (i.e., after three fill-ups). *Author collection*

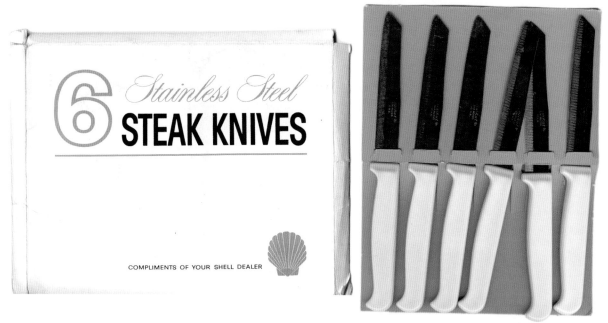

Price cutters, such as Spur, originated the coupon redemption promotion during the 1930s. Items similar to these were displayed on forecourts and redeemed for a set number of coupons. One coupon was provided after each fill-up. The free crockery appealed especially to the thrifty housewife and meant she could spend the money saved on some luxuries or treats. *Author collection*

Virtually every British gas station gave away glasses similar to these during the early 1970s in exchange for saved coupons. At one point it was estimated that more glasses were actually given away than sold by conventional outlets! *Author collection*

Mobil in Great Britain took the glass promotion one stage further in the early 1970s with mugs. Mobil ran book promotions very similar to those run by Pan-Am and by other United States oil companies during the 1930s. Mobil also ran a decorative salt and pepper sets promotion across Europe. *Richard W. Marjoram*

FREE! 25 BEAUTIFUL, FULL-COLOR WESTERN PHOTOGRAPHS

Great Salt Lake, Utah

The Alamo, San Antonio, Texas

You can easily collect them all,

because the West has been divided into different zones that distribute a different Scenic View each week. The zones cover about the distance you'll run on a tankful of Chevron Supreme. To be sure you get all 25 distinctive 9x12 color photographs,

Keep this check list with you!

- San Francisco-Oakland Bay Bridge
- Yosemite National Park, California
- Columbia, California
- Mount Shasta, California
- Kings Canyon National Park, Calif.
- Mission San Juan Capistrano, Calif.
- Lake Tahoe, Nevada-California
- Mount Hood, Oregon
- The Oregon Coast
- Olympic Nat'l Park, Washington
- Mount St. Helens, Washington
- Snoqualmie Falls, Washington
- Boulder Peak, Idaho

- Great Salt Lake, Utah
- Walpi Indian Village, Arizona
- Navajo Country, Arizona
- Hawaiian Waters
- Alaska Fishing Fleet
- Acoma Water Hole, New Mexico
- The Alamo, San Antonio, Texas
- Snowmass Lake, Colorado
- Chimney Rock, Nebraska
- Grand Teton Nat'l Park, Wyoming
- Glacier National Park, Montana
- Mount Revelstoke Nat'l Park, B.C.

Ask for FREE Scenic Views at CHEVRON GAS STATION / STANDARD STATIONS INC.

031 200M-5-46 LITHO IN U. S. A.

In June 1946, Chevron launched its "See Your West" color print promotion, and the prints changed each week. In order to ensure a complete set, customers had to refuel every week at either a company-owned Standard site or dealer-owned Chevron station. *Author collection*

THE STORY OF MAN IN SPACE

Gulf offered a curious hybrid book commemorating the Apollo 11 landing on the moon with the history of rockets and space travel, ironically with minimal Gulf branding! The book even provided advice on the widespread career opportunities at NASA with typical salary scales. NASA employed a large number of people in Florida, Texas, and Alabama, which were major Gulf markets. Perhaps Gulf wanted to capitalize on the post-landing euphoria. *Ian Walker*

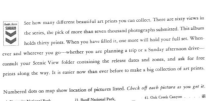

See how many different beautiful art prints you can collect. There are sixty views in the series, the pick of more than seven thousand photographs submitted. This album holds thirty prints. When you have filled it, one more will hold your full set. Whenever and wherever you go—whether you are planning a trip or a Sunday afternoon drive—consult your Scenic View folder containing the release dates and zones, and ask for free prints along the way. It is easier now than ever before to make a big collection of art prints.

Numbered dots on map show location of pictures listed. *Check off each picture as you get it.*

1. Yosemite National Park, Bridalveil Fall
2. Santa Catalina Island
3. Monterey Peninsula, Pinnacle Rock
4. Sequoia National Park, General Sherman Tree
5. Multnomah Falls
6. Mount Hood
7. Mount Adams
8. Mount Shuksan
9. Lake Pend Oreille
10. Natural Bridges National Monument
11. Virginia City, Nevada
12. Monument Valley
13. Keahiakahoe Cliffs
14. Black Sands, Kalapana Beach
15. White Sands National Monument
16. Big Bend, Texas
17. Pikes Peak
18. East Rosebud Creek, Montana
19. Devils Tower National Monument
20. Scotts Bluff National Monument

21. Banff National Park, Skoki Ski Lodge
22. Jasper National Park, Royal Canadian Mounted Police
23. Butchart's Gardens
24. Lake Tahoe
25. Redwood Highway
26. Mission San Diego de Alcala
27. Death Valley National Monument
28. Lassen Volcanic National Park
29. Rogue River
30. Wallowa Lake
31. McKenzie River
32. The Scenic Oregon Coast
33. Mount Rainier National Park
34. Mount Baker
35. Lake Chelan
36. Sawtooth Range
37. Coeur d'Alene Lake
38. Bryce Canyon National Park
39. Zion National Park, Great White Throne
40. California Wild Flowers

41. Oak Creek Canyon
42. Chiricahua National Monument
43. Apache Trail
44. Mission San Xavier del Bac
45. Carlsbad Caverns National Park
46. Vancouver Island, Malahat Drive
47. Harrison Lake
48. Snowmass Valley
49. Crater Lake National Park
50. Mesa Verde National Park
51. Glacier National Park
52. Grand Teton National Park
53. Yellowstone National Park, Old Faithful
54. Diamond Head and Waikiki
55. Niuatou Pali
56. Grand Canyon National Park
57. Canyon de Chelly National Monument
58. Saguaro Cactus
59. Hanalei Valley
60. Crater of Haleakala

DIRECTIONS FOR MOUNTING PRINTS*

1. Use scissors, photo trimmer, sharp knife or razor blade to remove flap of Scenic Art Print, along fold.
2. Lift glassine tape at an inner corner and peel from gummed strip by pulling slowly and at right angle away from binding.
3. Align edge of art mat with ruled line on stub. Press firmly onto gummed strip all the way across stub and rub to remove any wrinkles. After pressing and rubbing down, allow mat to stand for a few minutes so that mat may "set" before turning in album.
4. Prints may be removed at any time . . . for framing, or moving to another position in album . . . by "peeling" off. If, when print is removed, insufficient adhesive remains for additional prints, roll off residue with finger, utilize conventional adhesives.

* Best results are secured by mounting prints first on stubs in back of album and working forward.

NOTE: These Scenic Views are available only at Standard Stations, Inc., Authorized Distributors, and at dealers of Standard Oil Company of California, Standard Oil Company of Texas, Standard Oil Company of British Columbia Limited, and at Calso Gasoline Dealers in Rocky Mountain states. We regret that requests cannot be filled by mail.

STANDARD OIL COMPANY OF CALIFORNIA

knives at the gas station. Shell ran virtually identical steak knife promotions in America and Great Britain during the late 1960s. Glass promotions were phenomenally successful in Great Britain, largely thanks to the initiative taken by a Shell-Mex & BP secondary brand, National Benzole. The glass promotion, together with one for glass storage jars, did wonders for National Benzole's repeat-purchase sales and was quickly copied by every major oil company in Great Britain. Just as with trading stamps, people driving company-owned vehicles received benefits without having to pass on cash savings to the company. As previously mentioned, it was estimated at one point that more glasses were being given away at British gas stations than were actually sold in shops! Mobil cleverly ran coffee mug and salt and pepper shaker promotions, as well.

Collectibles and Commemorative Sets

Amoco was probably one of the first oil companies to offer commemorative stamp collections that could be pasted into special presentation books during the 1930s. This promotion appealed particularly to children and forced the parents to buy Amoco gas. Both Amoco and its dealers had to ensure that the stamps were constantly updated so that customers could complete their sets. Chevron used the same method in its "See Your West" promotion in 1946. Each week, Standard service stations and Chevron dealers offered a new scenic color print for that week only so the driver had to purchase gas at either station every week in order to ensure the set could be completed.

Sunoco had a successful U.S. presidents commemorative coins promotion in America, while Shell and Exxon ran highly successful

Shell built excellent repeat-purchase sales in Great Britain and Germany during the late 1960s and early 1970s with its commemorative coin collections. Drivers went out of their way to ensure they got the right coin with more frequent visits, which was exactly as intended. *Ian Walker*

Exxon ran a sweepstake competition during the early 1960s that offered either cash prizes or automobiles, trailers, boats, or camping equipment. It was aimed at high-mileage, company-owned vehicle users who welcomed the chance of winning something at no cost to them. All they had to do was fill up at an Esso station as frequently as possible for better chances of winning. *Author collection*

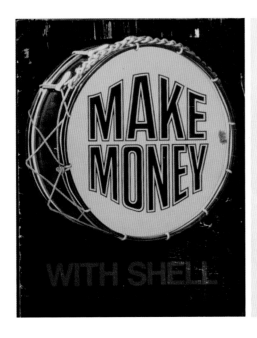

Shell completely undermined the Esso tiger campaign in Great Britain during the summer of 1966 by appealing to motorists' greed. Half a coupon was supplied with each purchase. The motorist's task was to find the matching half and redeem the pair for up to $250. The net result was smaller but more frequent purchases at a wider number of Shell stations. *Ian Walker*

Fabulous new toy!
Fun afloat...or on the shore!
Phillips 66 Power Yacht—$4.98!

Big 18-inch yacht—already assembled. Twin-battery motor powers this toy yacht through the water. (Two batteries are included.) Set the rudder so she'll circle back, or control her course from shore with a self-contained line! You can even organize your own boat races. Get your friends to join the fun. She's built of Phillips Marlex* plastic ... built to last! And you can charge it with a Phillips 66 credit card. *A Trademark

Runs on land, too! It has wheels for more fun—indoors or out! Plus custom lettering set. A great all-weather, all-year-round toy! Sold only at Phillips 66 stations or marinas.

Model Marina Pier is part of the kit ... Box converts to your own pier ... with pumps, pennants—the works—included! A great gift idea, too! Go first-class ... go Phillips 66!

PHILLIPS 66

Get yours early for Christmas! Only at Phillips 66 dealers!

Authentic, scale-model, all-steel Texaco tank truck ... actual size 25-inches long!

$7 95 value
$3 50 only
with free coupon from any Texaco Dealer

Here's how to get this custom-made "Buddy-L" toy Texaco Tank Truck delivered to your door for only $3.50 (certified retail value—$7.95). Drive in to any Texaco Dealer in continental U.S.A. Ask for a free coupon. Mail coupon with your check or money order. It's that easy to get this exclusive Texaco Dealer offer. Wonderful to give a child now. Great to lay away for Christmas gifts, too! **TEXACO DEALERS**

(Above two images) The collectible model was established by Texaco in the late 1950s with its tank truck promotions immediately before each Christmas. The motorist received a coupon after filling up and sent it with a check to a redemption center. Cities Service and Phillips 66 had similar promotions during the 1960s, and neither was as successful as the Texaco promotion. *Author collection*

EXCLUSIVE TEXACO DEALER OFFER:
Precision barometer, thermometer, hygrometer—by Honeywell, only $3.50 WITH FREE COUPON

$3.50

Barometer top dial gives barometric pressure—which indicates current weather trends. Thermometer, lower left, gives accurate room temperature. Hygrometer, lower right, registers indoor humidity. Precision-made and guaranteed by Honeywell—exclusively for Texaco.

Handsome for your home, office or schoolroom. Hangs on wall; stands on desk or table. Smart, brass-colored aluminum face; black plastic case. If you could buy this instrument anywhere else, it would cost at least three times as much. (This offer good only in U.S.A.)

Get your free coupon from any Texaco Dealer. Mail the coupon with your check or money order for $3.50. It's that easy. This exclusive offer is made to introduce you to Texaco's Climate-Controlled Sky Chief Supreme and Fire Chief gasolines—and Texaco Dealer service.

(Left) Texaco aimed at the adult collectible market during the early 1960s with an ornate barometer promotion that worked on exactly the same principle as the toy tank truck offer. The barometer fit in perfectly with typical suburban home interiors. *Author collection*

collectible coin promotions during the late 1960s and early 1970s in Europe, all of which worked on exactly the same principle as the Chevron promotion. Shell promoted Man in Flight and Historic Cars sets across Europe, and Exxon ran a series on British soccer teams. BP ran collectible coin promotions in France, as well. There are many stories of people driving from one gas station to another in hope of finding the correct coin to complete their set!

Gulf offered a lavishly illustrated book entitled *We Came in Peace,* complete with a set of five NASA color photographs to commemorate the Apollo 11 landing on the Moon in July 1969. The limited use of branding in gold seems to indicate it was produced very quickly to capitalize on the postlanding euphoria.

Exxon ran highly effective promotions of small collectible plastic Walt Disney and Tintin comic strip characters in France. Both promotions appealed to children and naturally forced the parents to buy gas at an Esso station!

Throughout the United States during the 1950s and 1960s, Texaco promoted special edition metal Buddy L tank truck models as Christmas presents for children. The customer received a coupon that was sent with a bank check to a redemption center. These models are eagerly sought after by collectors. Phillips 66 quickly responded with highly detailed plastic motor cruisers with electric motors made from its own plastic. Cities Service (later Citgo) offered plastic trucks with sports automobiles made by Ideal, a leading American toy manufacturer. During 1961, Texaco took a leaf out of the trading stamp catalogs and offered a decorative but highly practical barometer set, which was appropriate for a typical suburban home interior.

Sunoco, Sinclair, and Amoco each offered gas-pump-shaped transistor radios at special promotional prices during the 1960s, all of which are highly collectible today. The same applies to gas-pump-shaped salt and pepper sets that were supplied in all the major oil company liveries during the 1950s. Gas-pump-shaped coin banks are equally collectible.

Fill Up and Win

Exxon and Mobil both ran sweepstakes competitons in the United States during the early 1960s that offered either cash prizes or cars, boats, trailers, and camping equipment. As with trading stamps, these competitions were aimed primarily at high-mileage users, specifically salesmen driving company-owned automobiles, to induce repeat purchase and attract additional customers away from full-price or cut-price competitors.

Shell ran enormously successful "Pirate Treasure Hunt" campaigns on the West Coast during the late 1920s and early 1930s. Pump attendants and promotion girls, as seen here in 1930, were dressed up as pirates and gas stations were turned into pirate ships. Customers were given cryptic clues on where to find "treasure" (coupons in plaster scallop shells), which could be redeemed at Shell stations. *Author collection*

Initially, British gas station openings were family events, as shown here during the early 1960s, to attract and amuse everyone. Live music with dancers, like this Hawaiian band with hula girls, were very popular. *Richard W. Marjoram*

Shell responded to the immensely successful Exxon "Put a Tiger in Your Tank" campaign with an extremely effective repeat-purchase incentive in Great Britain during the summer of 1966 called "Make Money," which appealed to the customers' greed. Each time a British motorist bought Shell gas, he or she was given a "Make Money" envelope containing one half of a coupon for £100 ($250 in 1966), £10 ($25), £1 ($2.50), or 10 shillings ($1.25). The motorist had to find a matching half in order to win the cash prize. Customers quickly grew wise to the fact that they stood a better chance of finding the matching half with more frequent, though smaller, purchases and at a wider number of Shell stations. The Shell "Make Money" competition was subsequently revived in Great Britain during the early 1980s with equally successful results.

Special Events

Every oil company encouraged its managed outlets or dealerships to create special events for increased customer traffic. The Christmas event was a long-established tradition with pump attendants dressed as Santa Claus who gave away free gifts. The service building was adorned with model sleighs, reindeer, and multicolored lights. Shell was particularly notable for turning many of its company-owned stations on the West Coast into fantastic stage sets during the Christmas festivities in the late 1920s. Shell was equally famous for its Pirate Treasure Hunts when the stations were turned into pirate ships and the pump attendants were dressed up as pirates with eye patches! Customers and their children were given cryptic clues on where to dig for buried treasure on vacant lots. The lucky treasure seeker would find a plaster scallop shell containing a voucher that could be exchanged for a gift at a Shell station. Both events received very wide press coverage and created a great sense of fun and customer goodwill.

A change in management or ownership was the perfect excuse for a grand opening event with discount service vouchers and free gifts for the family. Great Britain became notorious during the mid-1960s and early 1970s for the widespread use of scantily clad promotion girls for gas station openings and gasoline promotions. One cut-price company, EP, offered the irresistible combination of gasoline at six old pence a gallon, one-tenth of the normal price, served by very attractive women in miniscule bikinis. The police often had to be called in to break up the traffic jams. Naturally, EP received free blanket press and TV coverage. Mobil dealers, while not immune to using scantily clad promotion girls for self-service gas station openings in Great Britain, also created family-oriented events with Hawaiian bands and hula dancers.

(Right) Mr. Poust's Atlantic station was a textbook example of how to run promotional events. In addition to the annual Christmas event, he also sponsored the Little League and had a big twentieth anniversary celebration, complete with clowns and free balloons for children. There were also beauty contests. *Author collection*

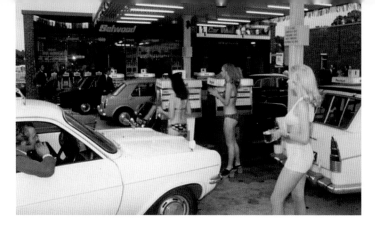

By the early 1970s, tough competition in Great Britain forced many dealers to use bikini girls offering glasses of beer to boost customer traffic at opening events. The change in attitudes towards women and drinking and driving would make such an event unthinkable today. *Richard W. Marjoram*

(Above) All oil companies encouraged their dealers to create special events for increased customer traffic. The Christmas event was the most popular and long-established one, as seen here at Mr. Poust's Atlantic station in Naugatuck, Connecticut, during the mid-1950s. Typically, the station roof had a Santa Claus display complete with sleigh and reindeer, as well as multicolored lights. One attendant was always dressed up as Santa doling out gifts to children. *Author collection*

5

Roadside Attractions

ALL RETAILERS USE THE BEST MEANS POSSIBLE to attract customers, whether with snappy logos, bright color schemes, or eye-catching storefront designs. Everyone is familiar with the highly distinctive McDonald's golden arches logo or the quaint Walgreens drugstore script. Gas stations are no different in this respect.

Some independent gas station dealers went the extra mile and created exaggerated, almost grotesque, attractions that a passing motorist could not fail to notice. These are commonly known as vernacular architecture, which highlights local tourist attractions, and regional architectural styles, or they reflect public preoccupations at a given time.

Gas stations in the shape of icebergs or giant coffee pots promised the motorist an ice-cold drink or a nice warm cup of coffee. The latter also had a political subtext. The Teapot Dome oil scandal came to light after the death of President Warren Harding in 1923. Albert B. Fall, the secretary of the interior, had provided access to the U.S. Navy's strategic oil reserves in Teapot Dome, Wyoming, in exchange for bribes. A number of witty dealers quickly built gas stations in the shape of giant teapots. This created a trend for giant measuring oil can-, gas pump-, and coffee pot-shaped gas stations.

Airplane-shaped gas stations were built in large numbers during the late 1920s and early 1930s across America. On one level, they reflected the public's growing fascination with air travel, which had been spectacularly demonstrated by Charles Lindbergh's solo Atlantic crossing in 1927 and Amelia Earhart and Howard Hughes' record-breaking exploits throughout the 1930s. On another level, the sheer incongruity of a full-size airplane with gas pumps at the side of the road could not fail to catch the eye of the passing motorist! On a more practical level, the wings provided excellent canopy cover for the gas pumps and automobiles. The most spectacular example was Art Lacey's B-17 bomber gas station on the outskirts of Portland, Oregon. Immediately after World War II, Art Lacey purchased a war surplus B-17 bomber at a knockdown price. After a few hair-raising attempts, he managed to install it on-site.

Egyptian mummy gas pumps and Arabian palace gas stations were equally topical reflections of events during the 1920s and early 1930s. Howard Carter and the Earl of Carnarvon discovered the fabulous treasure of Tutankhamen's tomb in 1922, which created a public fixation in Great Britain with all things Egyptian. Soon British cinemas and even cigarette factories were built in the style of Egyptian temples. A giant Egyptian mummy gas pump was erected on a gas station forecourt a short distance from the famous Egyptian-style Carreras cigarette factory in Mornington Crescent, London. In Los Angeles, Calpet built a series of Arabian palace gas stations that reflected the public's fixation with the movie stars Rudolph Valentino and Douglas Fairbanks as either romantic or daring Arab sheiks in silent movies.

In the Midwest and West, there was a particular pattern in the 1930s and 1950s for using giant figures in the shape of the legendary Paul Bunyan, cavemen, and even our old friend, the pump attendant, to catch the eye of passing traffic. Windmill-shaped gas stations were a common sight across America, more often created for sheer whimsy, but sometimes they highlighted the local association with Amish or Mennonite communities that were German (Deutsch) in origin, but mistakenly identified as Dutch, hence the use of the windmill motif!

Many enterprising dealers built eye-catching gas stations and motels, like this wigwam complex just outside Bardstown, Kentucky, to cater to increasing tourist traffic during the late 1930s, made possible by improved roads and paid holidays. The photograph was taken in July 1940. *Library of Congress*

Even major oil companies, like Gulf, went the extra mile to build extravagant, eye-catching gas stations, like this example in Miami Beach, Florida, which was photographed in April 1939. The lighthouse motif was purely and simply a gimmick, but it subconsciously promised a safe haven. The design fit in perfectly with a large number of brightly colored, elaborate art deco hotels, which are now protected buildings. *Library of Congress*

Cottage-style gas stations were built throughout the United States and Europe during the 1920s and 1930s, primarily as a means of diminishing the impact of an entirely new and incongruous retail phenomenon, but sometimes as an eye-catching gimmick. In the Midwest, quite a few retailers built fantastic gingerbread-type cottages that would not have been out of place on *Hansel and Gretel* or *The Wizard of Oz* sets. Phillips 66 and Pure used distinctive cottage designs right up to the mid-1950s, in the case of the latter. Cottage gas stations of half timber or stone construction with thatched or recycled slate roofs were widely built in Great Britain during the 1920s and 1930s, partly in response to campaigns by the *London Daily Express* and the Council for the Protection of Rural England (CPRE). They were also built to supply the increasing numbers of British automobile tourists from towns and cities that searched in vain for Ye Olde England, treating the English countryside more as a theme park than as a self-supporting entity. It is possible to speculate that this quest may well have inspired the construction of Williamsburg in Virginia during the late 1920s and early 1930s, Disneyland in California in the 1950s, and subsequently Walt Disney World in Florida.

Lighthouse-shaped gas stations could be found all along the eastern seaboard during the 1930s. On one level, the design was a

(Right) Giant figures, like this friendly Texaco gas pump attendant, were widely used by many gas stations across the United States to pull in passing trade. This photograph was taken in October 1966. *Author collection*

(Below) No passing motorist could fail to stop for a cool drink and a fill-up at this enticing iceberg, located on Route 66, just outside Albuquerque, New Mexico, which was photographed in July 1940. *Library of Congress*

form of escapism from the harsh realities of the Great Depression, and on another level, it symbolized a safe haven.

Radical, advanced architecture was equally eye-catching. The most celebrated example is the Phillips 66 gas station in Cloquet, Minnesota, designed by Frank Lloyd Wright (see Chapter 7). A number of gas stations were built in the United States, France, and Great Britain during the early 1960s that used the radical hyperbolic parabaloid roof, which used two of the four apexes to provide support for the whole structure. One example still survives in Great Britain, although it has now been converted into a diner. The radical designs reflected a period of high economic growth, stability, and optimism for the future, which was underscored by giant leaps made in space exploration.

(Left) Some dealers took tourist attractions to extremes, such as this fantasy sausage tree photographed in Florida during 1939. Other dealers in Texas used giant mythical jack rabbits to catch the eyes of passing motorists. *Author collection*

(Below) British dealers were equally adept at catching the eye of the motorist. This giant Egyptian mummy gas pump reflected the British public's fascination with Egypt after the discovery of Tutankhamen's tomb in 1922. The pump was photographed in York Way during the early 1930s, which was a short distance from the newly opened Egyptian-inspired Carreras cigarette factory in Mornington Crescent, London. *LAT Photographic*

(Above) Alexander Eschweiler's classic 1917 Wadhams Oil pagoda design was created purely to grab the attention of the motorist. The design was held in deep affection by Wisconsin motorists and was not replaced until the early 1950s, when this photograph was taken. *Charles Skaggs*

(Left) Smokey Wong's eye-catching pagoda canopy was obviously designed to pull in the tourist traffic passing through San Francisco's Chinatown. The photograph was taken in October 1966. *Author collection*

(Upper left) A recycled church? Nope. This attention-grabbing gas station was located in the Bavarian village of Leavenworth, Washington, and photographed during the mid-1960s. Architecturally themed villages first appeared during the 1920s, and the most notable example was in Williamsburg, Virginia. *Author collection*

(Lower left) Dealers in the Midwest and Pennsylvania situated close to Mennonite and Amish communities often built windmill gas stations in the mistaken belief they were Dutch rather than German—Deutsch—in origin. Tourists were often no better informed and delighted in the spectacle of people who shunned the trappings of the twentieth century. *Ernie Tomlinson*

This eclectic British cottage gas station, complete with art deco pylons, was built as part of a shopping center on the Great West Road in the outskirts of London, during the early 1930s. The gas station was located close to a number of fantastic art deco showcase factories, which clearly gave the architect license to indulge his fantasies! *LAT Photographic*

Enterprising dealers often used powerful combinations of cottage designs with neon lighting, which had a dramatic impact. This Associated gas station was photographed in the late 1930s. *Author collection*

Nobody could fail to notice this elaborate confection in the backwoods of Shannon County, Missouri, which was photographed in February 1942. While the log cabin was indigenous to the area, the elaborate fretwork reflected the mid-1930s craze for miniature golf courses with minutely detailed course markers and obstacles created with fret saws. *Library of Congress*

Art Lacey went the extra mile and actually bought a very cheap war-surplus B-17 bomber. The delivery flight, dismantling, and reassembly of this aircraft were the stuff of legend—hair-raising but often

hilarious. It soon became a tourist attraction just outside Portland, Oregon. The gas station has closed and the bomber is now extremely valuable and is being restored. *Author collection*

While this giant arch provided some protection for customers, there can be no question that its primary function was to grab the attention of passing motorists. This BP station was located in Montmélian in the

Savoie region of France and photographed in the mid-1960s. *Author collection*

(Left) This spectacular art deco tower gas station is located on the main Route Nationale road leading out of Nice, France. The inadequate fore-court made it virtually impossible for motorists to leave or rejoin fast-moving traffic safely. Formerly an antique market, the site is now a bakery. *Author collection*

(Top) This eye-catching futuristic Gulf station was located in the Lenox Square shopping mall, which opened in 1959, in the Buckhead district of Atlanta, Georgia. Such attention-grabbing designs were essential for drawing in customers and making shopping malls the success that they are. *BP Archive*

(Bottom) The hyperbolic parabaloid roof, supported by two of its four apexes, provided a unique opportunity for gas station design. It not only gave the dealer a progressive, forward-looking image, but it could not fail to be noticed by any motorist. This example, located near Doncaster, Great Britain, was built in the early 1960s and photographed in about 1970. The roof remains intact but is now part of a café diner. Other examples were built in the United States and France, but it is unclear how many have remained intact. *Alan Pond*

6

Good Neighbor

ANYONE OVER THE AGE OF FORTY-FIVE has fond memories of fill-ups at their local gas station. You were always greeted by name, the kids were offered sticks of gum or coloring books, the pump attendant politely enquired about the family pet or how you were doing at school, and made a methodical check of the automobile's condition. "The tire wear's a bit uneven, could be a problem with the tracking. You're due in next week for a lube job, so we could do it then, or if you can spare the time, we could fix it right now." I remember my sisters and I clambering for Esso tiger tails and forcing my mother to fill up at an Esso station rather than the local Shell station. What exactly influences such choices is difficult to establish. Was it the friendly, helpful staff who had a better idea of the automobile's condition than a woman driver, or was it simply a matter of convenience? In contrast, the man of the house might claim that location, prices, trading stamps, and free gifts were more important. Similarly, the station's appearance might be considered crucial to a woman, while the man pointed to ease of access and an efficient layout as deciding factors in his choice of gas station.

In fact, all of these requirements were equally valid and formed part of the complex equation that made up a neighborhood gas station. Initially, oil companies, particularly Atlantic Refining, placed a very high premium on appearance to placate concerned neighbors. Standard Oil of Indiana and Gulf, in particular, took a far more pragmatic approach with a less extravagant design and a greater emphasis on a convenient location for commuters. This is amply demonstrated by three 1920s Gulf sand brick stations on Magazine Street in New Orleans. They were placed approximately two miles apart from one another, all in the same direction away from the central business district leading towards the residential Garden District, which indicated that refueling was more convenient in the evening than in the morning.

The postwar housing boom enabled many people to become proud homeowners. They clearly wanted their key asset to appreciate in value and avoid any risk of it being devalued by unattractive or mismatched neighboring gas stations. This particularly affected women who stayed at home to raise their children. The housewife wanted a gas station that would fit in with the neighborhood, while the man needed a convenient station that provided ease of access and fast fill-ups. The ranch and coach house designs were good compromises for the short term, but the 1966 Mobil Pegasus design provided an outstanding, transcendent solution that has stood the test of time (see Chapter 10).

Civic Pride

Atlantic Refining introduced its elaborate city beautiful gas station design in Pittsburgh in 1915 (see Chapter 1) and subsequently in Philadelphia and across Pennsylvania, western New York state, and New England. The city beautiful style was an eclectic mix of the classical order and Beaux-Arts and was introduced in 1893 at the Chicago Columbian Exposition. It epitomized America's rising self-confidence and on a local level, it exemplified civic pride. The latter seems to have been the decisive factor in local council approval for the Atlantic design rather than actual compatibility with surrounding structures, particularly in historically important cities, such as Philadelphia and Boston. While the city beautiful design provided Atlantic with superb brand identity, it was very expensive to build (up to three times the cost of a conventional gas station) and often incongruous with its surroundings. It created a precedent for extravagant, ambitious designs worldwide.

Friendly, helpful service and a design that harmonized with the surrounding houses were the essence of a neighborhood gas station. Neocolonial designs, like this 1960s Sinclair station, were a big hit with women who appreciated the positive contribution to the neighborhood. *BP Archive*

Three New England oil companies—Jenney, Colonial Beacon, and Socony (later Mobil)—quickly responded in the early 1920s with their own elaborate designs that drew on New England's neocolonial architectural heritage. Colonial Beacon (later acquired by Exxon) built a chain of Palladian pavilions with distinctive green domes that became virtual trademarks for Colonial Beacon and were held in deep affection by local communities. Jenney and Socony built large numbers of red brick gas stations, primarily for wealthy residential neighborhoods, which were closely modeled on eighteenth-century New England pavilions and coach houses with elaborate doorways and sash windows. All three designs were far more compatible with their immediate surroundings because of their common heritage than the Atlantic city beautiful design, which was quietly replaced in the mid-1920s with a less obtrusive, cheaper neocolonial design.

Calpet (later acquired by Texaco) built a series of elaborately tiled Moorish-palace-style gas stations in Los Angeles during the mid-1920s that shared the same aspirational qualities as the Atlantic city beautiful design. They were oases in the midst of Los Angeles' chaotic development and provided a sharp contrast to Shell and Chevron's utilitarian prefabricated structures. Imperial Oil, Exxon's Canadian subsidiary, opened an elegant, well-proportioned gas station in Toronto in 1925 that exuded pride of ownership and set high standards for competitors to match.

In London, Great Britain, at least three highly elaborate, aspirational multistory garages with gas forecourts were opened in the mid- to late 1920s and are now protected buildings. Macy's Garage (now an Avis car rental depot) in Balderton Street bears some resemblance to the Selfridges department store around the corner on Oxford Street. The elegant semicircular canopied gas forecourt set very high standards for other British gas retailers and garages to follow. The same can be said for the Bluebird Garage in Kings

Jenney reached into New England's rich architectural heritage and responded with a dignified neocolonial design that blended in perfectly with virtually any residential neighborhood. This design could be built with either red brick or white clapboard timber. Jenney took great pride in its design and featured it prominently on the front cover of its Autoroute atlas for New England, as shown here. *Author collection*

Atlantic spent lavishly on its city beautiful gas stations, which probably cost at least three times more to build than a conventional station. This example, located in Roxbury, Massachusetts, was built between 1916 and the early 1920s and was similar to the Temple of Vesta in Rome. It was a smaller version of an Atlantic station opened in Philadelphia in 1915. These extravagant designs forced Jenney, Socony, and Colonial Beacon in New England to build ornate neocolonial or Palladian stations. *Author collection*

(Above) The Bluebird Garage on Kings Road in London, which opened in 1924, was the largest of its kind in Europe and was carefully designed to blend in with neighboring shops. The elaborate terracotta brick and wrought-iron front wall added considerably to the garage's dignified appearance. The garage has been sensitively redeveloped into the Bluebird Café: a gastronomic complex of restaurants, cafes, and gourmet food stores. *English Heritage, NMR*

(Right) Imperial Oil, the Canadian subsidiary of Exxon, built a number of gas stations throughout Canada that set very high standards. This example in Toronto, on the corner of King W and Strachan Streets, was built around 1925 and demonstrated sensitivity to surrounding houses and provided pointers for the new Exxon design being developed in the United States. *Author collection*

(Above) Macy's Garage on Balderton Street in London, built in 1926, was an outstanding example of civic pride. The semicircular gas forecourt was both elegant and highly practical. The multistory elevation was similar to Selfridges department store around the corner in Oxford Street. The garage is now used as an Avis car rental depot. *Author collection*

(Top left) Atlantic overcompensated by erecting lavish city beautiful gas stations even in industrial districts, as seen in this Boston, Massachusetts, location. The elaborate perimeter wall with lamp standards was an exact copy of a 1916 Atlantic station on North Street in Philadelphia. *Author collection*

(Bottom left) Bowser, a gas pump manufacturer, was keen to be seen doing its bit for improving the appearance of gas stations. This 1927 British advertisement ostensibly sold gas pumps for private use but prominently featured a dignified gas station design that Bowser provided for gas station dealers in the United States and Great Britain. *BP Archive*

Road, Chelsea (now Terence Conran's Bluebird Café), and the Lex parking garage (now NCP car park) in Brewer Street, Soho.

British oil companies and gas pump distributors were also acutely aware of the prestige of civic pride gas stations. Bowser, an American gas pump manufacturer, employed a four-color civic pride gas station design to sell its gas pumps. Pratt's, a British affiliate of Exxon, used a full-color illustration of a civic pride garage to advertise its gasoline.

Home Sweet Home

Gulf, Conoco, Texaco, and particularly Standard Oil of Indiana were principally responsible for the development of gas station designs for residential neighborhoods on the eastern seaboard and Midwest (see Chapter 1). By the mid-1920s, virtually every major oil company had residential gas station designs.

Oil companies were acutely aware of local community sensitivities about compatibility of gas station design, layout, safe access/departure ramps, and even the potential impact on property values. These enterprises simply could not afford to alienate regular customers on their doorstep. Standard Oil of Indiana developed the highly adaptable Joliet design in 1917 specifically for residential neighborhoods. Initially, the Joliet design consisted of a brick building, bare or covered with cement render depending on the location, and a flat-roofed canopy over both driveways. The front elevation had a very high entablature, which was strikingly similar to the Lincoln Memorial that opened in Washington, D.C., in the same year. The Joliet design was modified in 1921 with a pitched roof, plain red brick, and the canopy over one driveway rather than

(Right) The Joliet-type station was introduced by Standard Oil of Indiana in 1917. It was a remarkably flexible design that could be adapted for virtually any location. Many skeptics were won over by the design's acute sensitivity to its surroundings, as demonstrated by the extensive use of white brick in this 1920 Bay City, Michigan, location, combined with careful landscaping. *Author collection*

(Below) Standard Oil of Indiana's Joliet design was modified in 1921 with a pitched roof, bare brick, and the canopy covering one driveway rather than two, as shown in this Jacksonville, Illinois, photograph. The changes were for practical rather than aesthetic reasons. The modified Joliet design was equally popular and widely copied, most notably by Exxon. It became a virtual generic for gas station design in the Midwest and the eastern seaboard during the 1920s. *Author collection*

two. The modifications were more practical than aesthetic. The pitched roof prevented the accumulation of heavy snow and enabled rainwater to quickly drain. The bare brick required less maintenance than cement render, which cracked easily and required regular painting. The canopy over one driveway rather than two permitted high-sided trucks to refuel. The pitched-roof version of the Joliet design was widely copied by competitors, most notably Exxon, and became a virtual generic for gas station design during the mid-1920s in the Midwest and on the eastern seaboard. Standard Oil of Indiana, to its infinite credit, went to extraordinary lengths in the mid-1920s to allay residential neighborhood fears with a remarkable loose-leaf book containing testimonial letters and sample photographs. Most of the testimonial letters expressed doubts about a gas station next door to homes but were won over by sympathetic design, landscaping, and Standard of Indiana's good neighbor policy.

Standard Oil of Indiana's Joliet design and good neighbor policy were endorsed by C. E. Franks,

Texaco built hundreds of Denver-design gas stations nationwide during the 1920s, which became virtual trademarks, as shown in this 1929 advertisement. The combination of a pitched roof, a muted light green and cream color scheme, and extensive use of trellis work fit in perfectly with many new suburban housing developments across the United States. Note the absence of a canopy that had begun to fall out of fashion. The Denver design was clearly aimed at young, highly affluent, and discriminating motorists. *Author collection*

managing director of Wayne Pump and Tank's British subsidiary, in a series of shrewd articles for *The Service Station* magazine, a British publication, in July-October 1926. C. E. Franks, an American, set up Wayne's British subsidiary in 1923 and later became chairman/CEO of the parent company in Fort Wayne, Indiana, after World War II. The articles were apt observations of developments in the United States and especially of communities' response to them. This excerpt is from page 6 in the August 1926 issue:

Plan the building solid, substantial, and attractive, but not of the gingerbread-type. Bear in mind that it is a place of business. It should be designed in such a manner that it can be placed in the better residence districts without causing ill feeling to your neighbors.

Indeed, Wayne and Bowser published a series of gas station design booklets during the mid-1920s for oil companies or independent dealers in the United States and Europe to plan their own stations. Bowser's Treasure Island booklet showed a wide variety of designs, including gingerbread designs disparaged by C. E. Franks. Wayne, by contrast, particularly in Great Britain, was careful to be associated with aesthetically pleasing sites that won prizes. One outstanding example was the Park Langley garage in Beckenham,

Independent dealers were equally conscious of the need for designs that were in harmony with the location. The canopy of this upstate New York gas station, photographed around 1922, blends in perfectly with neighboring porches. The dealer offered his customers a choice of Kendall or Sinclair gasolines, which was a common practice until the early 1940s. *Author collection*

Kent, which was popularly known as the Chinese pagoda garage, but it was in fact based on a Japanese temple design. It was built as part of a housing estate by a property developer who had recently returned from Japan and was full of enthusiasm for Japanese classical architecture. Coincidently, Japanese-style gardens had just come back into fashion in Great Britain.

In the United States, Conoco made consistent use of its residential design, first introduced in 1917 (see Chapter 1), throughout the Rocky

Conoco first introduced this L–shaped, twin-canopy residential design around 1917 and continued to use it throughout the 1920s, as shown in this Boise, Idaho, photograph. The other canopy with two additional pumps is hidden in the background. The design had a buttress motif on the four corners of the building, which were also repeated on the canopy strut. Conoco, like Standard Oil of Indiana, made very careful use of landscaping to minimize the impact of the station. *Author collection*

(Above) Sinclair introduced its highly distinctive Castle design in the early 1930s. The false roof, crenellated Spanish colonial motif was also widely used in suburban shopping centers and housing developments. It was particularly ironic that Sinclair made the canopy a key feature of this design just as other oil companies were abandoning it. *Ernie Tomlinson*

Mountain region up to the early 1930s. Gulf introduced its "Sandbrick" design in 1917, which incorporated many features from the 1913 Pittsburgh design and retained it up to 1931. The Sandbrick design was far more consistent than the Standard of Indiana Joliet design and was used over a wider geographic spread from the Gulf of Mexico to Maine. The dark brown bricks were equally appropriate for both residential and business districts. There were two basic designs: one with a flat-roofed canopy over one of the driveways that was used for high-volume sites and the other was a sales kiosk with a gestural tiled awning for low-volume sites. Both designs were highly distinctive and immediately recognizable as Gulf stations. At least three examples survive to this day on Magazine Street in New Orleans. While none of them sell gas and have all been covered in painted cement render, it is remarkable how naturally the buildings blend in with their immediate neighbors.

Texaco launched its Denver design in the mid-1920s, and it was used nationwide by 1928 when Texaco was the first American oil company to sell gasoline in all forty-eight states. The design consisted of a cream-colored stucco building with a green gabled roof and a gestural green tiled awning immediately above the window. The Denver design bore a very close resemblance to suburban housing developments built across America and was, therefore, acceptable in virtually any residential location. Like Gulf, Texaco was absolutely consistent, and with heavy nationwide full-color advertising, made the Denver design a virtual trademark. Sohio, the leading Ohio marketer, introduced a substantial "Tudor" design in 1928 for its new super service stations that contained multiple lubrication bays that matched neighboring houses.

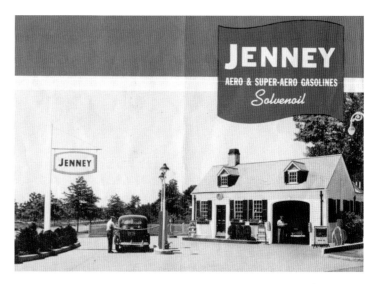

By the early 1930s, Jenney moved over to a more relaxed and elegant clapboard design similar to an eighteenth-century New England country house. In most instances, the lubrication bay entrance was through the side, in parallel with the pump island, rather than from the front. This is a later example taken from the front cover of a Jenney Road Atlas issued during the late 1930s. *Author collection*

Sinclair launched its iconic "Castle" design in the early 1930s. Like Texaco, Sinclair used both a cream stucco finish and green tiles. The latter were used to create a false pitched roof/crenelated effect rather than a gestural awning. The highly distinctive castle design gave Sinclair superb brand identity and harmonized with new suburban housing and shopping center developments. It relied, however, too heavily on the highly distinctive canopy, which was rendered obsolete during the mid-1930s by the popularity of trailer caravans. Exxon and Standard of Indiana introduced "Spanish Colonial" designs in the early 1930s that used the same false pitched

Standard Oil of Indiana launched its Spanish Mission design in 1932, which employed the same false-roof crenellated effect as the Sinclair and Exxon designs. This example was photographed in the early 1950s. Note how Standard Oil of Indiana used glazed cream-colored brick rather than cement render or stucco. *BP Archive*

(Below) Mobil successfully transposed its neocolonial design nationwide during the mid-1930s. This example, in Milwaukee, Wisconsin, was photographed in the early 1950s. The design was surprisingly easy to build and relied largely on red brick. The distinctive features were provided by mass-produced ornate door frames and fan lights. *Charles Skaggs*

(Above) This striking British garage in Park Langley, Kent, won a series of awards in the late 1920s for setting very high standards for British gas station design. Wayne, another gas pump manufacturer, featured it prominently in its trade advertising. The photograph was taken around 1931. *BP Archive*

roof/crenelated effect as Sinclair. Neither the Exxon nor the Standard of Indiana designs had canopies. The Exxon design, like the Sinclair castle design, used stucco and bore a striking resemblance to Los Angeles shopping centers from the late 1920s. Standard of Indiana, by contrast, used glazed cream brick. Exxon and Standard of Indiana made adept transitions to more modern and less domestic designs in the late 1930s (see Chapter 7). Like Richfield and Associated/Flying A on the West Coast, Sinclair clung on to the Castle design for too long and was overtaken by competitors.

Jenney and Mobil (created by the merger of Socony and Vacuum Oil in 1931) remained faithful to their New England roots and persisted with more relaxed versions of neocolonial architecture up to 1939. In the early 1930s, Jenney introduced a white clapboard design that incorporated an enclosed lubrication bay that looked similar to a boathouse. Mobil used its

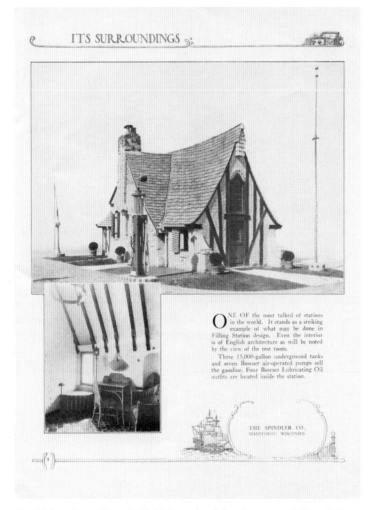

The Midwest was littered with blatant gimmick cottage gas stations that were built to attract passing trade. This example in Manitowoc, Wisconsin, was featured in Bowser's Treasure Island book from 1926. Other gas pump manufacturers, notably Wayne, frowned upon designs like these, as did most local civic societies. *Author collection*

neocolonial design nationwide in locations as diverse as Milwaukee, Wisconsin, and Los Angeles, California.

The Cottage

While gas stations were commonplace in America from 1913 on, they did not become widespread in Europe until the mid-1920s. The sheer novelty of these stations made them appear incongruous no matter where they were placed. In a sincere but misguided attempt to lessen their impact and to maintain the status quo, particularly in the outer suburbs and the countryside, the cottage-style gas station was created.

Standard Oil of Indiana unwittingly built the first cottage station in April 1918 at 429 Vistula Street in Elkhart, Indiana (see Chapter 1). The single-story building, complete with pitched roof, dormer windows, trellises, and window boxes, blended in perfectly with surrounding houses and provided a splendid example for subsequent designs.

The cottage style reflected a social conflict between the need for progress and nostalgia for the past. Cottage gas stations could be found in wealthy suburbs throughout the eastern seaboard and Midwest in the United States. A number of cottage gas stations were built on the Hutchinson River and Saw Mill River parkways in Westchester County, New York, during the late 1920s and early 1930s. These designs were later used in Long Island, New York, and the Pennsylvania Turnpike in 1940 and 1941. Some American oil companies and independent dealers used the cottage as a blatant gimmick with bright colors and exaggerated features. Pure Oil and Phillips 66 introduced highly distinctive cottage designs in the late 1920s, which, in the case of Pure, was used with some modifications up to the mid-1950s. Nobody could miss Pure's bright blue roof, nor Phillips 66's multicolored roof, green building, and prominent chimney breast. The Midwest was littered with gingerbread cottages that seemed to come straight out of stage sets for *Hansel and Gretel*!

European designs were created ostensibly to be in harmony with the immediate surroundings but in fact had to appease a very reactionary outcry in France and, particularly, Great Britain, in the short term. An even more insidious campaign by Adolf Hitler took place in Germany during the mid- to late 1930s. The *British Daily Express* newspaper and the Council for the Protection of Rural England (CPRE) ran vociferous campaigns in the late 1920s for cottage-style gas stations. *Vendre* magazine ran a similar campaign in France. Hitler encouraged the building of cottage-style gas stations as part of the Heimatschutzstil campaign that aimed to symbolize the idea of the German homeland through architecture. Heimatschutzstil effectively stopped any further construction of hypermodern international-style gas stations in Germany. BP developed a number of regional cottage designs in France during the early to mid-1920s that matched the indigenous architecture,

Westchester County in New York created a cottage gas station design for the Hutchinson River and Saw Mill River Parkways. This example in Ardsley was opened in1931. Note how even the gas pumps were encased in stone to create a rustic look. Similar designs were also used in Long Island and later on the Pennsylvania Turnpike in 1940 and 1941. *Author collection*

and at least one was created in Germany at the same time. Compagnie Industrielle des Petroles (CIP), the French subsidiary of Mobil, adopted the Normandy cottage for its corporate style and used it across France during the early to mid-1930s. Great Britain had the widest variety of kitsch pastiche gas stations masquerading as thatched cottages and country pubs mainly because gasoline was sold exclusively by independent multibrand dealers. Single-brand company-owned sites were virtually nonexistent there until the early 1950s. Fortunately, the *British Autocar* magazine and the *London Times* lobbied for functional, aesthetically honest gas stations that were introduced, primarily in urban areas, during the mid- to late 1930s (see Chapter 7).

Home Again

By the late 1940s, virtually every American oil company had a box super service station design with enclosed lubrication and wash bays. The vast majority of these designs used colored exterior porcelain enamel panels to ensure consistent brand identity and a minimum of maintenance. While the box design was highly functional and honest, its monolithic appearance dictated by the height required for cars on hoists often overshadowed surrounding buildings. This became increasingly apparent, particularly with new postwar suburban housing developments that were predominantly single-story bungalows or ranch-style houses. The gas station exterior porcelain enamel panels clashed with the brick, stone, wooden clapboard, or aluminum siding of the surrounding houses.

Cities Service opened this stepped service station in Hays, Kansas, in December 1954. The stepped design, with the sales office lower than the service bays, lessened the impact of an otherwise monolithic structure on surrounding single-story houses. The stepped design was quickly adopted by other oil companies in the United States and Europe. *Author collection*

Oil companies across America, particularly in the Midwest, gradually addressed these issues during the mid- to late 1950s. Cities Service, Conoco, Sinclair, Exxon, and Atlantic introduced stepped designs with sales kiosks that were lower in height than the service bays and floor to ceiling plate-glass windows, which created a more horizontal effect. The stepped designs were later used in Europe, particularly by Shell-Mex & BP (a joint marketing organization 60 percent owned by Shell and 40 percent owned by BP) and Exxon in Great Britain. Sinclair and Phillips 66, respectively, experimented with stone-clad gas stations in Illinois and Minnesota during the mid-1950s. These were later copied by Texaco in 1964 with its Matawan design.

Around 1958, the trend towards domestic-style gas stations gathered momentum and split into two distinct patterns: colonial heritage and contemporary suburban. Howard Johnson's, the nationwide highway diner chain, introduced its neocolonial coach house design with a miniature steeple in Massachusetts during the late 1930s, and subsequently went nationwide after World War II. The design was immensely popular with surrounding communities and assured the weary motorist of predictable service and meals. Sunoco opened a coach house–style gas station in Ohio in 1957 that was a close copy of the Howard Johnson's design. The station was the first of many to be built over the next twelve years, and Gulf opened a similar one in New Jersey in 1958. Sinclair, Mobil, and Atlantic, in particular, built a large number of neocolonial coach house gas stations during the 1960s and early 1970s. Both the Howard Johnson's and the oil company coach house designs were frankly more appropriate for theme parks than faithful architectural copies.

Shell introduced the ranch-style gas station in response to a local California planning committee request in 1958 for a gas station design that was compatible with a new housing development. The ranch design resembled a standard single-story house design that was built nationwide in the 1950s and 1960s. It consisted of two interlocking gabled roofs with a fake chimney stack bolted onto an otherwise conventional structure. Brick, stone, or tiles were substituted for porcelain enamel panels. It proved to be immensely popular with local residents and motorists alike and was rapidly introduced nationwide. Shell, like Mobil, was acutely aware of growing consumer unease about unsightly or mismatched gas station designs whipped up by Peter Blake's book, *God's Own Junkyard*, and Lady Bird Johnson, wife of President Lyndon B. Johnson, in 1964 (see Chapters 7 and 8). By the late 1960s, every American oil company had a domestic design.

Gas station design in Europe went through less upheaval during the late 1950s and 1960s. There were tougher local planning

Howard Johnson's, the highway diner chain, introduced its neocolonial design in Massachusetts during the late 1930s. This design was used nationwide in Howard Johnson's highly successful postwar expansion, as shown in this August 1950 advertisement. The design was immensely popular with both local residents and customers. It clearly inspired oil companies, too. *Author collection*

Gulf had a fairly restrained neocolonial design that was used in historically important locations, such as Cambridge, Massachusetts. Unfortunately, Gulf spoiled an otherwise acceptable design with the addition of a superfluous steeple in this New Jersey location, which was photographed in August 1958. *Author collection*

Atlantic completely embraced the neocolonial style from 1961 on and retrofitted it onto existing structures, as shown in this Fairport, New York, location in October 1963. In fairness, the roof line matched those of the surrounding houses, but the miniature steeple, the neo-Georgian doorway, and bow window were excessive. *Author collection*

Shell-Mex & BP Ltd (60 percent owned by Shell and 40 percent owned by BP) developed a highly flexible British modular design in the late 1950s. The neutral colors, stepped service bays, and horizontal emphasis were very similar to contemporary designs for schools, libraries, and community centers, which gave the Shell-Mex & BP design the aura of an essential local amenity. The design was popular with both the British public and the architectural press. This example was photographed in the early 1960s. *BP Archive*

and zoning laws that placed stringent controls on designs, building materials, and height, as well as detailed public enquiries/consultation. Another reason is large-scale European service station building programs did not begin until around 1955 and took account of recent changes in American gas station design and quickly moved over to the stepped service station design for a more harmonious effect. Painted cement render, bare brick, or large prefabricated panels were used for exterior finish. Porcelain enamel exterior cladding was never used in Europe. Shell-Mex & BP introduced a highly flexible flat-roofed modular design in Great Britain during the late 1950s that used prefabricated panels and brick, which adapted to virtually any location with a simple change in brick color. Fortuitously, the Shell-Mex & BP design was very similar to contemporary designs for libraries, community centers, and schools

in residential neighborhoods, which effectively identified it as an essential local amenity. At least one BP station in this design was built in Essex with a pitched roof that worked equally well. Exxon quickly copied the Shell-Mex & BP design. Company-owned service stations were positively welcomed in Great Britain during the 1950s by Ian Nairn, an architectural commentator, and Sir Colin Buchanan, a civil servant who later published *The Buchanan Report* in 1963 (comprehensive survey/long-term projection of the impact of the automobile on Great Britain). They approved of the designs because of the very high standards that were set for design, layout, and, most importantly, the absence of unnecessary point-of-sale advertising.

Shell was quick to reposition itself in America during the late 1960s as a caring, responsive oil company that addressed people's planning concerns on a local, if not case by case, basis. Shell ran heavyweight consumer press campaigns to show its acute sensitivity to local community needs that proclaimed the end of the box and the rise of the ranch. Just like in the period between 1913 and the early1920s, gas station design had again become an even bigger local consumer issue than either product quality or forecourt service. Mobil's Pegasus design, introduced in 1966, was the purest, most aesthetically honest, and internationally versatile response to design (see Chapter 7). Texaco introduced its Matawan design with prototypes in Matawan, New Jersey, and Long Island, New York, in 1964. The Long Island location, in particular, had a low, single-story design with extensive stone cladding that matched surrounding houses. Interestingly, the cantilevered canopy gables were in the shape of the hexagonal Texaco logo. Exxon in the early1960s quietly followed Shell's example and created variants of the ranch design. Chevron introduced its highly versatile "Hallmark" pitched-roof service station design in the late 1960s, which was compatible with residential neighborhoods or seaside communities. The Hallmark design was more pragmatic than Shell's ranch and could be easily adapted with heavy wood exterior cladding or large seashore rocks. ARCO/Atlantic Richfield (the companies merged in 1966) commissioned Victor Christ-Janer in 1969 to develop a retrofit design that could turn a porcelain enamel box into a "Cape Cod" salt-box design or similar that was compatible with surrounding houses. The Cape Cod salt-box prototype was

built in Rhode Island with a pitched roof and had a simple, pure elegance that outclassed the coach house design used elsewhere. Unfortunately, it was rejected by ARCO on the grounds of security (brick pillars restricted vision from the sales office), but more likely because it was too expensive and exposed the fatuity of the neocolonial coach house design.

One cannot escape the conclusion, albeit based on conjecture, that key (white, affluent, and middle-age) American consumers were looking for reassuring, constant, traditional designs in the midst of considerable social upheaval and change in the United States during the late 1960s and early 1970s. This is clearly demonstrated by Sinclair's "If You Know People Like These . . . " advertisement in 1968 and Shell's Ranch, New Canaan Tree, and Lexington Colonial advertisements between 1968 and 1970. Europe, by contrast, went through considerably less social unrest and embraced new gas station designs and self-service, in particular, remarkably quickly (see Chapter 8). This is best illustrated by Raymond Loewy's creation of a radical service station design called Most Advanced, Yet Acceptable (MAYA) for Shell in 1970 and 1971 for worldwide use. This was based on a brief with specifications drawn up by a specially created team of Shell marketing executives from around the world. A number of prototypes were built in Europe, notably in Italy and Great Britain. None were built in the United States.

(Far left) Shell took the good neighbor concept one stage further and demonstrated that it was caring enough to deal with environmental and heritage concerns on a case by case basis. All of these campaigns in 1969 and 1970 did wonders for Shell's corporate image. *Author collection*

(Left) Sinclair took a leaf out of Shell's book and promoted its neocolonial gas station design as part of its "American Conservation Series" advertising campaign in November 1968. *Author collection*

Shell rolled out its enormously successful ranch design nationwide in the early 1960s after the design, requested by a California planning committee, received widespread public acclaim. Shell sensibly saw this as a unique public relations opportunity and repositioned itself as an attentive and responsive good neighbor, as shown in this 1968 advertisement. Other oil companies quickly copied Shell's ranch design, but none created quite the same feel-good factor in its advertising. *Author collection*

You might even want to live here, if it weren't a service station.

When we put up a new Shell station, we start with the makings of a beautiful home.

Huge spans of glass. Elegant walls and pillars of white or red brick. Tasteful detailing.

We planned it that way—because a station is home to a Shell dealer.

It's where he welcomes his customers, offers his services, and sells Shell products.

That's why we put our trademark on the station. We want you to know exactly where a Shell dealer is when you need him.

Our ranch house designs are basic to our whole point of view about service stations.

We want them to blend in with the community.

And to look as if they belonged to the site.

There are over 24,000 Shell service stations across the country. And we want them all to look great—because it's great for business.

But there's another reason, too. This is where we raise our children. Make our home. We want it to look nice.

Sinclair experimented with stone cladding for its station exteriors to minimize their impact. This example was photographed in Joliet, Illinois, in July 1955. Phillips 66 later used stone cladding for some of its Midwestern stations, too. Texaco made the most widespread use of stone cladding with its Matawan design from the mid-1960s on. *Author collection*

(Below) Victor Christ-Janer was commissioned by ARCO in 1969 to adapt existing Atlantic stations to their surroundings. Christ-Janer created an elegant, understated Cape Cod salt box design in Rhode Island, which eliminated any cause for complaint. Sadly, ARCO chose not to proceed further, most likely because this design exposed the fatuity of the neocolonial style elsewhere. *Author collection*

This is the City of TOMORROW—

"Pedestrians—
Express Traffic—
Local Traffic—
—each will be given
a clear path by 1960"

—predicts NORMAN BEL GEDDES,
authority on future trends

"When traffic delays and confusion seem hopeless, remember that men of vision are working on the problem. Already traffic engineers are planning city streets and country highways free from stop and go . . . .

"1. Sidewalks will be elevated—you'll walk and shop ABOVE Main Street, actually cross OVER it.

"2. Local traffic will use the FULL width of the streets below—no sidewalks, no parked cars. Loading and unloading will be done INSIDE the buildings.

"3. High-speed, long-distance traffic will have its own elevated, one-way lanes, no stop lights or intersections."

...but TODAY,
4 miles in 5 are
Stop and Go

STOP-AND-GO driving is not only annoying, but also is the costliest kind you do.

One stop can waste enough gasoline to take you 5 city blocks . . . and 30 stops a day is the nation-wide average!

While traffic authorities are planning "The City of Tomorrow," Shell engineers have developed a fuel . . . Super-Shell . . . to meet to-

day's driving problem TODAY

They have found a way to re-arrange the chemical structure of gasoline . . . actually to balance it.

Automotive engineers term Super-Shell "motor-digestible," because at all speeds it is converted so QUICKLY, so COMPLETELY into power.

Save by the regular use of Super-Shell. A Shell dealer is near you.

SUPER-SHELL SHELL

7

The Shape of Things to Come

DURING THE MID- TO LATE 1920S, there was a marked tendency to shake off the shackles of the past, the memories of World War I, and look towards a bright new future. The public in America and Europe enthusiastically embraced new architectural styles, most notably art deco, and the international style to a lesser extent. Streamline moderne, a hybrid of art deco and the international style, was equally popular in the United States and Europe throughout the 1930s. Quite by chance, the one-stop super service station with integral lubrication/wash bays and customer restrooms was introduced around the same time in America. New, futuristic designs epitomized modern, up-to-date service and heralded a new age in gasoline retailing. Shell ran a nationwide press campaign in July through October 1937 entitled "The City of Tomorrow" that featured Norman Bel Geddes, a leading American industrial designer, with his futuristic streamline moderne city models.

Art deco and streamline moderne had an immediate, short-term impact. Art deco was a flamboyant, colorful, extroverted style that was absolutely ideal for commercial structures. Art deco was subsequently superseded by streamline moderne in about 1936 and 1937, which faded away by the late 1940s. The international style, by contrast, was highly disciplined, systematic, and above all, decreed that "form follows function." It had a slow start but a more profound long-term impact, particularly after World War II.

Art Deco

Art deco first appeared in Paris in 1925 at the Exposition Internationale des Arts Decoratifs et Industriels Modernes and was quickly adopted by Exxon, BP, and Desmarais Fréres for their French company-owned gas stations. The three designs were almost direct copies of the 1925 Exposition's art deco pavilions and were fairly restrained in appearance with discreet bas relief panels and fluting, although BP used very striking green, yellow, and black graphics. Art deco subsequently spread worldwide, particularly in the United States, thanks in part to the impact of the German science fiction movie *Metropolis* in 1926. *Metropolis* provided a spellbinding vision of a futuristic art deco city, largely based on the frenetic energy of Manhattan, and created a public sensation. Director Fritz Lang was an architect by training and perhaps realized film was the best medium for bringing his designs to life. Art Deco, thereafter, in a more extroverted, angular format, was rapidly adopted for cinema and shop design in America and Europe.

The 1929 Wall Street Crash and subsequent Great Depression ironically hastened the spread of art deco thanks to the construction of the art deco Empire State and the Chrysler skyscrapers in New York in 1930 and 1931. Both were built to inspire public confidence and as gestures of defiance in the face of a collapsed economy. These confidence-boosting efforts were repeated throughout the 1930s, most notably with the 1932 Los Angeles Olympics, the 1933 Chicago Century of Progress Exposition, the 1935 San Diego California Pacific International Exposition, the 1937 Cleveland Great Lakes Exposition, the 1937 Paris International Exposition, the 1939 San Francisco Golden Gate International Exposition, and the 1939–1940 New York World's Fair. Many oil companies had exhibition stands at these events, notably Texaco, Standard Oil of Indiana, Chevron, and Sohio. Each event was full of art deco architecture and provided much inspiration for gas

Shell cleverly promoted its product as tomorrow's gasoline for today's driving conditions in tandem with Norman Bel Geddes' vision for the future. This highly successful press campaign, between July and October 1937, enhanced both Shell and Bel Geddes' reputations for prescient, high-technology solutions. *Author collection*

Hollywood comes to Portland. Chevron looked to Hollywood not only for architectural inspiration, but even adapted the floodlit film premiere look for gas station openings, like this one in Portland, Oregon, in 1939 or 1940. Floodlights accentuated the streamlined modernity and drew large numbers of customers. *Author collection*

Exxon was quick to adopt art deco for its French company-owned gas stations and built large numbers of them between 1927 and 1939. The earliest stations, between 1927 and 1931, traded under the Eco/L'Economique brand name. The design incorporated an overhanging lip and a vertical or horizontal fluted frieze immediately below. Note the unusual layout of two completely enclosed refueling bays and a greasing bay on the extreme right in this late 1940s Strasbourg photograph. *Author collection*

Texaco gained considerable prestige from the Chicago Century of Progress Exposition advertising, which for a while masked its rather old-fashioned image. Texaco, the only gasoline retailer in all forty-eight states, was also quick to realize it could sell more gasoline by actively encouraging people to travel long distances with the assistance of its travel advice service. *Author collection*

No one could miss BP's eye-catching green, yellow, and black art deco graphics that provided instant recognition for its French gas stations. *Author collection*

station design. Hollywood also played a key role in the spread of art deco. The iconic Twentieth Century Fox art deco opening title/trademark set a gold standard. The fabulous Busby Berkeley sets provided much inspiration and a welcome escape from depressing reality, while the Buck Rogers science fiction series full of futuristic art deco rockets and cities encouraged people to look to the future with hope rather than dwell on the demoralizing present. Art deco, in short, projected a progressive, resolute image.

Art deco gas stations appeared in the United States from as early as 1931. Diamond DX Oil built a superb art deco station in Sapulpa, Oklahoma. Chevron adopted art deco as a house style in 1932 for prestige showcase stations near the 1932 Los Angeles Olympics venues and events.

Shell, the archrival of Chevron, was aware that its skeletal prefabricated crackerbox stations, introduced in 1915, were outdated and incapable of being adapted for enclosed lubrica-

Shell's art deco design was introduced in 1934 after trials with different designs. This prefabricated structure in Portland, Oregon, in 1936, with its distinctive, angular twin-humped canopy, provided the inspiration for Texaco's streamline moderne EM design of 1937. *Author collection*

tion/wash bays with customer restrooms. From as far back as 1930 and 1931, Shell had experimented with a number of different designs on the West Coast. In 1934, Shell took the plunge and built a series of showcase art deco gas stations in the Midwest and on the West Coast. The art deco design also incorporated a new cream color scheme with a red skirting board accentuated with a yellow pinstripe. The most elaborate Shell art deco station was in St. Louis, Missouri, on the corner of Linden and Vandenventer Avenues. This was a brick construction with terracotta tile cladding. Shell cleverly turned the exceptionally tall central heating chimney (dictated by local building ordinances) into an eye-catching tower. Elsewhere, all the Shell art deco stations were built with prefabricated porcelain enamel panels.

Shell faced formidable competition on the West Coast, particularly in Los Angeles, which is generally regarded as the world's most competitive local gasoline market. Intense rivalry from Chevron, Union Oil, Richfield, Gilmore, and Associated/Flying A forced any competitor to keep on its toes or go under. Each of these oil companies developed outstanding designs for prefabricated art deco gas stations. Los Angeles was a veritable hothouse for art deco gas station development. In fact, both the Shell and Richfield art deco designs clearly provided the inspiration for Walter Dorwin Teague's iconic streamline moderne Texaco EM design from 1937, albeit in a more rounded, streamlined format. Richfield and Associated/Flying A were immensely proud of their art deco stations and continued to feature them in both their advertising and road maps right up to the early 1950s.

Gulf built a number of art deco gas stations on the eastern seaboard in New Jersey, Pennsylvania, and Washington, D.C., between 1932 and 1935. These were brick with terracotta cladding. In the same region, Sunoco had a fairly restrained art deco gas station design of brick with white cement render. Standard Oil of Indiana built at least one experimental art deco gas station in Minnesota. An equally striking art deco gas station was built in Shreveport, Louisiana, around 1935 and clearly took its inspiration from the 1933 Chicago Century of Progress Exposition entrance. Other enterprising dealers made spectacular use of glass blocks for art deco gas stations.

Great Britain and France had a large number of individual art deco gas stations and garages inspired by cinemas and shopping centers. In Great Britain, there were virtually no single-brand, company-owned gas stations until 1950, so the spread of art deco and its hybrid, streamline moderne, was largely dependent on car distributors with gasoline forecourts, most notably Caffyns and Henleys. There were two outstanding clusters of art deco showcase factories in West London on the Great West Road and Western Avenue, which had a halo effect on gas station design in the immediate vicinity. CIP, the French Mobil subsidiary, adopted the more hard-edged American art deco style in the mid-1930s.

Streamline Moderne

During the early 1930s, there was unprecedented competition to raise air, land, and water speed records. Internationally, people

Richfield gave Shell a good run for its money with its flamboyant use of its Eagle trademark and extravagant canopies. Richfield was immensely proud of this design and persisted with it until the early 1950s. *Author collection*

Chevron's design seemed positively restrained by comparison with Richfield and Flying A. Standard made a deft, seamless transition to streamline moderne in the late 1930s and on to the international style in the late 1940s. *Author collection*

(Below) This experimental station in Minnesota, although owned and operated by an independent dealer, clearly had the active assistance of Standard Oil of Indiana. The dealer would not have been able to install the large three-dimensional crown, let alone the custom-made lamp standards, without the approval and financial assistance of Standard Oil of Indiana. *Minnesota Historical Society*

were fascinated by the excitement, risk, and drama surrounding record attempts, which at times were fatal and morbidly added to the thrill of the event. Daily newspaper reports, radio commentaries, and weekly cinema newsreels kept the public at fever pitch. Record breakers, such as Malcolm Campbell, Henry Segrave, George Eyston, and John Cobb became household names and were sponsored successively by Exxon, National Benzole, BP, and Mobil. At the same time, Auto Union and Mercedes Benz dominated European Grand Prix motor racing with their supercharged race cars. The Grand Prix race cars and the record-breaking airplanes, cars, and boats closely resembled each other with their low, smooth, streamlined appearance. Extensive wind-tunnel research had demonstrated that the reduction of wind resistance could actually increase a vehicle's speed. Commercial air travel was speeding up transcontinental trips and the silver streamlined DC3 airliner

was admired as a symbol of speed and progress. Anything streamlined had an immediate topical, modern appeal, even for everyday items like pencil sharpeners! Gulf sponsored Buckminster Fuller's radical streamlined Dymaxion automobile featured at the 1933 Chicago Century of Progress Exposition, and Texaco commissioned a series of equally radical streamlined tank trucks. As previously mentioned, Shell ran a nationwide double-page press campaign in July through October 1937 entitled "City of Tomorrow" featuring Norman Bel Geddes, a leading American industrial designer, with his futuristic, streamline moderne city models. This undoubtedly led to Norman Bel Geddes being commissioned by General Motors to design its Futurama pavilion at the New York World's Fair in 1939 and 1940.

The new exacting discipline of industrial design came to prominence with the breakthrough in the development of

The Wayne 60 computer pump was the epitome of modernity and marked the change to purchasing gasoline by value rather than volume. It was created by Van Doren and Rideout, industrial design consultants who were also responsible for the iconic Philco Bakelite radio, weighing scales, and refrigerators. *Author collection*

(Top) The 1933 Chicago Century of Progress gateway clearly provided the inspiration for this Shreveport, Louisiana, station. Like the Flying A design, this station was even more eye-catching at night than by day. *Author collection*

(Middle) Art deco provided versatile, eye-catching appeal, and a modern image for this Waukegan, Illinois, dealer. The fluted tower, a common art deco feature, turned the gas station into a prominent landmark, day or night. *Author collection*

(Bottom) British garages were quick to appreciate the crisp modernity of art deco, because it created an efficient, businesslike image that attracted customers. Art deco marked a positive move towards forward-looking styles rather than backward, pastiche styles. *LAT Photographic*

record-breaking streamlined vehicles. Industrial design had a far-reaching impact on manufacturing equipment, packaging, household appliances and utensils, airplanes, locomotives, automobiles, and even gas pumps. The German Bauhaus style, led by Walter Gropius and Ludwig Mies van der Rohe, pioneered both industrial design and international-style architecture during the 1920s. Both were based on the premise of form follows function and aesthetic honesty. Ironically, the analytical and systematic discipline of industrial design was disingenuously used in America to develop the streamline moderne style. In the long term it paved the way for high-quality design and architecture after World War II, particularly in the United States. All the major American industrial designers, including Walter Dorwin Teague, Norman Bel Geddes, Raymond Loewy, and Van Doren and Rideout, played a direct or indirect role in gas station design from the mid-1930s to the early 1970s.

Chrysler introduced its streamlined Airflow automobile in 1934, and while not a commercial success, the Chrysler Airflow did force its competitors to catch up and introduce similar models or get dismissed as old-fashioned. At the same time, it was becoming increasingly obvious that Texaco, the only American gas retailer in all forty-eight states, had a very old-fashioned, lackluster image. Texaco drastically needed to overhaul its image or be overtaken by Shell. The introduction of mass-produced streamlined

(Above) Streamlined record-breaking cars, sponsored by oil companies like BP, captured the imagination of the public and graphic artists alike. It also provided the inspiration for the streamline moderne style. *BP Archive*

(Below) Walter Dorwin Teague's iconic 1937 streamline moderne EM design for Texaco owed much to Shell and Richfield's art deco designs and was the first truly modern design to be used nationwide. The canopy was used only in the South and the West Coast, as seen in this 1949 photograph. Elsewhere the emphasis was placed on large, efficient forecourts with widely spaced pump islands. *Author collection*

automobiles and Gulf's sponsorship of Buckminster Fuller's streamlined Dymaxion automobile could only point Texaco in one direction: streamline moderne. Texaco commissioned Walter Dorwin Teague to develop a highly flexible modular gas station design, with or without a canopy, that could be adapted for a wide variety of different locations nationwide. Walter Dorwin Teague created the iconic streamline moderne EM design in 1937 that could accommodate as little as one service bay or as many as four; it looked equally good with and without a canopy, and could even include an octagonal sales office. Texaco's EM station with a distinctive twin-humped canopy looks strikingly similar to Shell's, in particular, and Richfield's art deco designs, albeit with softer, more rounded edges. While Shell and Richfield undoubtedly provided role models, Texaco was the first American oil company to introduce a truly modern gas station design nationwide. The Texaco EM design remained intact until the early 1960s. Shell built one experimental streamline moderne gas station in Evanston, Illinois. Gulf quickly responded with its own streamline moderne gas station design, affectionately known as the "Icebox," and used it for almost as long as Texaco. Chevron, Conoco, and Standard Oil of Indiana introduced even more curvaceous streamline moderne designs. All three designs were replaced in the late 1940s with squared-off, hard-edge designs. Tydol and DS, an independent marketer, used some superb streamline moderne designs in Minnesota.

In France, BP and Auto Gazo/Ozo created very striking streamline moderne designs undoubtedly inspired by the exhibition pavilions at the 1937 Paris International Exposition. BP's extremely wide reinforced concrete canopy design pushed French concrete technology, the best in the world, to the absolute limit. The Auto Gazo/Ozo streamline moderne design was used right up to the early 1960s. In Great Britain, streamline moderne design was championed by two car dealer chains: Caffyns and Henleys. Both were strongly influenced by key developments in their immediate surroundings. Erich Mendelsohn's superb international-style De la Warr pavilion in Bexhill-on-Sea opened in 1935 and had an immediate halo effect on gas station design in the surrounding area. Overnight, local gas stations and car dealers, notably Caffyns, abandoned traditional pastiche styles and opted for clean, functional, streamlined designs. Henleys was influenced by all the showcase art deco factories on the Great West Road in London, but instead opted for a more up-to-date streamline moderne design in March 1937.

It is important to note, however, that pastiche, retrograde gas stations continued to be built worldwide. Pure Oil was still building cottage gas stations in Ohio and Mississippi in 1936, and Mobil persisted with its neocolonial gas station design up to 1939. At the same time in Germany, Adolf Hitler was actively encouraging the construction of regressive Heimatschutzstil gas stations. While in Great Britain, in marked contrast to Henleys on the Great West Road, Cliftons opened a pastiche gas station on the South Circular Road in London in May 1937, two months after Henleys. The Cliftons station was in the style of a semicircular olde English barn, complete with exposed half timbers, dormer windows with leaded glass, and two large curved barn doors at either end.

Frank Lloyd Wright: A Unique Vision

Frank Lloyd Wright was a remarkable architect with a highly eclectic range of commissions and projects, and therefore impossible to place within any movement. He was simply in a class of his own. Wright developed a number of radical gas station designs for Rochester, New York, and Los Angeles, California, as far back as the late 1920s. They were simply ahead of their time, including the provision of gas pump hoses suspended from a canopy to allow easy refueling and maximum use of space. The idea was adopted and patented by a Japanese gas pump manufacturer, Tatsuno, in the early 1960s and is now the standard gas dispensing method in Japan.

Like the Swiss/French architect, Le Corbusier, Wright was intrigued by the impact of the automobile on town planning. He differed from Le Corbusier in the belief that towns and cities grew and agglomerated by meeting specific needs rather than by imposition. Wright saw the gas station as an oasis, which if it was successful, attracted other businesses and eventually created a

Gulf quickly introduced its own streamline moderne design, affectionately known as the icebox. The design made extensive use of porcelain enamel panels on a cinder block construction and remained virtually unchanged until the late 1950s. This Long Island, New York, photograph dates from the mid-1940s. *Author collection*

Direct Services (DS), a Minnesota independent marketer, produced a wonderfully exuberant streamline moderne design that could not fail to catch the eye of the passing motorist and raise a chuckle or two! It positively screamed modernity and quick service. *Minnesota Historical Society*

This was reputedly Britain's largest gas forecourt with twenty gas pumps, all Wayne 60s, on five islands when it was opened in March 1937. The Great West Road was famous for its showcase art deco factories, most notably the Firestone tire factory, and provided the stimulus for Henley's bold streamline moderne design. *LAT Photographic*

Standard Oil of Indiana had virtually abandoned direct ownership of its stations, but was forced by Shell and Texaco's aggressive marketing to create a few showcase streamline moderne stations, like this example that was photographed in 1941. After World War II, Standard Oil of Indiana used a more squared-off version of this design. *Author collection*

This remarkable streamline moderne design in Minneapolis made very intelligent use of a high-sided corner site. Note how the otherwise useless upper walls were deftly turned into a harmonious brand identity/advertising section, while the comparatively narrow sales office on the left merged seamlessly with the service bays on the right. *Minnesota Historical Society*

neighborhood. This was based on shrewd observation of Los Angeles' haphazard development during the early 1920s and the subsequent growth of food markets and shopping plazas in Los Angeles in the late 1920s, which often installed cut-rate gas stations to attract customers. Many of the points raised here are discussed in greater detail in Richard Longstreth's book *The Drive-In, the Supermarket, and the Transformation of Commercial Space in Los Angeles: 1914–1941*. A similar pattern emerged in Great Britain during the mid-1930s on the Great West Road in London. A highly eclectic gas station composed of art deco cottages with thatched roofs was opened before the completion of an art deco shopping parade immediately behind the station.

Frank Lloyd Wright finally realized his ideas for gas station design for a forward-thinking independent Phillips 66 dealer in Cloquet, Minnesota, in 1959. Unfortunately, local fire bylaws prohibited overhead gasoline hoses, so conventional gas dispensers had to be used instead. The design was both highly unorthodox and expensive. One trade publication estimated it cost two to three times more to build than a conventional service station design. Conversely, it stimulated a great deal of discussion within trade publications and oil companies, nationally and internationally, about the next step forward in gas station design. Phillips 66, while playing no direct part in the commission, discreetly incorporated some of the elements in its 1960s design.

Frank Lloyd Wright proposed overhanging gas pump hoses as far back as the 1920s to provide efficient refueling and save space. Tatsuno, a Japanese gas pump manufacturer, patented an overhead system in the early 1960s, and this is now the norm for all Japanese urban sites. These stations take up one fifth or less of the space of their equivalent elsewhere. *Author collection*

The International Style

The German Bauhaus movement had a profound impact upon all aspects of architecture and industrial design in Germany during the 1920s. The Bauhaus, through Walter Gropius and Ludwig Mies van der Rohe, promulgated the principles of aesthetic honesty and transparency with "the form follows the function" and "less is more" theories. This architectural style became known as the international style.

BV Aral and BP OLEX developed highly distinctive, functional, prefabricated service station designs in Germany during the late 1920s. Both designs were the essence of the Bauhaus ethos and

Frank Lloyd Wright finally realized his ideas for gas station design with this Phillips 66 station in Cloquet, Minnesota, in 1959. Wright had previously created a series of radical gas station designs that dated back to the late 1920s. They were simply too technologically far ahead of their time. This particular design was both unorthodox and up to three times more expensive than a conventional station. On the other hand, it caused much comment and thought. *Minnesota Historical Society*

were outstanding examples of standardized prefabrication technology and the machine-age aesthetic. These designs were, in part, dictated by the rapid recovery/expansion of the German economy after 1924 (which was strikingly similar to California in 1914) and the pressing need for cost-effective, quick construction methods. The cost of a BV Aral or BP OLEX station was one third that of an equivalent brick or stone structure. The designs were of all-steel construction with prefabricated steel frames and panels. They could be assembled in as little as eight days and had the added advantage of being easy to disassemble. Both designs were built in large numbers throughout Germany in the late 1920s and early 1930s. The BV Aral design inspired Arne Jacobsen's iconic 1937 service station at Skovshoved, Denmark.

Shell's German corporate headquarters, the Shell Haus, built in Berlin in 1930 and 1931, was the epitome of the international style, along with several experimental Shell gas stations that opened in the late 1920s and early 1930s. In Germany, Exxon responded by building experimental international-style gas stations in Kassel during the late 1920s and Hamburg-Rothenbaum during 1932. The Hamburg-Rothenbaum design by Karl Schneider bears some resemblance to Mies van der Rohe's 1929 Barcelona Pavilion. Both the Shell and Exxon designs were of conventional brick construction with cement render. Adolf Hitler's rise to power in 1933, his contempt for the Bauhaus style, and his promotion of the backward Heimatschutzstil design prevented any further developments. Ironically, the worldwide spread of the international style was actually hastened by the mass exodus from Germany in 1933 of prominent architects, such as Gropius, Mies van der Rohe, and Mendelsohn.

Sohio, the dominant marketer in Ohio, introduced the experimental prefabricated portable station in 1932. The "Sohio" station, although more angular in appearance and without a canopy, was identical in every other respect to the BV Aral and BP OLEX German designs. It was very easy to assemble and disassemble. Porcelain enamel steel panels were extensively used. The Sohio design received rave reviews in the American architectural trade journals. For reasons that have never been fully explained, the custom-made pumps, rather than the service station structure, were featured in the landmark Museum of Modern Art Machine Art exhibition in 1934, curated by Philip Johnson, doyen of the international style in America. The Sohio portable station was a one-off experiment, but it formed the basis for all subsequent Sohio service station designs during the 1930s.

Advocates of the international style in Great Britain were helped immeasurably by the progressive stance of the *London Times* and *Autocar* magazine. Both publications were perturbed by the profusion of kitsch with pastiche service stations masquerading as cottages or Palladian pavilions. A *Times* editorial from August 20, 1932, crystalizes this:

It is for the young architect or engineer of the present day to prove . . . that they can be designed to look like petrol stations and nothing else . . . no modern appliance offers so clear a chance for the production of a new beauty.

Arne Jacobsen's iconic 1937 station was inspired by BV Aral and BP OLEX's German designs. The elegant, tapered, single-column and circular canopy anticipated Mobil's 1966 Pegasus design, while the bold, sharp angularity of the service building was copied by Gasolin in Germany during the 1950s. The station survives to this day in Skovshoved, Denmark. *Struwing*

Erich Mendelsohn's superb 1935 international-style De la Warr pavilion at Bexhill-on-Sea, Sussex, was the final catalyst and created a halo effect. Overnight, local garages and car dealers, notably Caffyns, abandoned pastiche, retrograde styles and adopted contemporary designs. An identical pattern developed on the Great West Road, Brentford, London. The best example of an international-style service station in Great Britain was Golly's Garage on Earls Court Road, London, that opened in 1938. Its understated elegance and open-plan lubrication bay owed much to Erich Mendelsohn's department store designs from the late 1920s and Mies van der Rohe's flexible living/dining room design for the Tugendhat house in Brno, Czechoslovakia, in 1932.

The most influential international-style gas station was designed by Arne Jacobsen, the eminent Danish architect, and opened in Skovshoved, Denmark in 1937. The pure, simple elegance of the

(Above left) The 1932 American Sohio portable international-style station incorporated all the best features of BV Aral and BP OLEX's German prefabricated designs. The design was virtually identical for later permanent prefabricated Sohio stations, as seen here. *BP Archive*

(Above middle) This experimental BP gas station in Wiesbaden, Germany, designed by Dr. Lothar Gotz in the mid-1950s, had subtle echoes of Mies van der Rohe's postwar American work. It received widespread praise and some aspects were incorporated in subsequent German BP designs. *BP Archive*

(Above right) The 1966 Mobil Pegasus design was immensely flexible and could be retrofitted onto existing structures anywhere in the world. Compare this photograph with the AGIP advertisement. Note the effective use of the Pegasus circular logo and see how the elegant canopy and circular lamp standards with the muted color fit perfectly into a rural setting. *Richard W. Marjoram*

Golly's Garage was the epitome of the international style and opened in Earls Court Road, London, during 1938. The canopy made extensive use of glass bricks to allow extra daylight. The design was highly reminiscent of Eric Mendelsohn's 1920s German department stores, while the open, semicircular lubrication bay reflected Mies van der Rohe's flexible living/dining room layout for the Tugendhat house in Brno, Czechoslovakia, in 1932. *English Heritage/NMR*

circular canopy with the tapered pylon echoes the interior of Frank Lloyd Wright's Johnson Wax building in Racine, Wisconsin, anticipates Eero Saarinen's 1950 pedestal chair and table, and was possibly the inspiration for Eliot Noyes' Pegasus canopy for Mobil in 1966. The bold, sharp angularity of the service building was copied by Gasolin in Germany during the 1950s. Arne Jacobsen's long-standing interest in road transportation, aviation, and gas station design dated back to the late 1920s. He took a large number of photographs of German gas stations, notably the BV Aral design. Bertram Goldberg, a Chicago architect, designed an equally remarkable international-style gas station for Standard Oil of Indiana in 1940. It was located in Chicago on the corner of LaSalle and Maple Streets. It made striking use of floor-to-ceiling plate-glass panels with a central core of rough-hewn sandstone slabs that enclosed customer restrooms and storage. The roof was actually suspended on steel wire from two steel masts with a simple neon "GAS" sign. The simple elegant design was equally eye-catching day or night. Richard Neutra, an Austrian immigrant who had worked with Erich Mendelsohn, designed an international-style gas station for a Norwalk gasoline retailer in Bakersfield, California, in 1947. The sharp, uncompromising lines clearly provided the inspiration for Chevron's early 1950s design, immortalized in Ed Ruscha's pop art painting.

Marathon Oil, a Midwest marketer, developed an international-style gas station design in the late 1940s that was retained until the early 1960s. The front elevation resembled a landscape-format picture frame divided into three distinct segments–a triptych.

The design was dictated more by industrial design's efficient logic than the whimsical elegance of Jacobsen and Bertram's designs. The

West German government appointed Dr. Heller to coordinate the design of autobahn (superhighways) gas station/service areas in the early 1950s. Although designed by individual architects, the autobahn gas stations conformed to a standard layout. The individual international-style designs showed the influence of both Alvar Aalto and Mies van der Rohe. As previously mentioned, Gasolin built an experimental international-style gas station in Germany in the mid-1950s that owed much to Jacobsen's design. At about the same time, BP commissioned Dr. Lothar Gotz to design an experimental international-style gas station in Wiesbaden, Germany. The design was the quintessence of postwar international style and mirrored exactly the appearance of Mies van der Rohe's Lake Shore Drive apartments in Chicago (i.e., black frame with light-colored brick or plate-glass infill). The raised sales office and elegant staircase reflect Mies van der Rohe's Farnsworth House, built in Fox River, Plano, Illinois, between 1946 and 1950. Dr. Gotz's design was widely praised by architectural journals and adopted, in part, by BP for subsequent German gas station designs. Joseph Fujikawa, a member of Mies van der Rohe's team, designed a gas station in 1966 for a residential complex on Nuns' Island (Ile des Soeurs) near Montreal, Canada, that was adjacent to Expo '67, the Canadian World's Fair. The gas station consisted of two modules: one for car servicing and the other for sales/customer restrooms with a central pump island corridor. The design was a mirror image of Mies van der Rohe's work in the Midwest during the 1940s and 1950s and was elegant and unobtrusive, but unfortunately rather impractical.

Eliot Noyes' iconic Pegasus design for Mobil in the mid-1960s owed much to Jacobsen and Gotz's pioneering designs for its distinctive

Gasolin built at least one experimental gas station in the international style in Germany during 1955. It owed much to Arne Jacobsen's 1937 Skovshoved design. Many key elements, such as the floating canopy and the sharp angularity of the sales office, were subsequently used by the parent company, BV Aral, in its 1960s design. *Author collection*

Joseph Fujikawa, a member of Mies van der Rohe's team, designed this gas station as part of a residential complex on Nuns' Island (Ile des Soeurs) adjacent to the Expo 1967 World's Fair in Montreal, Canada. A greater emphasis was placed on unobtrusive elegance rather than pure functionality, which is a comment often made about van der Rohe's later work. *Author collection*

functional elegance. The Mobil Pegasus design was developed in the face of mounting political and public pressure, led by Lady Bird Johnson, wife of President Lyndon Johnson, to get rid of ugly gas stations and excessive point-of-sale advertising. There were even rumors at the time that prominent gas station identification pole signs and logos might be outlawed, which would severely hinder brand differentiation. Eliot Noyes' brief was to develop a gas station design as an instantly recognizable brand in its own right that could be identified immediately as a Mobil gas station without identification pole signs or logos. Noyes realized this could be achieved with the addition of unique custom-made gas pumps, canopies, and lamp standards. He was inspired by AGIP, an Italian oil company that relied entirely on elegant custom-made gas pumps, lamp standards, and a superb identification logo of a fire-eating, six-legged black dog. AGIP had extremely high brand recognition in Italy and amply demonstrated what could be achieved with a minimum of logos and point-of-sale advertising. The Mobil Pegasus design set new standards with its iconic circular canopies and cylindrical silver and black gas pumps, sympathetic use of brick, black window and door frames, light blue restroom doors, a putty grey color scheme for ancillary equipment and significantly, an illuminated white disc with the Pegasus logo. The Mobil Pegasus gas station design gained widespread plaudits from major design publications and was spectacularly successful with American and international customers alike. It is probably the single most consistent and apt expression of the international style ethos in a commercial context.

AGIP, an Italian oil company, amply demonstrated that very high brand recognition could be achieved with high-quality custom-made pumps, lamp standards, and the intelligent use of brand logos, as shown in this 1964 advertisement. This provided the inspiration for Eliot Noyes' classic Mobil Pegasus design of 1966. *Author collection*

Form Follows Function

THE GAS STATION HAS EVOLVED over the past ninety years through a complex interplay between changing automobile requirements, consumer demands, traffic patterns, taxation, and competition. This chapter examines the sometimes contradictory factors that brought this about and why the seemingly obsolete canopy came back into use.

Some of the best locations for gas stations were on main routes for catching commuters on their way to or from work. A convenient location with safe entrances and exits is absolutely critical. That being said, a good location is entirely dependent on local demographics and traffic patterns. A change in either can make it redundant virtually overnight. Forecourt ergonomics play a vital role in determining a gas station's success, particularly during busy periods. Every dealer wants to ensure he can refuel as many automobiles as quickly as possible during the busiest times without causing traffic congestion. Interestingly, large numbers of blue-collar motorists at the end of factory shifts forced price cutters to come up with the most efficient layout, parallel rows of gas pumps, during the mid-1930s.

High gasoline taxes in Europe during the 1960s encouraged dealers to examine ways of cutting costs and passing them on to customers. Self-service provided the logical answer. Dealers had to weigh the benefits of low-maintenance building materials versus the need for integration with the surrounding architecture, often with some loss in cost-effectiveness. Porcelain enamel panels provided the gas station with absolutely consistent brand identity, ease of maintenance, and because of their extensive use in bathroom fittings, a hygienic image. Conversely, porcelain enamel panels were incompatible with residential neighborhoods that were of brick or wood construction.

Strict national and local government controls have always guaranteed that the motorist gets what he pays for at the gas pump. Nevertheless, motorists' whims and insecurities played a crucial role in the move from blind piston pumps to visible glass cylinder pumps. The computer pump changed consumer purchasing habits from purchasing by volume to purchasing by value. The gas pump globe not only provided additional advertising but also enabled night service when illuminated by an electric bulb. It came into its own during the late 1920s with the introduction of premium grade gasoline when it provided the motorist with clear grade identity.

Location, Location, Location

Dealers and oil companies alike have always had to draw up complex equations for finding the best site. Key considerations are medium- to long-term growth potential affected by local businesscs/industries, expansion or decline of residential neighborhoods, transit and commuter traffic, and the impact of new routes, particularly interstate highways.

Some of the best locations for gas stations were on main routes leaving towns, in order to catch homeward-bound commuters who had more time for refueling in the evening than during the frantic morning rush (see Chapter 6). Dealers and oil companies placed a higher premium on a constant flow of traffic that could be found on main arterial roads or feeder routes for interstate highways or toll throughways rather than rush hour peaks in the morning and evening. Research by Exxon in the early 1950s indicated that between 0.75 to 1.25 percent of all passing traffic would actually pull into a gas station. It was imperative that Exxon gas stations were visible from at least 200 yards with clearly accessible entrances

Porcelain enamel panels came into widespread use in the early 1930s with the introduction of the super service station with enclosed lubrication and wash bays, as seen in this Ohio photograph from 1932–1933. Porcelain enamel panels provided an absolutely consistent brand identity, a modern and progressive image, required virtually no maintenance, and implied hygienic restrooms. They were, however, incompatible with residential neighborhoods. *Author collection*

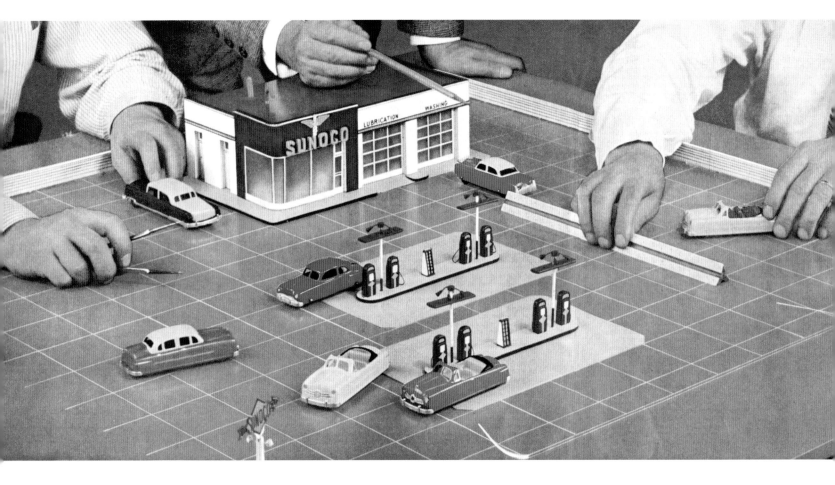

Every oil company in the United States and Europe after World War II developed highly efficient forecourts to maximize through traffic and minimize congestion. Scale models were indispensable for planners to optimize a site's potential. *Author collection*

and exits. The entry and exit ramps had to be at a 45 degree angle to the sidewalk with a minimum width of 30 feet. Other prime locations were midway between residential neighborhoods and shopping centers, but these have now been made redundant by supermarkets selling cut-rate gas under their own labels. Sites to be avoided were near schools (often prohibited by local ordinances), railroad crossings, traffic lights, on hills, and anything that obscured the sight of oncoming traffic.

There are two classic examples of the change in traffic patterns in New York and New Orleans after World War II. Many neighborhood gas stations were made redundant by the move to the Levittown suburban housing development on Long Island, New York, during the early 1950s. The integration of schools in New Orleans during the early 1960s caused "white flight" to the suburbs where white children were in the majority at local schools. The introduction of the I-10 elevated highway next to the New Orleans central business district provided a fast and direct commuting route to the suburbs, which made most gas stations on Magazine Street and St. Charles Avenue superfluous.

Protection versus Isolation

From the mid-1920s on, there has been an ongoing debate about the pros and cons of canopies versus maximum forecourt efficiency. For the first ten to fifteen years, the canopy was an indispensable part of American gas station design. It provided protection from rain and snow and provided additional advertising space. Initially, gas pumps were placed either within the sales office or just outside, which only allowed automobiles to be refueled from one side. National Supply stations, acquired by Chevron in 1914, was the first company to place gas pumps on the outer edge of the canopy to enable automobiles to be refueled from both sides. It was quickly copied by Shell with its Class A crackerbox stations launched in 1915, and later by Standard Oil of Indiana with the Joliet station in 1917.

By the mid-1920s, many oil companies and oil industry experts began to question the benefits of canopies. They added up to 25 percent to the cost of building a gas station, tended to concentrate and restrict forecourt traffic, and unless they had a ceiling height of at least 12 feet, they could not be used by high-sided trucks, which were major customers. The cumbersome trailer-caravan finally caused the canopy to disappear during the mid-1930s, except in the South and on the West Coast. Texaco was the first major oil company to introduce a gas station design, the Denver, without a canopy during the mid-1920s. They were quickly followed by Phillips 66 with its cottage design introduced in 1927. While the latter was possibly the first oil company to introduce pump islands, Exxon was the first major oil company to develop widely spaced pump islands that maximized forecourt efficiency and minimized congestion. This was no doubt hastened by the nationwide popularity of trailer-caravans during the 1930s, which required large areas to maneuver and potentially caused forecourt congestion.

Exxon had two pump-island sizes, 9 feet long for two pumps with a lamp standard but no oil rack and 14 feet long for two pumps with two lamp standards and an oil rack. The pump islands had to be at least 20 feet apart to prevent congestion. Pump islands were placed 12 feet away from the edge of the fore-court and were ideally 30 feet from the service building in order to allow the motorist to gain access to the second pump island by driving around the automobiles refueling at the pump island closest to the entrance. Tank truck offloading points had to be 20 to 25 feet away from either pump islands or service bays to prevent obstruction. This forecourt format was copied by every major oil company in America during the late 1930s and in Europe after World War II. It remained the standard layout until the widespread introduction of self-service in Europe during the late 1960s and early 1970s.

At about the same time that Exxon developed its widely spaced pump island forecourts during the mid- to late 1930s, price cutters in the Midwest, most notably Gaseteria, came up with the ultimate in forecourt design: parallel rows of gas-pump islands. This format was dictated by large volumes of blue-collar motorists at the end of factory shifts who needed to be served as quickly as possible with the minimum of congestion. This format, called the starting gate, was adapted from mass-transit bus garages that had been using it since the early to mid-1920s. The starting gate format was used by Shell, Exxon, and Mobil for very high-volume sites in New Jersey during the early 1950s. Sunoco also used the format for one site in Ohio, and it was adopted for many throughway gas stations, as well. Where feasible, the starting gate is now the standard format for self-service gas stations.

The canopy came back into use with the introduction of self-service in Europe. While it provided protection from rain and

The starting-gate format, parallel rows of pump islands, as shown in this Chicago photograph from the 1950s, is the most efficient forecourt layout. Price cutters in the Midwest developed it during the mid-1930s to refuel large numbers of blue-collar motorists quickly at the end of factory shifts. *Author collection*

snow, its role was subordinate to a highly efficient forecourt layout that maximized through traffic.

Pumping Icons

Gas pumps have been around for just over one hundred years, and by 1909–1910, they were sufficiently accurate and reliable for curb-side retailing. At this time, the most common type of gas pump was the manually operated blind piston pump, which simultaneously pumped and measured the gasoline via a vertical brass tube whose inner dimensions were exactly one or five U.S. gallons. The piston plunger was raised on a ratchet that counted off the quantity dispensed via a small dial. The largest manufacturer and the pioneer, dating back to 1885, was S. F. Bowser of Fort Wayne, Indiana.

According to a Bowser brochure from August 1908, there were also pressured systems. These were probably hydrostatic systems that relied on water pressure to dispense the gasoline via a flow meter. The gasoline floated on top of water in an underground storage tank, which was connected to an elevated water tank with a ball cock, identical in function to a household water supply system or a toilet cistern. While it is impossible to prove conclusively, it is fairly certain that Atlantic used this system for its elaborate city beautiful stations in Pennsylvania and New England. An identical system was introduced in Great Britain during 1911 by

"Always Accurate"

Visible Pump

Whenever you need gasoline drive to a Fry equipped Service Station operated by Jimmy the Courtesy Man. You will find Jimmy in all parts of the world. Undoubtedly he has a gasoline station right near your home. You will know him by his smile and his Fry Visible Pump. For Jimmy will have no other.

Guarantee Liquid Measure Company
Rochester, Pa.

Jimmy sells gasoline from the Fry Visible Pump because he knows it to be accurate, dependable and fool-proof. He knows such features will increase his gallonage by establishing confidence with you and millions of other motorists. Buy from Jimmy. He operates a Fry. There is one close by. Buy from a Fry. Millions do.

Fry Equipment Company, Limited
401 Royal Bank Bldg., Toronto, Ont.

(Left) Visible gas pumps were an instant hit with motorists during the 1920s simply because the motorist could see what he was actually paying for. In fact, visibles were no more accurate than blind piston pumps, thanks to strict certification and annual checks. Fry, similar to most manufacturers, ran heavyweight advertising campaigns in *The Saturday Evening Post* promoting the benefits of "visible" pumps to motorists. *Author collection*

(Opposite, top) This photograph, taken in July 1949, of the Sinclair station on the corner of South Main and Alvarez Streets in Jacksonville, Florida, shows an excellent location catering to two different types of customer: local residents and through traffic, effectively segregated by two pump islands at right angles to one another. The location is clearly visible to oncoming traffic. The well-laid-out forecourt with its wide entrance and exit ramps maximized through traffic and minimized congestion. *Author collection*

(Opposite, bottom) During the mid- to late 1930s, Exxon developed highly efficient forecourt grids that maximized through traffic and minimized congestion, as shown in this 1939 Pittsburgh photograph. Pump islands had to be at least 20 feet apart, a minimum of 12 feet from the boundary and 30 feet from the service building. *Author collection*

(Below) Canopies were quintessential gas station features until the mid- to late 1920s when they fell out of fashion, apart from in the Deep South and the West Coast. The canopy provided strong brand identity and weather protection, amply demonstrated in this Saginaw, Michigan, photograph from around 1924. Conversely, canopies added 25 percent to the cost of construction and were a hindrance to high-sided trucks and impeded forecourt traffic. *Author collection*

TEXACO Oasis... *for modern caravans*

45,000 TEXACO DEALERS
STAND BY
TO SERVE YOUR CAR

Every one of them offers you a gasoline that he has chosen to build his business upon . . . Texaco Fire-Chief, not just "regular" gas. Yet it costs no more than the gasoline you are now using.

He has put his judgment behind this gasoline because he knows that it has been developed as an emergency-duty fuel to give his customers quick response . . . that all slow-burning elements are removed . . . that it delivers full power on the road in less than $\frac{1}{100}$th of a second.

He knows that it is made to compensate for changes of season and of climate in various parts of the country. Quick starting and quick firing—anywhere.

Furthermore he knows this. When he cleans off your windshield or measures your tire pressure he does not feel he is doing you a favor. He knows he is doing himself a favor by bringing you back again to do business with him.

Try a Texaco Dealer next time!

TEXACO DEALERS

This message is published in behalf of more than 45,000 independent Texaco Dealers by The Texas Company . . . makers of Fire-Chief Gasoline, New Texaco Motor Oil, Havoline, Marfak and more than 350 Industrial Lubricants.

Texaco Dealers invite you to tune in Eddie Cantor in "Texaco Town" Every Wednesday Night—Columbia Network—8:30 EST 7:30 CST 9:30 MST 8:30 PST

EMERGENCY DUTY GASOLINE AT NO EXTRA COST. A good reason for stopping at Texaco Dealers. Originally developed for fire-engine and ambulance service, Texaco Fire-Chief has won millions of users by its livelier starting and road performance.

"STAYS FULL LONGER." Thank America's farmers for remarkable oil-purifier, Furfural, made from farm crops. Furfural-refined, New Texaco Motor Oil is free from oil impurities that result in excessive engine wear. It gives full lubrication with less oil used.

YOU MAY SAVE $100 BY SAYING "MARFAK." Don't say "grease it," ask for Marfak . . . a sturdier, longer-lasting chassis lubricant. Used car dealers tell us that proper lubrication can add $50 to $100 to a car's trade-in value. Let us Marfak your car.

The nationwide popularity of trailer caravans during the 1930s, of which 200,000 were sold in 1937 alone, forced a drastic rethinking of forecourt layouts and the demise of the canopy, apart from in the Deep South and the West Coast. *Author collection*

(Above) Every major oil company adopted Exxon's widely spaced island format, as shown in this Cities Service Chicago location during the 1950s. This would remain the norm until the introduction of self-service. *Author collection*

Bywater Petrol Storage Ltd. The proprietor, Darol Bywater, had lived and worked in the United States for a number of years previously. It is pretty clear that Bywater was inspired by what he had seen in America.

Initially, gas pumps were fairly skeletal in appearance with no provision for brand identification. Gradually, they became enclosed with cast-iron or sheet-steel cabinets that were painted in bright colors, predominantly red, with brand decals or enamel plates. Gilbert and Barker (now known as Gilbarco) introduced the first gas pump in 1912, the T-8, with an electrically illuminated globe that provided additional advertising and nighttime service. Gilbert and Barker, like Bowser and Wayne, also marketed blind piston pumps that used compressed air to raise the piston plunger.

Visible gas pumps with large calibrated glass cylinders date back as early as 1901 but did not come into widespread use until just after World War I, due to the steep rise in gasoline prices due to shortages. Seeing the actual fluid measured off reassured the motorist he or she was getting the full measure of this increasingly

expensive commodity. In actuality, the visible pump was no more accurate than the blind piston pump that continued to be manufactured until the late 1920s. Visible pumps were very eye-catching because of their height that allowed the gasoline to flow by gravity into automobiles, especially with dyed gasoline: bright orange for Gulf No-Nox, red for Esso, blue for Sunoco, and green for Cities Service Koolmotor. Some specialist manufacturers, particularly Fleckenstein, supplied retrofit visible conversion kits for blind piston pumps. One particular twin-cylinder system provided a virtually continuous flow. As one cylinder emptied, the other filled up. This system was adopted throughout Europe, albeit with smaller-capacity twin cylinders, each of one imperial gallon (1.2 U.S. gallons) capacity for Great Britain or five liters capacity (1.321 U.S. gallons) for the rest of Europe. American visible pumps were initially supplied via hand-operated pumps, but by the mid-1920s, were increasingly replenished via electric pumps or compressed air.

Continuous-flow electric gas pumps appeared in the mid- to late 1920s, initially with flow meters. There was, however, one

Canopies came back into fashion with the introduction of self-service in Europe, as seen in this Aveley, Essex, site in Great Britain during the late 1960s. Retailers quickly discovered that customers were reluctant to serve themselves without some protection from the weather. *Alan Pond*

example manufactured by Milwaukee from as early as 1913. The sheer force and speed of the electric pumps created special problems with tanks, air vents, filters, meters, and nozzles that were not entirely resolved until the early 1930s. These pumps sped up gasoline sales and dispensed eighteen to twenty gallons a minute compared with five to ten gallons a minute for visibles and paved the way for elaborate forecourt service during the early 1930s. Bowser introduced the Xacto Sentry in 1928 with a positive displacement meter that became the standard method of measurement still used today. Essentially, the positive displacement meter uses four or five separate pistons in cylinders attached to a crankshaft, just like an automobile motor, that measure the exact quantity of gasoline dispensed.

Computer pumps were launched by Wayne in 1933 and transformed people's buying habits, from purchasing by volume to purchasing by value. Automobiles became progressively lower in height after World War II and gas pumps were reduced accordingly, so the computer display was at the driver's eye level. These pumps

were known as lo-boys. Hydrant systems came into widespread use during the 1950s and used one semisubmersed electric pump in an underground storage tank to supply up to six gas pumps, known as dispensers, that contained only the positive displacement meter and computer. Toward the end of the 1950s, pumps and dispensers were further reduced in height with panoramic display meters with large ad plates for brand/grade identity and were sometimes known as panorama pumps. Effectively, panorama pumps made gas pump globes redundant. During the early 1960s, panorama pumps and dispensers were introduced with narrow bases, known as T pumps or dispensers because of the silhouette. Technically, gas pumps changed little after the mid-1930s, apart from the introduction of hydrant systems for high-volume sites during the late 1930s, the automatic shutoff nozzle in 1940, and the blender pump in 1956. The introduction of the electronic computer display in the early 1970s and EPA vapor-recovery systems and multiproduct dispensers in the mid- to late 1970s were significant but still relied on the same electric pumps and positive displacement meters.

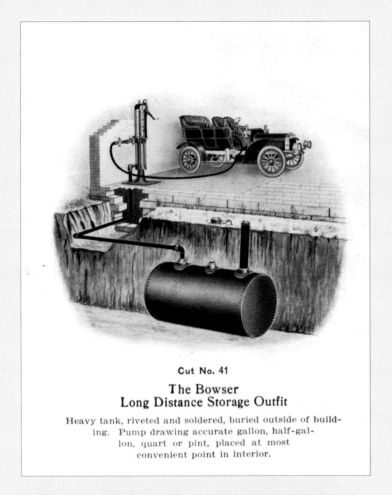

Cut No. 41

**The Bowser
Long Distance Storage Outfit**

Heavy tank, riveted and soldered, buried outside of building. Pump drawing accurate gallon, half-gallon, quart or pint, placed at most convenient point in interior.

(Above) Prior to 1909 and 1910, Bowser "blind" piston pumps and tanks were aimed primarily at wealthy private motorists and companies with vehicle fleets. The illustration appeared in a rare August 1908 Bowser catalog. The Bowser cut 41 pump was advertised from as early as June 1906 and was still in production fifty years later! *Author collection*

(Right) By 1916, Wayne supplied blind piston pumps were encased in steel cabinets complete with electrically lit globes that turned the gas pump into a self-advertising package, exactly like a Coca Cola bottle or Camel cigarette pack.
Author collection

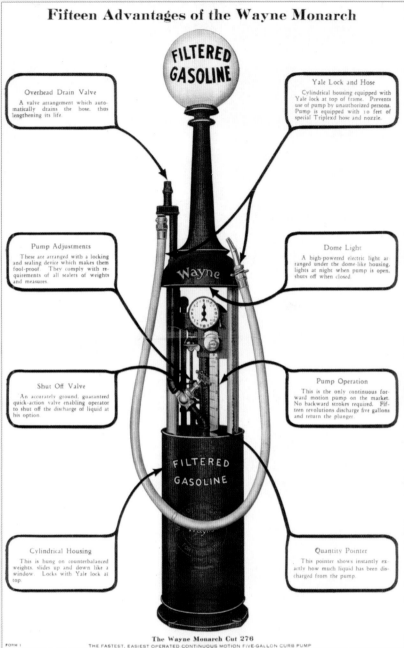

Fifteen Advantages of the Wayne Monarch

The Wayne Monarch Cut 276
THE FASTEST, EASIEST OPERATED CONTINUOUS MOTION FIVE-GALLON CURB PUMP

Shining Beacons

Gas pump globes were introduced in 1912 with the launch of the Gilbert and Barker T-8 gas pump that had a cast-iron pole supporting a white milk-glass globe with an electric light bulb that provided additional publicity and made night service feasible. Other gas pump manufacturers, most notably Bowser, quickly introduced gas pumps with globes.

The earliest gas pump globes were either spheres or pill-shaped. They were generic with only "Gasolene" or "Gasoline" etched on both sides. Many of the pill-shaped globes had an additional opening at the top with a metal cap, known as "chimney top" globes, which prevented the buildup of heat from the electric light bulb.

Around 1915 and 1916, Socony, Atlantic, Gulf, Texaco, Sohio, and Standard Oil of Indiana introduced pill-shaped gas pump globes with two-color silkscreened or etched logos. Standard Oil of Indiana later experimented with an unusual oval-shaped globe that resembled a football. Just before the 1920s, metal-frame globes were introduced with two removable glass lens inserts held in place by circular pieces of notched wire. These became the most common type of gas pump globe throughout the 1920s and 1930s because they were so easy to update with a simple change of lens

continued on page 140

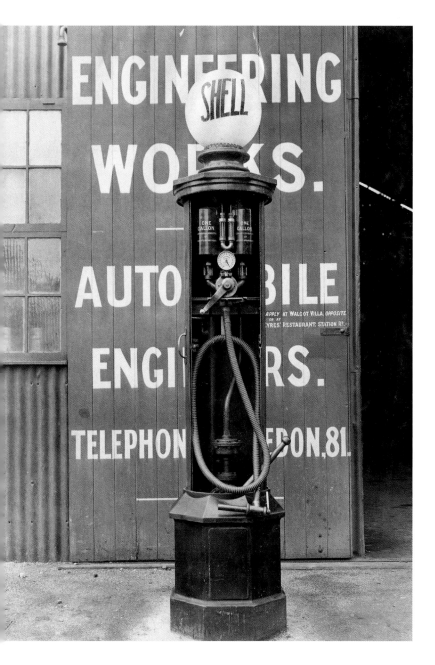

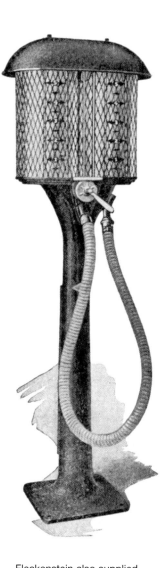

Shell introduced the twin-cylinder visible gas pump in Great Britain in October 1921 and had it manufactured to specifications by at least three different companies. As one gallon cylinder emptied, the other filled up. The brass cylinders were later replaced by glass bottles. Shell continuously improved its specifications throughout the 1920s and worked very closely with British, French, and German manufacturers. *BP Archive*

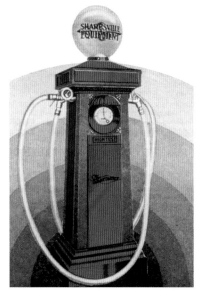

Flow meter dispensers supplied by compressed air or water pressure systems (from as early as 1908, in the case of the latter) were a fairly common sight on the eastern seaboard and in the Midwest during the 1920s. Farr Hydraulic systems, Aqua, and Erie were leading suppliers. The Sharmeter, featured here, was made by the Sharpsville Boiler Works and was a typical example. *Author collection*

Steep gasoline price rises after World War I hastened the widespread introduction of visible pumps in the United States because the motorist could actually see what he or she was paying for. Tokheim was at the forefront of this trend. *Author collection*

Fleckenstein also supplied visible kits that could be retrofitted to blind pumps. The twin-cylinder visible-dispensing method, featured here, became the standard throughout Europe, largely thanks to Shell, albeit with smaller-capacity cylinders. *Author collection*

(Right) The Wayne 861 gas pump, launched in 1932, with its highly distinctive art deco clock face made circular dials obsolete and started a trend for more decorative pumps with square or rectangular dials. *Author collection*

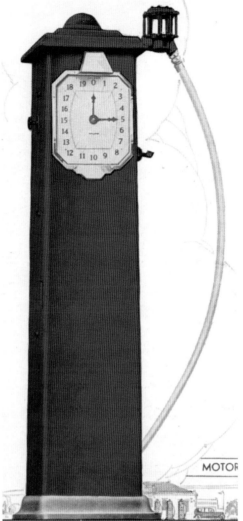

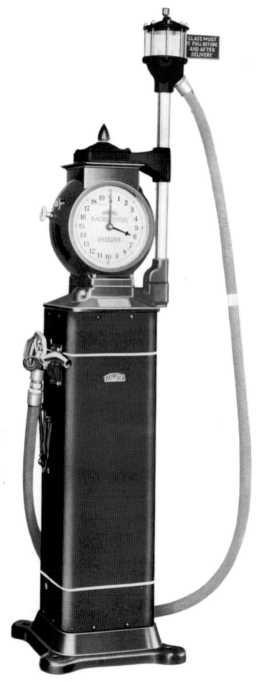

The invention of the computer pump by Wayne in 1933 revolutionized purchasing habits. People bought by value rather than volume. The Wayne 60, the second Wayne computer pump that was introduced in 1934, caused a sensation with its radical appearance created by Van Doren and Rideout, who were industrial design consultants. *Author collection*

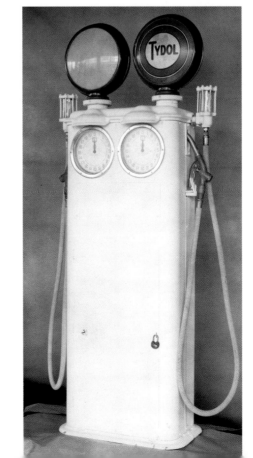

The Bowser Xacto Sentry dispenser, launched in 1928, transformed measuring technology. The positive displacement meter offered an unrivalled accuracy at any speed and is still in use to this day. Initially, the Bowser Xacto Sentry was sold as a dispenser supplied directly by a hand pump or remotely by an electric pump or compressed air. By 1930, the Bowser Xacto Sentry was a fully integrated pump/meter unit. *Author collection*

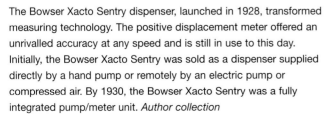

Gilbert & Barker (now known as Gilbarco), like many manufacturers, marketed single and twin electric gas pumps. Exxon was a large customer for the Gilbert & Barker 105 Dual Extended twin pumps because pump attendants found it easy to get customers to change up to ethyl from regular gas. *Author collection*

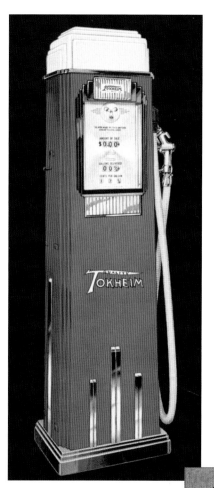

Tokheim, amongst others, quickly introduced elaborate art deco computer pumps. This pump, like the Wayne 60, was a perfect match for flamboyant art deco gas stations, especially those in Los Angeles. *Author collection*

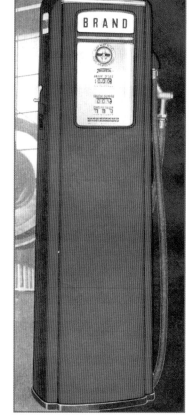

After World War II, gas pump manufacturers progressively lowered the height of gas pumps to match that of automobiles, enabling the driver to see the computer at eye level. These pumps were known as lo-boys, which used either a retractable hose or, more commonly, a hose retained by a spring-loaded hawser. *Author collection*

The Wayne 70, introduced in 1937, started a trend toward more functional and streamlined designs and was epitomized by the 1938 Gilbarco Calcometer 96 and Tokheim 39 (pictured here) models. All models showed the influence of industrial design with an emphasis on form following function. The Gilbarco Calcometer pump, in particular, demonstrated the impact of mass production with quickly detachable panels. *Author collection*

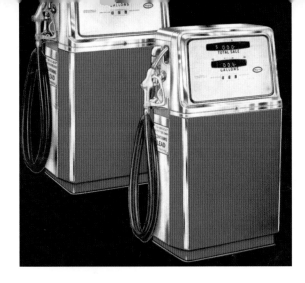

(Left) During the late 1950s, Wayne, like most manufacturers, introduced even lower models, known as panorama pumps, with computer displays and large ad plates to extend the width of the pump. Panorama pumps effectively made gas pump globes obsolete. The Wayne 400 series was available with and without overhead lighting cowls. *Author collection*

(Below) Panorama pumps with narrow bases were introduced in the early 1960s and were sometimes known as T-pumps because of the silhouette. The Gilbarco Trimline model featured is from 1963. *Author collection*

Beckmeter, a British manufacturer, introduced radial arm pumps in March 1946. The radial arm could be rotated 360 degrees and enabled the pump attendant to extend the hose conveniently over the top of the automobile. The model featured was a later version introduced in 1950. Radial arm pumps were built by all British manufacturers and were the norm in Great Britain until the early 1960s. They were also built by Ljungmans, a Swedish manufacturer. *Author collection*

During the mid-1950s, Tokheim, similar to other United States manufacturers, introduced lo-boy models with wider computer display windows that imitated the wider wraparound automobile windshields. The actual computer numerals were no larger than on previous models. *Author collection*

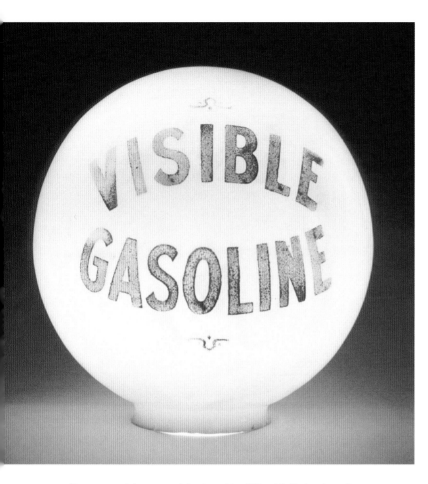

Gas pump globes were introduced by Gilbert & Barker (now known as Gilbarco) in 1912 with a T-8 blind piston pump. The globes were made from white glass, known as milk glass, and cast from molds. Initially, globes were purely generic with "Gasolene" or "Gasoline" etched or stenciled onto the globe. Generic globes were a common sight up to the mid-1920s. *Michael Karl Witzel/Coolstock*

continued from page 135

inserts. This became critical with the introduction of premium grade gasoline in 1925 and the launch of the new Pegasus logo for Mobilgas in 1934. There were also pill-shaped glass globes with lens inserts attached by two lead studs that were used by Sinclair and Texaco up to the 1950s. There were postwar French examples, as well.

The most stunning, eye-catching globes were shaped globes blown in molds by skilled glass blowers. The two earliest and most eagerly sought after shaped globes were the Red Crown globes introduced by Standard Oil of Indiana in the early 1920s and the White Eagle globes launched by White Eagle Refining around the same time in the Midwest. There were quite a few variations in both designs. These in turn undoubtedly provided the inspiration for Shell to launch its iconic scallop-shell-shaped globe around 1928. Shell went on to introduce a considerable number of variants of the scallop shell shape around the world.

Shell was quick to take note of Standard Oil of Indiana and White Eagle's shaped globes and introduced the iconic scallop-shaped globe around 1928. Shell went on to introduce many different versions around the world, and they remained in use as late as the early 1970s in Great Britain and the Netherlands. In view of this, collectors have to use extreme caution when purchasing Shell globes. *Author collection*

British multibrand gas stations were veritable showcases for highly sophisticated molded gas pump globes throughout the 1930s with shapes ranging from shells, coal sacks (synthetic gasoline from coal), clover leafs, diamonds, triangles, hands, aces, shields, and three-dimensional Ds (for diesel fuel). Each one tried to outshine the rest of the competing globes on the same forecourt.

Plastic frames with glass lens inserts were introduced during the 1940s, but the golden age of gas pump globes had already passed. They simply did not fit in with the new international corporate identity programs. Shell, Standard Oil of Indiana, and particularly Texaco were the only major oil companies to persist with globes up to the late 1950s in the United States. Globes became the exclusive preserve of small regional marketers and price cutters. Plastic injection-molded globes were later introduced as low-cost alternatives to hand-blown glass globes. Gas pump globes were still in widespread use in Great Britain and the Netherlands up to the early 1970s when self-service replaced attended service.

Pump and Save

Self-service as we know it today first emerged in Sweden fifty years ago, but its antecedents date back to around 1915. Self-service is divided into two methods: prepayment and postpayment.

For "pulling power" at point-of-sale use

CINCINNATI GLOBES

The attention compelling designs of Cincinnati Globes stop motorists . . . There's no chance of overlooking the clean cut lettering, the lasting color effects, the super-brilliance of Cincinnati Globes . . . The master workmanship of these sturdy, durable, good looking globes, their trade "pulling power", and their economical cost, has caused them to be preferred by the leading marketers . . . Write for prices . . . Learn the dollar for dollar value offered by Cincinnati Globes — in small or large lots.

THE CINCINNATI ADVERTISING PRODUCTS COMPANY
YORK and COLERAIN AVE.
CINCINNATI, O., U. S. A.

The last word in all glass globes

Permanent, not painted designs — separate replaceable faces — more economical — higher illuminating power.

This finer-looking globe is a blood-brother of the famous Cincinnati Metal Frame Globe . . . Both have replaceable faces with the design fired-into, and part of the glass . . . The weakness, heretofore, in all glass globes has been in the design . . . For while it is possible to paint a design, it is not possible to fire ceramic colors directly on an all glass globe at the necessary heat of more than 1000° *without* the globe col-

lapsing . . . This weakness is overcome in Cincinnati All Glass Opal Globes by the use of separate convex faces which permit firing ceramic colors into glass . . . The Cincinnati method produces a permanent design which is not possible by any known process when design is placed directly on all glass globe . . . And separate faces are economical, too, in that broken faces may be replaced without going to expense of buying entire new globe . . . Write for full data on Cincinnati All Glass Opal Globes . . . They are economical to buy and use:

CINCINNATI GLOBES
SELL MORE GASOLINE AND OILS

Cincinnati Globes were one of many United States manufacturers that produced large numbers of metal band globes with glass lens inserts during the 1920s, as shown in this July 1928 advertisement. The metal band globe was the most common type, largely because it was so flexible. In the event of grade or brand identity change, the detachable glass lenses could simply be replaced with new ones.
Author collection

(Left) During the early 1920s, Standard Oil of Indiana introduced eye-catching crown-shaped globes that remained an essential part of its marketing until the late 1950s. Shaped globes required highly skilled glass blowers who knew exactly how much air to blow to form the shape inside a mold. There were many variants and the date of this example is unknown. *Michael Karl Witzel/Coolstock*

(Below) White Eagle Refining (later acquired by Mobil) introduced its highly distinctive eagle-shaped globes at about the same time as Standard Oil of Indiana launched its crown-shaped globes. There are a few variants, which are all very rare and eagerly sought after by collectors. *Michael Karl Witzel/Coolstock*

Prepayment via coins with the self-service pumps first appeared in the United States around 1915 with purpose-built pumps, and it appeared in Great Britain during the mid-1920s with bolt-on devices. It was designed primarily as an emergency night/after-hours service. The British bolt-on devices could only be used on certain types of gas pumps and were very easy to defraud with foreign coins, washers, or buttons. Both the purpose-built pumps and the bolt-on devices were impossible to adjust for wildly fluctuating prices prevailing at the time and posed a dangerous fire hazard when inexperienced users overfilled automobile gas tanks. Coin self-service briefly reappeared with electric computer pumps in New York State during the mid-1930s but was quickly abandoned over concerns about fire safety. This, however, marked a turning point for self-service for three different reasons. First, the quantity of fuel dispensed could be adjusted; second, it was a discretionary purchase; and third, discount pricing was used as an incentive. The latter was a guiding principle in all subsequent self-service development.

The fire hazard risk was finally resolved with the introduction of the automatic shutoff nozzle in 1940, which prevented automobile gas tanks from being overfilled. The automatic shutoff nozzle came into widespread use after World War II when it was developed as a labor-saving device with a latched ratchet. This enabled the pump attendant to wipe the windshield and check the fluid levels and tire pressures while the automobile was being filled automatically with gasoline. The

(Above) Injection-molded plastic globes were introduced during the mid-1950s and were mainly used by small regional cooperatives and marketers and refiners in the Midwest. They were later used by Texaco and price cutters in Great Britain. *Michael Karl Witzel/Coolstock*

(Right) There were also pill shaped globes with glass lenses attached by a pair of lead studs. This example dates from the mid-1930s. Texaco and Sinclair, in particular, were the main users of this type of globe in America. Total and Caltex used them in France during the 1950s. *Michael Karl Witzel/Coolstock*

143

Start *This* To Work For You Day and Night

"The Help Yourself Way To Gasoline"—

The new vending gasoline pump which enables the autoist to serve himself without disturbing you from your work or sleep. He simply drops required coin into slot and gets the proper amount of gasoline to the very ounce.

Most convenient and economical device ever invented for the handler and user of gasoline.

Write today for particulars regarding this and other Hull Garage Service devices.

Hull Pump & Tank Co.
INCORPORATED

Box 2001   Owensboro, Ky.

"Salesman Wanted Everywhere"

Hull was one of the first United States manufacturers to introduce coin-in-the-slot self-service pumps. This advertisement appeared in 1916. It provided the motorist with the convenience of twenty-four-hour service and enabled the garage mechanic to complete repairs or sleep without interruption.
Author collection

safety aspect became implicit. Ironically, this same device paved the way for the large-scale development of self-service and the demise of the pump attendant.

Postpayment self service had a limited success in America during the late 1940s and early 1950s and did not become well established until it was systematically developed by a Swedish co-op in the late 1950s. In Sweden, just as the rest of postwar Europe, automobile ownership expanded from the previously exclusive preserve of white-collar professionals to skilled blue-collar workers. The latter, in particular, were keen to receive good value for money. Sweden had a well-established network of consumer unions or cooperative societies that enabled their members to buy groceries, consumer goods, and even gasoline at discount prices. One consumer union, IC, realized that the food supermarket self-service format could be adapted cost-effectively for selling gasoline. Fortuitously, Ljungmans, a Swedish gas pump manufacturer, had just developed a data transmission/recording system for municipal councils. It permitted council truck drivers to refuel trucks at any time, and the finance department could keep track of consumption and expenditure. The IC consumer union was able to adapt this system for retail use. By their very nature, consumer unions or cooperative societies are wholly dependent on consensus and collaboration with the members. Self-service would not have succeeded without the members' active participation and feedback. The Swedish experience was a crucial factor in convincing other European countries that self-service was viable.

(Right) Coin-operated self-service gas pumps spread to Great Britain by the mid-1920s when this photograph was taken. Coin-operated service was developed primarily as an emergency night or after-hours amenity.
Getty Images

NEW OPACO

Safety-Fill

PATENTS PENDING

NOZZLE

with automatic shutoff Feature

PREVENTS SPILLING, WASTING GASOLINE

Self-service, as we know it today, would have been impossible without this crucial safety device, the automatic shutoff nozzle, which was introduced in the United States during 1940. A pressure sensor automatically cut off the flow as soon as it detected blowback from the automobile tank. The automatic shutoff nozzle came into widespread use after World War II, ironically as a labor-saving device with a latched ratchet.
Author collection

The move to self-service in Great Britain during the 1960s was hastened by increases on gasoline and employee taxes introduced by the Labour government between 1964 and 1970. The Selective Employment Tax (SET), introduced in 1966, was essentially an employee poll or head-count tax. The greater the number of employees a business had, the higher the tax. Enterprising dealers found that they could run a highly efficient self-service operation with two cashiers rather than six pump attendants, pay less SET tax, and increase turnover. Alan Pond, the British self-service pioneer, quickly discovered that self-service gas stations required employees with fundamentally different abilities, such as food supermarket managers who were

used to handling large volumes of cash and bank tellers who had proven people/cash handling abilities.

Consensus and collaboration were essential for developing self-service gas stations in Great Britain from 1963 on. Alan Pond and BP went to exhaustive lengths discussing self-service gas station proposals with local communities, planning departments, and fire authorities. BP even took these groups to Germany and Sweden to see self-service in action. Alan Pond issued regular local newsletters to give the community a greater sense of involvement. This was in stark contrast to early experiments with post-payment self-service in the United States during the late 1940s and 1950s.

Many of the early American self-service pioneers were brash publicity-seeking mavericks who antagonized local communities,

(Above) European housewives on tight budgets played a pivotal role in the development of self-service, as shown in this Malmo, Sweden, photograph from around 1965. Research indicated that women could be relied upon to follow the step-by-step instructions in exactly the same way as they did with cooking recipes. Men proved to be a bigger problem. They ignored the instructions, had difficulties, and were reluctant to repeat the experience. *Alan Pond*

Britain's first self-service gas station was opened in April 1963 by Turnbull's Garage in Plymouth. The station had an unusual circular layout with nine widely spaced pumps and sold Shell gasoline at a discount to attract customers. Note the blue-collar workers with the old car in the foreground, who were key self-service customers. British retailers, rather than major oil companies, were at the forefront of developing self-service prior to the late 1960s. *Getty Images*

In April 1964, BP set up a network of Munztank (coin-operated) self-service gas pumps across West Germany for night/after-hours service. They were very popular, especially among taxi drivers. Their ease of use and exemplary safety record convinced local British planning and fire authorities that self-service was viable. *Author collection*

authorities, and competitors. This was especially true in California and New Jersey. Elsewhere, particularly in the South, self-service sites were often in unsafe neighborhoods, were badly laid out, and sold little-known cut-rate brands. They offered little incentive for the passing motorist. None of the major oil companies were prepared to consider self-service for the American market until it had become firmly established in Europe during the early 1970s. One of the deciding factors may have been how easily British women adapted to it, contrary to all expectations. By the early 1960s, it was clear that Swedish women were perfectly happy to serve themselves in exchange for saving money. This was, however, put down to the egalitarian, progressive attitude of Swedes in general. Oil companies were less optimistic about the British market, which was still fairly narrow-minded and class ridden in outlook. British women adapted far more easily than men simply because they were prepared to read the instructions carefully in the same way they followed a recipe. British men, by contrast, were notorious for failing to follow instructions, getting into difficulties, looking like idiots, and refusing to repeat the experience.

Self-service brought about fundamental changes in site dimensions and forecourt layouts, as well as the reintroduction of the canopy. Alan Pond was largely responsible for developing the Four Square self-service format in Great Britain during the late 1960s that relied on multigrade blender pumps for maximum forecourt efficiency. Four widely spaced blender pumps, each located next to a canopy support, enabled the customer to get the exact grade required from any one of four locations. If necessary, they could drive around the back of an automobile being refueled nearest the entrance. The Four Square with a six-pump variant for higher-volume sites was the norm in Great Britain until the late 1980s. Historically, it was more desirable to have a fairly wide frontage with a shallow depth for attended service for a landscape format. The most efficient self-service format, the starting gate that consisted of parallel rows of gas pumps, completely changed this with the portrait

Contrary to all expectations, British women, like their Swedish counterparts, were equally willing to use self-service in exchange for saving money, as seen in this Ealing photograph from the swinging 1960s (around 1969). *Alan Pond*

Manor garages in Southampton opened the second British self-service site in July 1964, and Mobil provided technical support. The site, while very eye-catching, was poorly laid out with a long row of pumps that caused congestion, a common problem with early self-service sites. The optimum self-service layout would only be achieved after a good deal of trial and error. *Richard W. Marjoram*

Alan Pond, the British self-service pioneer, developed the Four Square forecourt layout, which had four widely spaced multigrade blender pumps that provided maximum convenience and minimum congestion. This remained the norm in Great Britain until the mid- to late 1980s. This Harlow, Essex, site that opened in the summer of 1966, with six pumps, was the first example. *Alan Pond*

By the early 1970s, BP became renowned for its highly efficient British self-service stations. This Whale Bridge, Swindon, site, photographed in 1972, clearly demonstrates the benefits of the Four Square layout with maximum choice of refueling points, maneuverability, and fast through traffic. *Austin J. Brown*

Shell went one better with this starting-gate format self-service station near Reading, Great Britain, that was photographed in 1972. The starting-gate format, while requiring a far deeper site, has an efficiency rating of 90 to 95 percent compared with 65 to 75 percent for the Four Square format. *Austin J. Brown*

format that featured a relatively narrow frontage and extended depth. Overnight, some prime locations for attended service became redundant for self-service because they were too shallow. The canopy had previously been a liability, especially with automobiles towing trailer-caravans or high-sided trucks, but it came back into its own with the introduction of self-service. Oil companies quickly discovered that motorists were reluctant to get out of the automobile and serve themselves without some protection from the rain or snow.

By the early 1970s, BP, Shell, Total, and ARCO had highly efficient Four Square or starting-gate self-service forecourts in Great Britain, largely thanks to the pioneering efforts of Alan Pond. Exxon and Mobil took slightly longer to implement similar layouts. While Exxon was at the forefront of developing electronic self-service gas pumps in Great Britain, this was often at the expense of efficient self-service forecourts, which was particularly ironic in view of its highly efficient pump island grid developed

during the late 1930s for attended service. Mobil had introduced its superb Pegasus corporate identity program in 1966 with its iconic cylindrical pump, but because of its shape, it could not accommodate the incremental blender, which was vital for maximum self-service efficiency. Mobil instead used less efficient linear layouts with single-grade pumps. Mobil later replaced the Pegasus pump in Great Britain during the mid-1970s with electronic Gilbarco Highline multigrade blender pumps.

Self-service completely changed gasoline retail. Gasoline sales were no longer a low-profit adjunct to highly profitable car servicing and tire/battery sales. Instead it was the primary focus with cigarettes, candy, soft drinks, snacks, convenience groceries, and car washes (space permitting) that provided additional profits. Car servicing bays were torn down and the vacant space was turned into additional self-service islands. Car servicing and tire/battery sales reverted to either automobile franchise dealers or specialist chains, such as Firestone, Midas, and Jiffy Lube.

Exxon, similar to all major oil companies, adopted self-service in Europe during the early 1970s. This attractive site, photographed in 1971, was located in Richmond, Great Britain. However, the angled pump island format, known as the echelon, was inefficient. The site was later redeveloped with a more efficient Four Square layout. *Author collection*

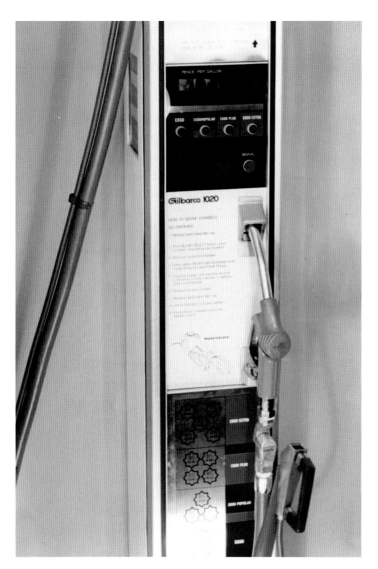

(Above, left and right) Gilbarco test marketed the 1020 electronic blender dispenser at this Shepperton, London, site in March 1971. The pumping units were at the center of both islands and special miniature VDUs were attached to the nozzles for the customer's convenience. The Gilbarco 1020 was test marketed at four different British sites. The experience gained from the 1020 led to the development of the highly successful Highline series in the mid-1970s. *Author collection*

(Two images on left) In July 1972, BP introduced Llewellyn Lewis LuLu 7 electronic multigrade dispensers at this well-laid-out Four Square site in Reading, Great Britain. All of the electronic systems relied on large central computers in sales offices for grade selection, quantity, and value of product dispensed. Electronic gas pumps finally came into widespread use after the invention of the microchip in the mid-1970s made them cost-effective. *Austin J. Brown*

French supermarket chains, most notably Carrefour, used cut-rate self-service sites to attract customers to large out-of-town hypermarkets in the early 1970s, as seen in this photograph on the outskirts of Paris in October 1971. They were quickly copied by other supermarket chains across Europe and fundamentally changed European gas retailing. *Alan Pond*

Electronic self-service blender gas pumps were introduced by Exxon in Bath, Great Britain, during January 1971. Price changes could be made at the flick of a switch rather than having to change four to six pumps manually. The Westcourt system combined Westinghouse overhead electronic VDUs with Tokheim hydraulics/dispensers, as shown in this Streatham, London, photograph from late 1971. *Author collection*

(Above) This ARCO self-service station photographed in Cowley, Great Britain, in December 1971, maximized efficiency with a combination of Westcourt electronic pumps and a Four Square layout. ABCO, ARCO's British predecessor company, had a very close working relationship with Alan Pond. *Richard W. Marjoram*

(Right) Alan Pond briefly used girls on roller skates as a promotional gimmick to take customers' payments to the sales kiosk and return with their change at the Harlow site. A Los Angeles self-service station during the late 1940s had previously used female cashiers on roller skates. *Alan Pond*

Coast to Coast 1920-1941

THE 1920S WITNESSED A SIGNIFICANT EXPANSION of oil companies' marketing territories within the United States and Europe. In 1929, Texaco became the first American oil company to sell gasoline in all forty-eight states. Socony, Standard Oil Company of New York (later Mobil), and Shell were not far behind. Sinclair, Gulf, Tydol, and Pure became seminational marketers.

Shell's expansion eastwards was of particular concern thanks to its instantly recognizable trademark and outstanding corporate identity. Shell was ruthless in imposing its brand and corporate identity immediately upon any business it acquired. Competitors quickly nicknamed Shell the yellow peril. Shell was the catalyst for change and spurred major oil companies to adopt instantly recognizable brands, logos, and color schemes. By the same token, Shell was equally prepared to learn from other oil companies. Shell quickly recognized the excellent brand identity provided by Standard Oil of Indiana's crown shaped gas pump globes and introduced the scallop shell shaped globe during the late 1920s.

It has been alleged that Shell invaded Socony's (later Mobil) New England territory in April 1929 in revenge for a destructive kerosene price war in India. In fact, Shell's expansion eastwards was dictated by demographics. During the 1920s and up to the early 1950s, the East Coast was still the United States' most populous area with a large, almost continuous population rather than the scattered communities on the West Coast and, to a lesser extent, the Midwest. The East Coast promised Shell greater long-term growth, albeit with tough competition. Purely by coincidence, Shell's major East Coast competitors were Exxon, Socony, and Vacuum, which competed fiercely with Shell in Europe and the Far East. None, however, could match Shell's instantly recognizable scallop shell logo and color scheme and suffered from a lack of brand consistency with Exxon selling under at least nine local brands in Europe. Mobil, formed by the merger of Socony and Vacuum in 1931, marketed under at least seven brand names in America and five different brand names overseas. It was no coincidence that Shell became the dominant marketer in Europe, with the exception of Germany and Switzerland, by the end of the 1930s. Having such a formidable international competitor in its own backyard must have forced Exxon and Mobil to realize the urgent need for single, instantly recognizable brands allied with strong corporate identities.

Shell, Exxon, and BP, a relative newcomer, rapidly expanded their marketing operations across Europe. In fact, Exxon had a far stronger presence in Europe than in the United States. Vacuum Oil (later Mobil) sold gasoline in central Europe and France, while Gulf and Texaco marketed in Belgium, the Netherlands, and Scandinavia. Three major European oil companies emerged during this decade: BV Aral in Germany, Compagnie Francaise de Raffinage in France, and AGIP in Italy. The latter two were directly government controlled. All three oil companies had significant shares of their national gasoline markets.

Exxon gradually introduced the curbside gas pump and storage tank across Europe between May 1920 and April 1923 and was quickly copied by its competitors. At the same time, Exxon launched drive-in gas stations in Great Britain and France. A vociferous British motor trade lobby, however, prevented the development of oil-company-owned, single-brand

Night vision. Shell experimented with a number of eye-catching art deco gas station designs during the early 1930s. Careful lighting made these designs even more attractive at night, as seen in this Portland, Oregon, photograph taken in circa 1932. The Shell San Francisco skyscraper inspired this design, and the indented tapering column motif was retained in subsequent designs. *Author collection*

Dapolin, Exxon's German subsidiary, launched curbside pumps and storage tanks in April 1923, and by 1925, about 1,000 Dapolin curbside pumps were installed across Germany. Dapolin pumps could be found outside garages, hotels, boarding houses, and hardware stores, as seen here in the Rhineland province circa 1925. The Indian chief logo, in particular, and the red triangle sign provided excellent publicity. *Author collection*

UNITED STATES

During the early 1920s, Gulf, Standard Oil of Indiana, Texaco, Shell, and Chevron had the most consistent, instantly recognizable gas station designs in the United States. As previously mentioned, Gulf and Standard Oil of Indiana, in particular, set the pattern for adaptable brick construction designs that were particularly suitable for residential neighborhoods. Shell and Chevron had highly functional, cost-effective, prefabricated designs. The Standard Oil of Indiana Joliet design had an immediate impact across the United States, while the Shell and Chevron prefabricated designs had a more far-reaching impact long-term both in America and Europe.

Once the drive-in gas station had become an established fact, neighbors and consumers became less rigid about its appearance. Inevitably, the Gulf Sandbrick and the Standard Oil of Indiana Joliet designs lost their impact, and other oil company designs overtook them.

Gas station designs became progressively more functional and looked to contemporary styles like art deco and streamline moderne for inspiration (see Chapter 7). Competition brought forth a lot of innovation. Texaco, with its national coverage, created a preference for cream or white stucco exteriors in the late 1920s. Sinclair, more significantly, caused a revolution with its enclosed lubrication bays. As the canopy disappeared, the pole sign became more important for station identity. Both Shell and Exxon had a far-reaching impact throughout the 1930s with their well-planned service station buildings and highly efficient forecourts. Texaco leapfrogged them both with its iconic streamline moderne EM station in 1937 that frankly borrowed heavily from Shell's design. Gulf and Standard Oil of Indiana quickly responded with their own streamline moderne designs in the late 1930s, which both oil companies retained until the early 1960s.

Gulf

Gulf introduced its Sandbrick design in 1917, which retained key features from its original 1913 Baum Boulevard gas station in Pittsburgh. The principal economic attractions of this design, as previously discussed in Chapter 6, were widely available with dark brown brick, off-the-shelf cornice moldings, and simple construction that enabled it to be installed in virtually any location without modification. No one could object to its dignified, low-key appearance,

gas stations in Great Britain until after World War II. Gas station design in Great Britain was more varied but consistent with developments elsewhere.

By the mid-1920s, most oil companies in the United States had well-established, consistent gas station designs and were the main gasoline retailers. In Europe, particularly Great Britain, automobile dealerships and service garages with drive-in gas forecourts were the most common gas retailers and remained so until the mid-1950s. It took slightly longer to establish consistent national gas station designs in Europe. Moreover, these remained national, rather than international, in style and appearance until after World War II. Different designs, building materials, and different color schemes were used for each European country. While the canopy began to fall out of favor in America during the late 1920s, it remained a key feature in European gas station design, particularly in Germany, until 1939.

The Wall Street Crash of 1929 and subsequent Great Depression had a catastrophic impact on the world economy and employment. Many oil companies were forced to reappraise their markets, consolidate profitable activities, dispose of loss-making assets, and withdraw from some territories. The 1930s was a ruthless decade, but it was one that ultimately defined gas station design and oil company marketing strategies for the next thirty years in America and subsequently Europe.

and the sheer consistency of Gulf's Sandbrick design provided unrivaled brand identity.

Gulf introduced a new logo in 1921 that consisted of an orange disc with "GULF" in blue capital letters, which considerably improved its brand identity as it expanded across the United States. Gulf and Texaco, in particular, were the fastest growing oil companies during the early 1920s. Gulf was also one of the first oil companies to introduce a premium grade, No-Nox, around 1925, which was manufactured by a catalytic process using aluminum chloride. By the mid-1920s, Gulf had two Sandbrick designs for low- and high-volume sites.

The low-volume site was essentially a small flat-roofed sales office with a tiled awning that ran around the office just above the

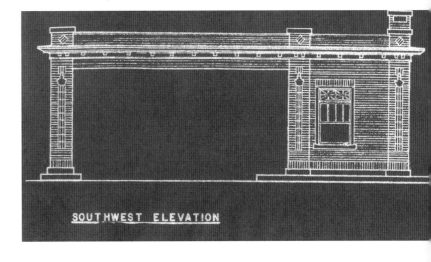

SOUTHWEST ELEVATION

(Below) By the early 1920s, Gulf modified its Sandbrick design for two different formats: a canopied design for high-volume sites and a sales kiosk with a tiled awning for low-volume sites. The dignified, low-key design fit in virtually anywhere and provided superb brand identity for Gulf. This station was probably located in Texas and photographed during the late 1920s. *Image Archives/Alan Reff*

(Above) This 1925 Gainesville, Florida, Gulf Sandbrick gas station blueprint shows the absolute consistency of Gulf's design across the Deep South. The only difference between this design and the photo below are the bracket lamps and the gazebo extension around the canopy. The Sandbrick design became obsolete as canopies fell out of favor and white stucco became popular during the late 1920s. *Courtesy of Vic and Karen Maidhof*

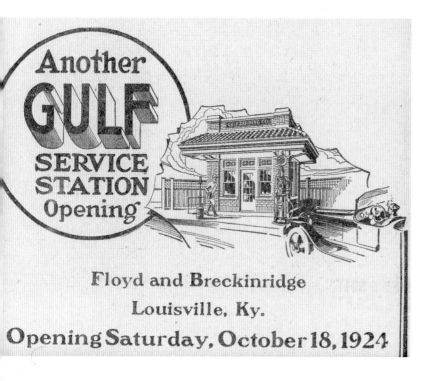

(Above) Gulf's distinctive logo and low-volume gas station design featured prominently in this Louisville, Kentucky, grand opening advertisement from October 17, 1924. Note how the tiled awning covered only the gas pump rather than the forecourt. *Author collection*

(Right) Gulf introduced its Sandbrick gas station design in Louisville, Kentucky, during 1917, as seen in this 1921 Bowser advert. The Sandbrick design retained many features from the original 1913 Pittsburgh gas station, notably the use of widely available dark brown brick and a simple, highly distinctive design that was easy to build. *Author collection*

windows. Two gas pumps were located on either side of the sales office. The high-volume site had a sales office with a very wide canopy, typically 22 feet across, which enabled two automobiles abreast to be refueled from two rows of gas pumps for a total of four pumps.

Gulf's Sandbrick canopy design appeared somewhat dated by the late 1920s, especially in comparison with Texaco's white stucco Denver design, which did not have a canopy, and Sinclair's recent introduction of enclosed lubrication bays provided food for thought. Gulf finally introduced an art deco design around 1932 that used molded, glazed, cream terracotta bricks. It is unclear as to how many Gulf art deco stations were actually built, due to the severity of the Great Depression and the subsequent impact of the 1935 Standard Oil of Indiana Iowa Plan where Standard relinquished direct control of its gas stations by leasing them to the managers, which was copied nationwide apart from on the West Coast (see Chapter 3).

Texaco's iconic streamline moderne EM station was designed by Walter Dorwin Teague in 1937 and provided the final catalyst

for Gulf to launch a highly functional, modern design that was affectionately known as the icebox, which Gulf used virtually unchanged until the early 1960s (see Chapter 7).

Standard Oil of Indiana

Standard Oil of Indiana's Joliet design, introduced in 1917 and subsequently modified in 1921, has been exhaustively discussed in Chapters 1 and 6, but this design set the benchmark for gas stations, especially in residential neighborhoods, up to the mid-1920s.

Standard Oil of Indiana was the dominant marketer in the Midwest and maintained this through a number of shrewd moves. It was one of the first oil companies to introduce molded glass gas pump globes in the shape of crowns, which provided superb brand identity and were quickly copied by competitors, most notably Shell and White Eagle. Standard Oil of Indiana also had the exclusive rights to tetraethyl leaded gasoline in the Midwest between 1926 and 1930, which enabled it to compete very effectively against Texaco and Shell. Standard Oil of Indiana acquired control of Pan-Am and Amoco during the late 1920s but operated them as separate entities until the early 1950s. In June 1926, Standard Oil of Indiana introduced a new trademark, a solid blue circle surrounded by two concentric blue circles that were vertically bisected by a blue torch, which was used until the late 1940s. Standard Oil of Indiana later introduced a dark blue rectangular pole sign with "STANDARD SERVICE" in white capital letters. Inevitably, the Joliet design was superseded by competitors' more up-to-date designs in the late 1920s, most notably Texaco's white stucco Denver design and, more significantly, Sinclair's greasing palaces.

Standard Oil of Indiana introduced its "Spanish Mission" (otherwise known as Spanish colonial) stations in 1932 in response to Sinclair's castle Spanish colonial design (see Chapter 6). As previously mentioned, Standard Oil of Indiana formulated the Iowa Plan in 1935 to avoid anti-chain-store taxes. It relinquished direct control of its gas stations and leased them to station managers. Aggressive marketing by Shell and Texaco in the late 1930s forced Standard Oil of Indiana to introduce a new streamline moderne design, which was retained, albeit in a less curved format, up to the early 1960s (see Chapter 7).

Texaco

Texaco was most closely identified with two particular gas station designs during this period: the Denver style that was introduced during the mid- to late 1920s (see Chapter 6) and the iconic EM streamline moderne station that was launched in 1937 (see Chapter 7).

Texaco was a formidable marketer with four distinct advantages: an instantly recognizable trademark (the red star with a green "T"), access to abundant supplies of low-cost Texas crude oil, national distribution with four-color advertising in nationally available magazines, and superb advertising campaigns with simple messages. Texaco built consumer confidence and repeat purchases by emphasizing consistent, predictable products and services from coast to coast. No other oil company could hope to match this apart from Shell or Mobil.

The key attraction of Standard Oil of Indiana's Joliet design was its sheer adaptability. The Joliet design could be modified to fit in with virtually any location, such as this red brick apartment block in Detroit, Michigan, in spring 1920, yet retain its brand identity. *Author collection*

The Standard Oil of Indiana Joliet design was subsequently modified with a pitched roof for the effective dispersal of rain and to prevent the accumulation of snow. The modified design was better suited to high-sided trucks as the canopy now extended over one driveway rather than two, as seen here in Chicago, Illinois, in 1922. *Author collection*

Standard Oil of Indiana introduced its Spanish Mission, also known as Spanish colonial, design in response to Sinclair's design in 1932. Note the crenellated effect created by the false tiled roof. Unlike Sinclair, Standard Oil of Indiana used glazed ivory bricks, as shown in this Franklin and Third Avenue South, Minneapolis photograph from the mid-1930s. *BP Archive*

No extra price

Everywhere . . . on highways of every State, stands the Texaco pump, a symbol of high test quality. Motorists who have regularly used "premium" motor fuels, who willingly paid 3¢ to 5¢ extra, now prefer the *new* and *better* Texaco Gasoline. For Texaco stands *every* test. It forms a dry gas. It starts easier — it accelerates quicker and, mile after mile, it delivers a full measure of honest power. Try Texaco today. Learn the real meaning of " high test."

THE TEXAS COMPANY, TEXACO PETROLEUM PRODUCTS

The NEW and BETTER

TEXACO GASOLINE

By the late 1920s, Texaco was prominently featuring its Denver gas stations in all its advertising, as shown in this detail from an April 6, 1929, advertisement. The subdued pistachio green and cream color scheme, combined with the extensive use of lattice screens, worked particularly well in new suburban neighborhoods. The Denver design set new standards and made both Gulf and Standard Oil of Indiana's designs look old-fashioned. *Author collection*

The green-roofed and white stucco Denver stations were a vital part of Texaco's corporate identity and were featured prominently in its advertising during the late 1920s and early 1930s. Texaco clung onto this design for too long and tried to adapt it for enclosed lubrication/wash bays, which tarnished its formerly pristine corporate image. Shell's experimental art deco gas stations brought this into even sharper focus and forced Texaco to come up

There is anecdotal evidence that Texaco introduced its elaborate Oaklawn gas station design as far back as 1916, as seen here in an April 22, 1922, advertisement, but this has been impossible to corroborate. The Oaklawn design was quickly superseded by the simpler, more versatile Denver design in the mid-1920s. *Author collection*

with a radically new design in 1937. The streamline moderne EM station was designed by Walter Dorwin Teague and borrowed heavily from Shell's designs, albeit in a more rounded format. At the same time, Texaco introduced its highly distinctive banjo pole sign that was widely copied by competitors.

Sinclair

Sinclair was established in 1916 and did not have a consistent design for its company-owned gas stations until the late 1920s. For a brief period, Sinclair was the industry trendsetter. Sinclair launched the super service station, known as a greasing palace, in the late 1920s and subsequently introduced a highly distinctive Spanish colonial design. Affectionately known as the castle, it inspired Standard Oil of Indiana and Exxon (see Chapter 7). Sinclair quickly lost all its influence by clinging to one outmoded feature, the canopy, and was content thereafter to sit back and follow other oil companies' initiatives, often ten years late.

Sinclair initially used a classical style similar to that used by banks, complete with stone facing, for some of the earliest greasing palaces, but it quickly moved over to a fairly anonymous design with a white stucco exterior and a steeply angled false-roof motif (see Chapter 3). Sinclair subsequently built two prototype gas

(Top right) Texaco adapted the Denver design with arched doorways, windows, and a miniature steeple, as in this one photographed in Miami during 1933. This made a complete mockery of an honest, widely accepted design and harmed Texaco's formerly pristine brand image. By contrast, Texaco advertising was still very modern. This exact same thing would happen thirty years later. *Author collection*

(Bottom right) Unfortunately, Texaco's Denver design was poorly suited for enclosed lubrication bays that had been recently introduced by Sinclair in the Midwest. The highly distinctive pitched roof and twin column design worked against the harmonious integration of lubrication bays. The photograph was taken in New Jersey around 1931. *Author collection*

stations in Samson and Sheffield, Alabama, which led to the castle design. Ironically, the most distinctive feature of the subsequent castle design, the gabled canopy, was placed at the rear of the first prototype station in Samson as a lubrication bay roof. The station in every other respect was as unremarkable as the one in the Midwest. The second prototype, built in Sheffield, had the lubrication bay in front on the left-hand side of the building. It retained the highly distinctive gable motif that was an even more eye-catching feature than the relatively anonymous gas pump canopy. In retrospect, it is easy to see why Sinclair didn't want to give up its highly distinctive canopy design because of the efforts to get it right. The castle design, with its highly distinctive gabled canopy with a crenelated effect, was built in large numbers during the early 1930s throughout the Midwest, the South, and the eastern seaboard. The canopy, its most distinctive feature, became a liability with the widespread popularity of trailer caravans. By August 1937, Sinclair featured a gas station without a canopy in an advertisement aimed at trailer caravan owners.

Texaco's expansion nationwide was helped immeasurably by superb simple and direct advertising campaigns, like this one from June 7, 1924, which were just as consistent as "the volatile gas" and "the clean, clear, golden colored oil" they were advertising. Texaco was probably the first oil company to make effective use of pole signs. *Author collection*

The elaborate crenellated canopy was the most distinctive feature in Sinclair's Castle gas stations, as shown in this superb illustration from a 1936 map. Ironically, this same feature became a liability with the nationwide popularity of trailer caravans in the mid-1930s, and Sinclair lost many customers.
Author collection

Shell

Shell built hundreds of its instantly recognizable yellow and red prefabricated crackerbox stations along the West Coast from the top of Washington to the southernmost tip of California throughout the 1920s. As previously mentioned, the crackerbox design was first introduced in 1915. Both the stations and gas pumps were embellished with an instantly recognizable yellow scallop shell logo highlighted with red pinstriping and "SHELL" in capital letters. The West Coast stations were supplied by a well-established infrastructure of pipelines, bulk storage depots, and oil refineries.

Shell adopted an entirely different strategy in its expansion castwards that began in 1923. Shell discovered it was quicker and cheaper to establish a strong presence in the Midwest and East Coast by acquiring existing gas station networks and local oil companies with bulk storage depots and oil refineries. This inevitably led to a plethora of different gas station designs that were

only linked by the Shell logo and yellow and red color scheme. In retrospect, Shell's strategy was very shrewd. From 1928 on, all major oil companies were forced to follow Sinclair's example and either extend the existing structures with enclosed lubrication and wash bays (a less satisfactory option) or build a new service station from scratch. In 1930, Shell had virtually nationwide coverage and required a service station design with enclosed lubrication and wash bays and customer restrooms that was suitable for most local climate conditions and locations across the United States. Between 1930 and 1934, Shell experimented with a number of prototype designs. Around this time, Shell realized that its scallop shell gas pump globes (introduced around 1928) and bright yellow gas pump color scheme provided ample brand identity. It also recognized that the prominent yellow and red station color scheme was less acceptable in communities with a strong architectural or historic significance, particularly on the East Coast. Shell used a cream-colored

Note how Sinclair moved the open-sided lubrication bays forward to the left of the sales office of this Sheffield, Alabama, station, circa 1928. The crenellated wall with the bracket motif was repeated in triplicate to form a canopy for the gas pumps in the Spanish colonial Castle design. The open lubrication bays would be an essential feature, as well. *Author collection*

Sinclair pioneered the development of enclosed lubrication bays, which quickly became known as super service stations. This photograph, along with the following two, trace the evolution of Sinclair's iconic Spanish colonial Castle gas station. The distinctive lubrication bay roof at the rear of this station in Samson, Alabama, circa 1928, was the inspiration for Sinclair's Castle gas pump canopy introduced in the early 1930s. *Author collection*

scheme for all its prototype stations and introduced the same color scheme for all its existing stations in 1934. The color scheme was accentuated with red wainscoting and a yellow pinstripe in 1935.

Initially, Shell used its San Francisco art deco headquarters for inspiration. This can clearly be seen in a prototype station that opened in Portland, Oregon, around 1932. The sales office, with a canopy over the gas pumps, bore a striking resemblance to the San Francisco headquarters' tower. The design had a strong European influence with the vertically indented frieze around the canopy, the North African–style filigree windows on the side of the service building, and the tapered, indented pilasters that were more decorative than structural. The latter were inspired by one of the gateways to the 1925 Paris Art Deco Exposition. The enclosed service bays and customer restrooms were in a separate building at right angles to the sales office and gas pumps. Chevron used an identical layout at this time.

Around 1933, Shell used a more sharp-edged and angular art deco style for another gas station in Oregon that bore a close resemblance to other West Coast art deco gas station designs. This prefabricated design with porcelain enamel panels had highly distinctive twin sharp-edged humps above the canopy that clearly provided the inspiration for Walter Dorwin Teague's iconic 1937 EM streamline moderne Texaco station. This Shell design retained the tapering, indented pilaster motif and used a horizontal frieze with four parallel red lines. The canopied sales office with gas pumps was still separate from the service building, though this was now behind and parallel to the sales office. This design was still a common practice on the West Coast at the time.

Shell built an experimental gas station in Toledo, Ohio, around 1935, with a glazed terracotta brick construction that used the same tapered, indented pilaster motif as the West Coast prototypes. This particular station had a stepped effect and the sales office was lower than the service bays and customer restrooms. Equally striking were the floor to ceiling glass windows in the sales office, which became an integral feature of all postwar gas station designs. The tall chimney was turned into a design feature as a tapered, indented pilaster. All of the aforementioned features were used for a showcase Shell gas station that opened in St Louis, Missouri, during 1937.

Shell's experimentation ended with an art deco gas station that opened in Marysville, California, in early 1935, and had a single service building that contained the sales office, a service bay, and customer restrooms. This design retained the tapered, indented pilaster; twin-hump motif; and horizontal red line frieze for the sales office bay window. The Marysville station design became Shell's standard model nationwide until 1941.

Exxon

Exxon, or Standard Oil of New Jersey as it was known at the time, did not officially embark on any company-owned gas station building program until 1924. The reasons were twofold. Exxon regarded itself primarily as a refiner and wholesaler that had large supply contracts with other ex–Standard Oil Trust companies, notably Socony and Standard Oil of Kentucky. The other reason was as the largest entity from the breakup of the Standard Oil Trust of 1911, Exxon was concerned that the Federal Trade Commission (FTC) would intervene if it became directly involved in gasoline marketing in its territory. Fierce competition from Texaco and Gulf throughout their territories in New Jersey, Maryland, and the South forced a change in policy and fortunately the FTC did not intervene. Unofficially, Exxon owned around eleven gas stations mainly in Baltimore, its most important market, since 1917. In 1922, Exxon built a company-owned station in front of one of their Baltimore bulk storage depots, which was an inspiration for stations built after 1924. The elegant design essentially was a red-brick arched canopy with natural orange terracotta roof tiles, which vastly improved the otherwise shabby setting.

The year 1924 was momentous for Exxon. First, it introduced a large-scale company-owned gas station building program with a consistent design, which for all intents and purposes was a straight copy of the Standard Oil of Indiana Joliet design. The Exxon version, however, used a cream and off-white color scheme that was very eye-catching when combined with the natural orange terracotta roof tiles. Secondly, it introduced a new instantly recognizable Standard logo that consisted of a red circle and horizontal bar. Thirdly, Exxon pioneered the use of tetraethyl lead for premium gasoline. The latter had to be withdrawn after careless handling of concentrated tetraethyl lead caused a number of deaths. Leaded

Shell experimented with a series of art deco designs during the early 1930s on the West Coast. The earliest designs bore a close resemblance to Shell's San Francisco skyscraper, as seen here on Broadway and Wheeler Street in Portland, Oregon, around 1932. Similar to other West Coast gas stations, the service bays and restrooms were in a separate building. Shell used a cream color scheme for all these experimental designs, which was subsequently adopted for all Shell stations in 1934. *Shell International Petroleum Company*

Shell launched a more hard-edged art deco prefabricated design with a canopy around 1933, which was widely used on the West Coast, and is seen here in Oregon. Note the highly distinctive twin-humped canopy, which was almost certainly the inspiration for Texaco's 1937 streamline moderne EM station. The service bays and restrooms were still in a separate building and now behind the sales kiosk. *Shell International Petroleum Company*

Shell built at least two experimental art deco gas stations in the Midwest with glazed terracotta blocks, as seen here in Toledo, Ohio, around 1935. Note the floor-to-ceiling sales-office window that was a common feature after World War II and the decorative heating chimney. All of these features were used in a large showcase station in St. Louis in 1937. *Shell International Petroleum Company*

gasoline was reintroduced under the new premium brand name Esso in 1926 after stringent health and safety guidelines had been put in place. During the mid- to late 1920s, as Shell expanded eastwards, Exxon examined all its weakest links. Exxon merged its subsidiary, Standard Oil of Louisiana, which operated in Louisiana, Arkansas, and Tennessee, into its mainstream operations and dispensed with the Stanacola brand name. Humble Oil, its Texas subsidiary, remained an entirely separate entity and did not become totally integrated until 1959. In 1929, Exxon acquired Beacon Oil, subsequently known as Colonial Beacon Oil, which gave it a springboard to expand northwards in New York and New England. During the previous year, 1928, Exxon set up Standard Oil of Pennsylvania to fill in the southern gap between New Jersey and Maryland. Unlike in New England, Exxon embarked on a large gas station construction program in Pennsylvania. This coincided with Sinclair's introduction of enclosed lubrication bays.

A series of photographs taken in Pittsburgh during the summer of 1939 traced the development of Exxon's gas station designs over a ten-year period, which showed much experimentation. Initially, Exxon adapted its existing sales office design to incorporate lubrication and wash bays with mixed results. Exxon then came up with an interim Spanish colonial design that was virtually indistinguishable from the Sinclair castle design. This was replaced around 1932 with an alternative, more distinctive Spanish colonial design that relied on a combination of indented pilasters, like the Shell design, and a false terracotta tile roof that created a crenelated effect (see Chapter 6). In conjunction with this modified design, Exxon developed highly efficient forecourts with widely spaced pump islands that maximized through traffic and eliminated congestion. Exxon's forecourt layout set the industry standard for the next forty years and was copied by every oil company. The Spanish colonial design became closely identified with the new Esso company brand name and oval logo

Exxon, as Standard Oil of New Jersey, erected this exquisite arched canopy gas station in front of a bulk storage depot on Harford Avenue in Baltimore in June 1922. At this time, Exxon had no formal network of company-owned gas stations, but it unofficially owned around eleven gas stations. This design inspired Exxon's subsequent company-owned gas station program in 1924. *Author collection*

that was launched in June 1933. It was replaced around 1937 by an elegant understated design that drew much inspiration from the international style.

Chevron

Throughout the 1920s, Chevron made widespread use of the highly distinctive red, blue, and white prefabricated design that was acquired from National Supply Stations in 1914. The design remained virtually intact until 1930.

Chevron introduced a red, white, and blue chevron logo to provide better sign identity in 1930. It was only after World War II that Chevron realized Chevron could be used as a distinctive brand name in its own right and ultimately as a corporate name.

Things changed dramatically in the early 1930s with the large-scale adoption of enclosed lubrication bays by competitors, the growing popularity of art deco, and the impending 1932 Los Angeles Olympics. Chevron's prefabricated design was virtually impossible to adapt for enclosed lubrication bays and lacked the necessary gravitas for the prestigious 1932 Los Angeles Olympics.

In response to these developments, Chevron introduced an elaborate prefabricated art deco sales office design. This had highly distinctive gable ends, which resembled the altar window of an English country church. This design was flexible but only viable with the lubrication bays and customer restrooms in a separate building, which was common practice on the West Coast. By the mid-1930s, Chevron eliminated the cumbersome gables that enabled the sales office, lubrication/wash bays, and customer restrooms to be combined in one service building. Chevron then moved on to streamline moderne style in the late 1930s (see Chapter 7). During the same time, Chevron expanded eastwards under the brand name Calso into Nevada, Colorado, Wyoming, Montana, North Dakota, and South Dakota.

Mobil

Mobil was created by the merger of Socony and Vacuum Oil in 1931 to form Socony-Vacuum Oil Company. Both oil companies had extensive networks of gas stations across America that, like Shell, had been acquired on a piecemeal basis, resulting in a patchwork quilt of different designs. Socony was the more dominant gasoline marketer of the two with major acquisitions of Magnolia Oil in Texas and General Petroleum in California. Vacuum Oil owned the world famous Mobiloil brand; sold its gasoline under the Mobilgas and Navigas brands; and acquired White Star, White Eagle, and Wadhams Oil in the Midwest. Wadhams Oil had a highly distinctive Chinese pagoda design that was not phased out until the early 1950s.

Socony was the leading gasoline marketer in New York and New England, and by the early 1920s, it introduced a discreet

(Top right) Exxon introduced its highly distinctive Spanish colonial design around 1932, as seen here in Baltimore, which became very closely associated with the new oval Esso logo launched in June 1933. The tall indented pilasters were strikingly similar to a 1928 Los Angeles shopping center design and similar to the ones used by Shell in its 1932 Portland, Oregon, station. The false roof and crenellated effect was very similar to Sinclair and Standard Oil of Indiana's designs. *Author collection*

(Bottom right) Exxon had a tall, free-standing canopy design with a head room in excess of 12 feet for high-sided trucks and the sales kiosk was located some distance away for maximum maneuverability, as shown in this Baltimore photograph. Note the Standard circle and bar logo, the silver Esso pumps, and the Standard motor oil banner that point to a date of 1926 or later. *Author collection*

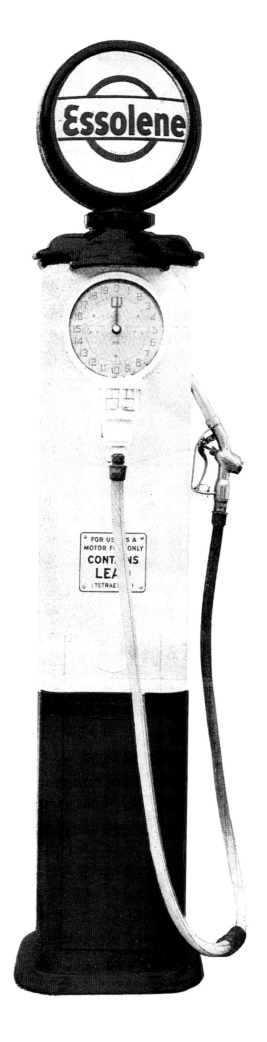

In June 1933, Exxon introduced the new oval Esso logo, Essolene regular grade, and bold pump color schemes that did wonders for its brand image. *Author collection*

white clapboard house design for rural and suburban sites. A neocolonial red brick house design was used for more prestigious locations. Both the clapboard and neocolonial designs were surprisingly adaptable for enclosed lubrication and wash bays.

A new logo was introduced in 1934 that consisted of the Socony shield with the highly distinctive red Pegasus flying-horse trademark Vacuum Oil had used in South Africa since 1913 for its gasoline. The Socony brand name was retained for New York and New England, while the Mobilgas brand name was used elsewhere. Surprisingly, the new logo also contained the acquired companies' names, Magnolia, General, White Star, White Eagle, and Wadhams, as well.

During the mid- to late 1930s, Mobil worked closely with consulting architect Frederick G. Frost to create a super service station with enclosed lubrication and wash bays that retained some of the distinctive Socony neocolonial elements and also looked highly functional. The early designs were dressed with white stucco and had red brick cornerstones or stone facings, while the service bays were surmounted by neocolonial pediments. The later designs had porcelain enamel cladding that incorporated a neocolonial pediment in bas relief. These were gradually introduced across America, but Mobil didn't have a truly consistent national gas station design, corporate identification, or gas pump color scheme until after World War II. Mobil also experimented in the late 1930s with very eye-catching porcelain-enamel-clad drum gas stations with cylindrical sales offices. The drum design was modified and built in key locations after World War II.

EUROPE

Large-scale drive-in gas station construction did not begin in Europe until the mid-1920s after the widespread introduction of the gas pump and storage tank during the early 1920s. While the latter had been used in isolated cases in Great Britain, France, and possibly Sweden before World War I, it was largely thanks to the pioneering efforts of Exxon across Europe that the gas pump and storage tank was adopted. Competitors were forced to respond immediately or go under.

The European market was fiercely fought between Shell, Exxon, and BP. Shell had the singular advantage of unique, instantly identifiable trademarks: the scallop shell and consistent use of a yellow and red color scheme (see Chapter 2). Not surprisingly, Shell was the European market leader, with the exception of Germany and Switzerland, by the end of the 1930s. Shell and BP formed a joint marketing and distribution company in Great Britain, Shell-Mex & BP Ltd (60 percent owned by Shell and 40 percent owned by BP), in 1931, which came into effect in 1932. The partnership was dissolved in 1976.

Exxon marketed gasoline under at least nine different local brand names in Europe during the early 1920s (see Chapter 2). Even as late as 1939, Exxon could not match Shell for absolute brand and corporate identity consistency across Europe. This perhaps explains Exxon's subsequently rigid corporate identification, gas station design, packaging, and pump color schemes throughout Europe in the 1950s.

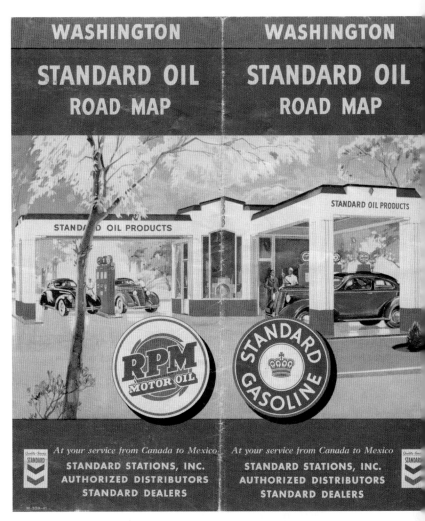

An elaborate, prefabricated art Deco design was introduced by Chevron during the early 1930s. Its most distinctive features were the narrow blue, white, and red gables that bore a close resemblance to an English church altar window. These were later dropped so that the sales office, service bays, and restrooms could be located in one building rather than two. *Author collection*

Chevron built a very large number of these distinctive prefabricated stations between 1914 and 1930, when this photograph was taken, by which time the design had become obsolete and overripe for redevelopment. *Author collection*

Toward the end of the 1930s, Chevron introduced a prefabricated streamline moderne design for both its company-owned and dealer-operated sites. The design was notable for the lubrication bay on the diagonal rather than parallel to the sales office. The photo was taken in New Mexico during the early 1940s. *Author collection*

BP, established in 1909 as the Anglo-Persian Oil Company, was a distant third behind Shell and Exxon in Europe. BP made up for this with outstanding corporate identity, gas station designs, and feel-good advertising campaigns tailor-made for each country. BP's European marketing strategy epitomized cross-fertilization of ideas and paid dividends in the long term.

CIP, Mobil's French subsidiary, was the only other American-owned oil company in Europe with a consistent gas station design.

It initially was a Normandy cottage and subsequently art deco, which are both discussed at length in Chapters 6 and 7.

Exxon

Exxon's British affiliate, the Anglo-American Oil Company (which became a wholly owned subsidiary in 1930), introduced curbside gas pumps in May 1920 that dispensed Pratt's gasoline, one of Exxon's nine European local brands. Exxon was prevented from selling

(Left) In 1934, Socony-Vacuum united its eight marketing operations with the superb Pegasus logo and Mobilgas brand name; although the Socony brand continued to be used in New England until 1939. Note the diversity of the station designs. Powerful nationwide full-color magazine campaigns during the late 1930s turned Mobilgas into a household name and inspired much affection for the flying horse. *Author collection*

(Above) Mobil retained and adapted their white clapperboard design for super service stations in rural New England. Both Mobil designs had identical ornate doorways. Note how this design complemented the clapboard houses in the background. The photograph was taken in Watkins Glen, New York, in May 1949. *Author collection*

(Right) By the mid-1930s, Mobil reconfigured its neocolonial red brick design with service bays as an integral feature and introduced it across the United States. Both Mobil designs had identical ornate doorways. This photograph was taken in Elmira, New York, around 1949. *Author collection*

U.S.A. GOES MOBILGAS

IT'S AMERICA'S MOST POPULAR GASOLINE!

WHY?

BECAUSE MOTORISTS LIKE
THE EXTRA THRIFT
AND POWER MOBILGAS GIVES!

IMAGINE a testing ground of 1,675,644,000 acres. Millions of test drivers! That's where Mobilgas has been proved best. In actual use on the highways of America! In the cars of millions of U.S.A. motorists! Every day, 1½ million of these motorists stop for Mobilgas. They've found Mobilgas IS different...IS better! The lightning-quick power of this gasoline makes their cars alive, alert...*fast* on the pick-up. Its even firing keeps their motors running smooth as silk. *And every gallon* gives extra satisfying miles! Mobilgas *has earned* its popularity by its fine performance under every possible driving condition.

Aren't the things which have made this gasoline U.S.A.'s favorite the very things you want for *your* gasoline dollar? Drive in today at the famous Flying Red Horse Sign and fill up with MOBILGAS!

MOBILGAS AND MOBILOIL

SOCONY-VACUUM OIL COMPANY, INC.

AND AFFILIATES
MAGNOLIA PETROLEUM CO.—GENERAL PETROLEUM CORPORATION

directly to the motorist by a tough British motor trade lobby but circumvented this by selling directly only to taxicabs and trucks from forty-nine Angloco gas stations spread across Great Britain. The Angloco gas station designs and layouts provided much inspiration for British gas station development during the 1920s. The sales building design was very similar to that of Exxon's 1924 model, right down to the use of a cream and off-white color scheme and orange terracotta roof tiles. Shell built at least one station that operated on an identical basis but quickly leased it to a dealer to avoid any ill will from the motor trade. Independently owned multibrand gas stations were the norm in Great Britain until after World War II.

Exxon had better luck in France with its recently established subsidiary, L'Economique S.A., and traded under the brand name Eco, which introduced curbside gas pumps in November 1920 and opened a series of company-owned gas stations in 1921. The early stations made extensive use of prefabricated cast-iron columns and steel panels, the canopies had a fluted glass fringe, and the overall appearance was very similar to a French railroad station. This was replaced by an art deco design of a conventional brick construction covered with an off-white cement render in 1926 and 1927 (see Chapter 7), which remained largely unchanged until 1939.

Exxon's German subsidiary, Deutsche-Amerikanische Petroleum Gesselschaft (DAPG), traded under the brand name, Dapolin, and introduced curbside gas pumps in April 1923. It was followed quickly by its Italian subsidiary in the same year. Dapolin had an outstanding Native American chief logo that provided superb brand identity, but it had to be dropped in favor of a transitional solid red circle and horizontal blue bar logo adopted across Europe. Dapolin launched its company-owned drive-in gas stations in 1927 that differed considerably from the British Angloco and French Eco designs. The German Dapolin design had a severe appearance highlighted by four parallel horizontal ribs that ran

Exxon, like Shell, used bolt-on canopies for its low-volume dealers in Germany during the 1930s, which provided excellent brand identification, as well as weather protection for the attendant and motorist. This site was located in Groschonau and photographed around 1935. *Author collection*

The canopy and the pole sign box were the most interesting features of this 1935 German Standard station located in Gorlitz. Hitler's repudiation of modern architecture forced Exxon and Shell to introduce more conventional designs after 1933, which increasingly relied on the canopy as the focal point. *Author collection*

Dapolin, Exxon's German subsidiary, launched its company-owned gas stations in 1927. The German design was very severe with four horizontal ribs around the sales office and canopy pillars, quite unlike the British or French designs. The red circle and blue bar logo was adopted throughout Europe in the late 1920s and used in conjunction with local brands until 1931. *Author collection*

The typical mid-1930s dealer-owned Standard station in Germany depended totally on the custom-made gas pumps, nicknamed Big Bens, and the Standard panels for brand identity. Like Shell, Exxon dealers supplied free handbooks full of product information, useful maintenance tips, and travel advice. This example dates from 1938. Note the transitional circular Esso logo. *Author collection*

around the sales office and canopy pillars. The station was built with brick and covered with naturally colored cement render that resembled Portland stone. Exxon experimented with at least two international-style gas stations in the late 1920s and early 1930s, but Hitler's rise to power stopped any further experiments with futuristic designs (see Chapters 6 and 7). After 1933, Exxon played safe with fairly conventional designs in Germany and used bolt-on canopies as the main brand identification for its dealer-owned gas stations. Exxon, like all German oil companies, had a distinctive custom-made gas pump affectionately known as Big Ben.

Shell

The Shell logo in Europe was a stylized red and black or yellow and red scallop shell without any script. It remained unchanged until 1948 (see Chapter 2). Scallop shell gas pump globes were introduced across most of Europe during the late 1920s and early 1930s, apart from France and Germany, which persisted with round globes. Shell did not begin any large-scale gas station construction in Europe until the late 1920s. It seemed to have relied initially on networks of independent dealers with curbside gas pumps. Shell's policy clearly changed when Exxon introduced its French art deco company-owned gas stations in 1926 and 1927 and subsequently launched drive-in gas stations in Germany during 1927.

The first European company-owned Shell gas stations were probably built in Germany during 1928. As previously discussed, the German Shell designs were cutting-edge international-style designs. These were constructed of conventional brick and covered

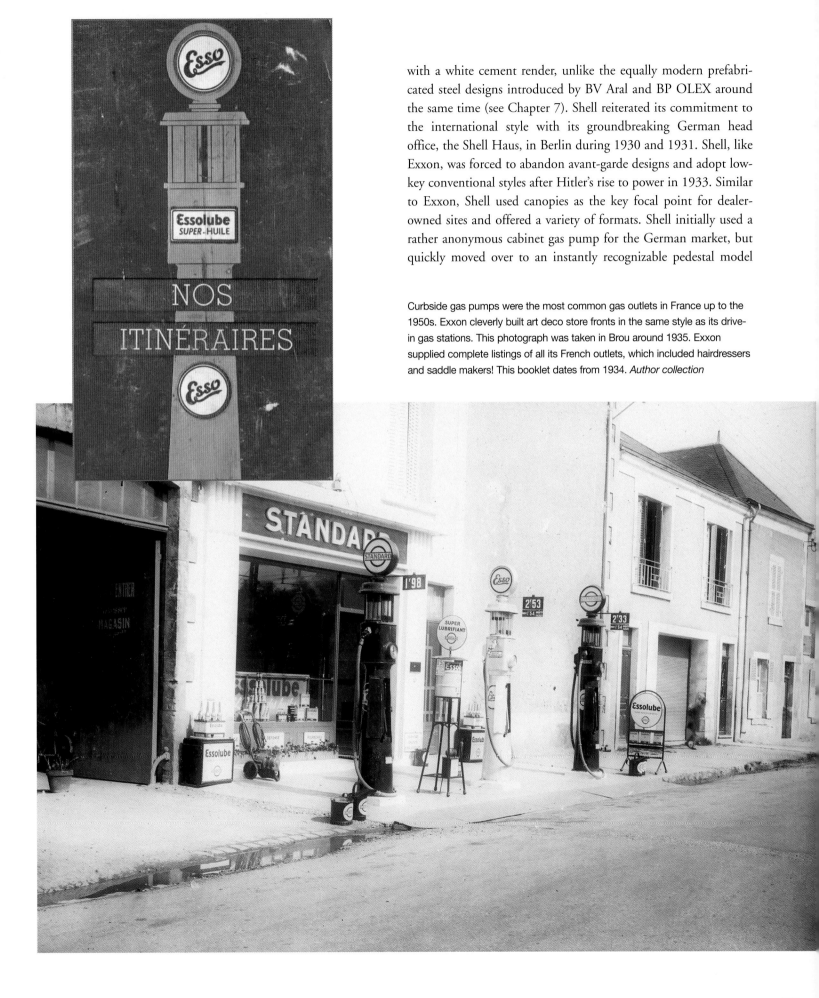

with a white cement render, unlike the equally modern prefabricated steel designs introduced by BV Aral and BP OLEX around the same time (see Chapter 7). Shell reiterated its commitment to the international style with its groundbreaking German head office, the Shell Haus, in Berlin during 1930 and 1931. Shell, like Exxon, was forced to abandon avant-garde designs and adopt low-key conventional styles after Hitler's rise to power in 1933. Similar to Exxon, Shell used canopies as the key focal point for dealer-owned sites and offered a variety of formats. Shell initially used a rather anonymous cabinet gas pump for the German market, but quickly moved over to an instantly recognizable pedestal model

Curbside gas pumps were the most common gas outlets in France up to the 1950s. Exxon cleverly built art deco store fronts in the same style as its drive-in gas stations. This photograph was taken in Brou around 1935. Exxon supplied complete listings of all its French outlets, which included hairdressers and saddle makers! This booklet dates from 1934. *Author collection*

RELAIS SHELL

(Above) Shell built a number of extremely flamboyant oil-can-shaped gas stations across France during the late 1920s and early 1930s in contrast to Exxon and BP's comparatively restrained designs. Uniquely, French Shell gas pumps were white with a red checkerboard globe and remained until 1939. *Author collection*

(Left) Super Shell premium grade gasoline replaced Shell Dynamin across Europe during 1938 and was publicized in France with this booklet, which provided details on places to visit, regional cuisine, and Super Shell outlets. It was very similar in style to the British Shell Guides. *Author collection*

with a round globe during the early 1930s, which was affectionately known as the iron maiden.

Shell built a series of extremely flamboyant gas stations in the shape of giant yellow oil cans across France during the late 1920s and early 1930s. They were extensively publicized in press advertising and road maps and were a very effective counterbalance to Exxon and BP's French company-owned gas stations. Unlike the rest of Europe, French Shell gas pumps were white with a red checkerboard globe. Shell had a number of futuristic international-style gas stations with very wide cantilevered roofs in Austria and a slightly more restrained design was used in the Netherlands. Both

(Below) This eye-catching pedestal gas pump, nicknamed the iron maiden, was introduced by Shell in Germany during the early 1930s. Similar to most of Europe, a bright yellow and red pump color scheme was used. Germany, like France, persisted with round gas pump globes up to 1939. Note the two alternate scallop shell logos on the yellow shield and the oil can. *Author collection*

designs used large three-dimensional capital letter logos on top of the canopies that were later incorporated in Shell's postwar American box service station design.

BP

BP, owned by the Anglo-Persian Oil Company, quickly became established in three key European markets (Great Britain, Germany, and France) during the early 1920s. At this time, Great Britain's gasoline market was larger, by volume, than those of Germany and France combined but this later changed. By the end of the 1930s, the three markets were roughly equal. Initially, Germany was the most significant for BP. OLEX, a recent BP acquisition, was at the forefront with its instantly recognizable castellated dome kiosks with integral gas pumps, known as a tankhaus. OLEX had a highly distinctive yellow and blue color scheme that BP retained up to 1947. In fact, OLEX had opened Germany's first drive-in gas station at its head office in Berlin during 1922 and was the catalyst for Exxon to introduce curbside gas pumps in Germany in April 1923. The German economy made a rapid recovery from 1924 on, and the motor vehicle population grew at an astonishing rate. It literally tripled from 300,000 in 1924 to 900,000 in 1928! The German motor vehicle population increased by one third again to 1,200,000 in 1929. BP OLEX met this burgeoning demand with highly innovative prefabricated international-style gas stations that were very cost-effective and easy to assemble (see Chapter 7). In spite of Hitler's rise to power in 1933, BP OLEX continued with its international-style gas stations. A few were built in the late 1930s with pitched roofs to match the surrounding architecture.

Société Générale des Huiles de Petrole (SGHP), BP's French subsidiary, introduced a highly original green and yellow color

(Above) The flamboyant oil can gas stations were prominently featured in a French Shell corporate advertising campaign during 1930. This advertisement, number 15, appeared on December 27. *Author collection*

(Left) A more restrained international-style design was used by Shell in the Netherlands during the 1930s, as seen here in Scheveningen. Curiously, the Dutch design used very small glass panes, perhaps to harmonize with the windows of surrounding houses. Sinks were built in either side of the canopy pillar for elaborate forecourt service, which was made possible by the extensive use of electric gas pumps in the Netherlands. *Shell International Petroleum Company*

BP's German subsidiary, OLEX, had a network of instantly recognizable castellated dome sales kiosks with integral gas pumps, known as a "tankhaus," during the early 1920s. This was the first OLEX tankhaus, which was opened in 1922, at Raschplatz in Hanover. OLEX also introduced the first German drive-in gas station at its Berlin headquarters in the same year. *BP Archive*

This eye-catching yellow and green art deco design was introduced by BP across France during 1926 and 1927 in response to Exxon's stations. The accompanying barrel label photograph shows the color scheme. The art deco design made maximum use of available light with a sky-lit canopy. The combination of this striking design and the bold color scheme, introduced in 1923, put BP at the forefront of French gasoline marketing. The photograph was taken during the early 1930s. *BP Archive*

BP OLEX also built international-style brick and concrete structures, which were absolutely consistent and provided instant brand recognition. The extensive use of bare brick, rather than a white cement render, forestalled any criticism by the Nazi regime. Occasionally, pitched roofs were placed on top of the canopy for greater harmony. The photograph was taken in the late 1930s. *BP Archive*

scheme in 1923 that really put BP on the map in France. It worked brilliantly with gas pumps, gas stations, advertising, and publicity material. BP in Switzerland quickly adopted it. The green gas pumps were introduced in Great Britain during 1927 to forestall any criticism of the countryside being spoiled by garish gas pumps. BP registered the green and yellow color scheme as an international trademark in 1928. As previously mentioned, BP OLEX persisted with a yellow and blue color scheme in Germany up to 1947.

BP had a number of French gas station designs that reflected regional architectural styles but became most notable for its highly distinctive yellow art deco gas stations that were introduced in 1926 and 1927 around the same time as Exxon launched its design. These stations were later superseded by a steamline moderne design with an extremely wide cantilevered canopy in the late 1930s (see Chapter 7). BP consolidated its corporate identity with its iconic shield logo, introduced in 1930, which worked equally well in France's green and yellow or Germany's yellow and blue color schemes (see Chapter 2).

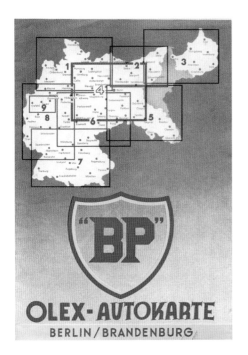

A yellow and blue color scheme was used by BP OLEX for its custom-made pumps, gas stations, and the BP shield logo, introduced in 1930, until 1947. All other BP markets used a distinctive green and yellow color scheme launched in France during 1923. *Author collection*

Prefabricated gas stations were cheap, easy, and quick to assemble in as little as eight days. They cost one-third of the price of a conventional brick or stone structure. BP OLEX, similar to its rival BV Aral, built large numbers of these prefabricated international-style stations throughout Germany during the 1930s. This photograph was taken during the late 1930s. *Author collection*

10

Global Priority 1945-1973

THE 1950S AND 1960S WERE REMARKABLE for an extended period of unprecedented affluence, optimism, and sustained economic growth in the United States and Europe. British Prime Minister Harold Macmillan summed it up best in the 1959 British general election: "You've never had it so good!"

This period was notable for highly memorable slogans and jingles, including "The Esso Sign Means Happy Motoring," "Go Well, Go Shell," "Trust Your Car to the Man Who Wears the Texaco Star," Mobil's "Flying Horsepower," and most memorable of all, Exxon's "Put a Tiger in Your Tank." Shell, Exxon, Mobil, and BP were renowned for both anticipating trends and being proactive. Texaco and particularly Gulf lost momentum. Neither oil company could match the frequent changes or the innovation of Shell, Exxon, and especially Mobil gas station designs. The Standard brand and its phonetic connotations became a liability for both Exxon and Chevron as they expanded nationwide. Both companies ultimately opted for noncontentious brands and corporate names of Exxon and Chevron respectively. Standard Oil of Indiana had the unique advantage of a large, long-established subsidiary, Amoco, and could afford to take a more long-term "wait and see" approach.

Motorists were gripped by Detroit's horsepower race and planned obsolescence and eagerly awaited Harley Earl or Virgil Exner's latest tail-finned extravagances, which invariably consumed even more gasoline than the models they replaced! Apart from the Suez Canal Crisis of late 1956 and early 1957 when gasoline rationing was temporarily introduced across Europe, gasoline consumption increased annually by 4 to 5 percent, and sometimes as high as 8 percent. Oil companies built large numbers of gas stations to meet increasing demand and sell ever-growing supplies of gasoline from large, new oil refineries. Inevitably, oil companies had to dispose of surplus gasoline on the spot or wholesale market,

which created a substrata of aggressive, minimal-service cut-rate gas stations across America and Europe.

The 1950s marked a key turning point for international gas retailing for a number of crucial reasons. Single-brand retailing was now universal, and the American super service station model with integral lubrication and wash bays was adopted worldwide. For the first time there were consistent international brand logos, color schemes, advertising campaigns, and gas station designs. The 1950s was probably the first decade when international corporate identity, as a distinct discipline, was truly implemented for gasoline or any other retail business.

Broadly speaking, gas station design worldwide was highly functional and predominantly used white or light pastel shades. In all instances, the sales office window was substantially increased in size, often from floor to ceiling, to provide greater visibility for value-added items and advertising displays. In the United States, porcelain enamel panels were used everywhere for ease of maintenance, durability, and consistent brand identity. Prefabrication was still the norm on the West Coast with the porcelain enamel panel as an integral structural unit. In the Midwest and the Atlantic seaboard, porcelain enamel panels were used as exterior cladding over a brick or cinder-block construction. In Europe, painted cement render was the standard exterior coating. Shell-Mex & BP Ltd. built a series of prefabricated super service stations in Great Britain during the mid-1950s but later reverted to conventional construction methods. Towards the end of the 1950s in America, there was a gradual swing back to styles that could integrate with residential neighborhoods (see Chapter 6). The canopy was virtually abandoned by international oil companies but remained an integral feature for gas stations in the South and on the West Coast in the United States. It was also retained in Germany by BP, Aral, and Gasolin (formerly known as Leuna). The canopy reappeared

This Esso station was photographed near York, Pennsylvania, during late 1952 and was a classic example of the cheaper three-window diagonal sales office design that required less skilled construction and eliminated the use of custom-made windows. This particular design was also used in Canada and particularly in Great Britain. *Author collection*

This March 1957 De Soto advertisement brilliantly summed up America's love affair with the automobile: the exaggerated tail fins and ever increasing horsepower; and, indeed, the consumer society—if you've got it, flaunt it! *Author collection*

with the introduction of self-service in Europe during the late 1960s and early 1970s.

Gas pumps became progressively lower in height and had widescreen computer displays, known as panorama or lo-boy pumps. The gas pump globe virtually disappeared, apart from in Great Britain and a few die-hard American regional marketers.

In the United States, major oil companies faced increasing pressure from cut-rate, minimal-service chains, Hess being an excellent example of the latter. While elaborate forecourt service was some compensation, customers needed other inducements to keep them coming back. Most American gas stations offered trading stamps that could be saved and redeemed for household items. Sperry and Hutchinson's green stamps were the most popular. Trading stamps later played a pivotal role in British gas retailing during the 1960s and early 1970s (see Chapter 4).

Toward the end of the 1950s, automobile ownership became more widespread in Europe, particularly among skilled and semi-skilled blue-collar workers. The latter were naturally very keen to receive good value for their money. The blue-collar worker was to become a key factor in the growth of cut-rate gas stations, trading stamps, and self-service in Europe during the 1960s.

Three key developments in retailing during the 1950s had a strategic impact on both gas station design and gas retail markets. The American self-service food supermarket came into its own and was rapidly introduced worldwide. A Swedish co-op, IC, realized in the late 1950s, that the self-service format could easily be adopted for gas stations. Self-service gas stations subsequently became the dominant feature in Europe during the early 1970s (see Chapter 8). In the United States, the out-of-town shopping plaza with multiple supermarkets, chain stores, department stores, and large parking lots was introduced during the mid-1950s. American oil companies installed high-turnover gas stations within or adjacent to these shopping plazas. These gas stations had up to

(Right) Shopping plazas on the outskirts of town first appeared in America during the mid-1950s and provided the shopper with convenient one-stop shopping and ample free parking. This precipitated the decline of the town center. Oil companies, such as Atlantic, installed high-volume gas stations within or adjacent to shopping plazas to supply increasing demand. This photograph was taken in De Witt, New York, on June 21, 1970. *Author collection*

ten parallel pump islands, known as the starting-gate format, which enabled very fast through traffic. The French hypermarket in the early 1970s pulled all of these disparate elements together, was quickly copied elsewhere, and had a devastating long-term impact on gas sales in Europe, which is still being felt to this day.

Exxon

Exxon launched the Esso brand name and oval logo in the United States in 1933 and rolled it out internationally during the mid- to late 1930s after a lengthy transition from nine local brands in Europe. The two exceptions were Imperial, Exxon's Canadian subsidiary, which adopted the Esso brand in the late 1940s, and Atlantic, Exxon's Australian operation that was acquired in 1935, which finally converted to Esso in the mid-1960s. Exxon was at a marked disadvantage to the long-established, instantly recognizable Shell brand. Shell made blanket use of a unique logo, a scallop shell, and a yellow and red color scheme. There was, however,

Increasing gasoline surpluses created a substrata of aggressive, minimal-service cut-rate chains. Price cutters, like Hess, had highly efficient forecourts with parallel pump islands, known as the starting-gate setup, that maximized through traffic. The layout of the station was copied by major oil companies. This site was photographed in Fort Lauderdale, Florida, during 1967. *Author collection*

MERRY CHRISTMAS FROM YOUR SERVICE STATION

That's right. You can get a bike from your service station. You can get almost any famous name-brand gift—if you shop at stores that give S&H Green Stamps. Service stations, supermarkets, drug stores, department stores—even beauty parlors. All kinds of stores give America's most valuable, most reliable stamps. They're fine stores that give good value, too. Remember, the more you shop at the S&H sign—the more extra gifts you get at Christmas time!

Trading stamps were used by all major American oil companies to win back customers from price cutters and build repeat purchase throughout the 1950s and 1960s. This advertisement appeared in December 1964. Trading stamps also played a pivotal role in British gas retail markets. *Author collection*

Exxon was immensely proud of its highly functional gas station design, which was built in very large numbers throughout North America and Europe during the 1950s. The design was featured prominently in both its advertising and maps. This scene appeared in a 1959 French advertisement. It became very difficult to distinguish between North American, French, Italian, and German Esso stations. *Author collection*

considerable variation in Shell logo styles, pump color schemes, globes, and gas station designs worldwide.

Exxon exploited Shell's lack of consistency by systematically developing a stringent corporate identity and a streamlined, highly functional gas station design in America during the mid-1940s. Both elements formed the cornerstone of Exxon's massive international gas station building program in the mid-1950s.

Exxon effectively launched the American super service station model in postwar Europe. It used consistent grade identification: Esso

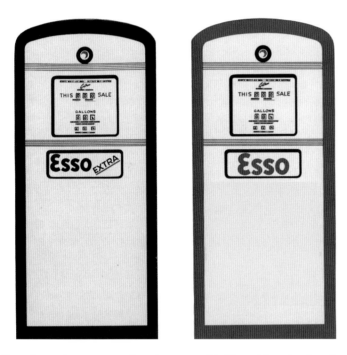

Exxon's consistent pump color schemes provided instant brand and grade identification in America from December 1939 on and in Europe after World War II. Great Britain used only the red and white color scheme prior to 1962. *Author collection*

for regular grade gasoline with red and white pumps and Esso Extra for premium grade gasoline with blue and white pumps. Exxon shrewdly built identical gas stations at high-profile, prestige locations, such as Paris Orly airport in France in 1953; the Winter Olympics at Cortina d'Ampezzo, Italy, in 1956; and the Brussels World Fair in Belgium during 1958. These sites generated customer goodwill and a great deal of press publicity. It became virtually impossible to distinguish between Esso stations in America, France, Germany, Belgium, or Italy. These gas stations were prominently featured in Esso advertising (refer to this chapter's opening image) and Esso maps in America and Europe. Just as in the early 1920s, Exxon set a new trend in Europe that competitors had to match or get left behind.

Exxon's stringent and absolutely consistent corporate identity program set the benchmark for other multinational oil companies to follow. Mobil was the only other oil company to match and ultimately surpass it in the long-term with its Pegasus design in 1966.

Ironically, just at the point that Exxon had absolutely consistent brand and corporate identity across Europe, it encountered severe problems in America with the Esso brand name as it expanded westward. As previously mentioned, Esso is the phonetic spelling of "SO," the initials for Standard Oil. Standard Oil of Indiana and Chevron successfully prevented the use of the Esso brand name within their assigned territories in the Midwest, the West Coast, and certain states in the South (after Chevron's acquisition of Standard Oil of Kentucky in 1961). Exxon was forced to trade under a variety of local brands (e.g., Carter, Pate, and Oklahoma in the familiar oval logo) with an inevitable diminution of brand identity. Exxon's Texas subsidiary, Humble, became the holding company for all Exxon operations in the United States in November 1960 and was featured on all gas station fascias. Enco, which stood for Energy Company, subsequently replaced the Carter, Oklahoma, and Pate brands. Even so, Exxon still could not run nationwide full-color press campaigns,

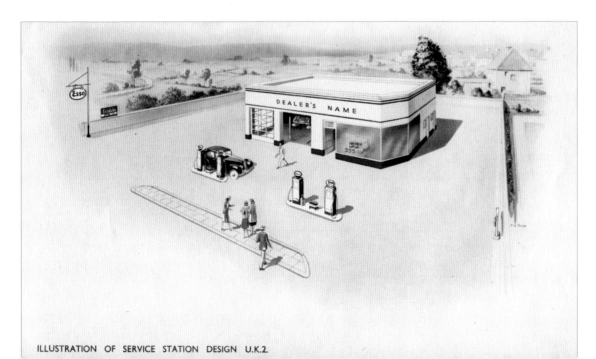

This gas station design was featured in a 1951 British Exxon design handbook and was used by Exxon worldwide up to the early 1960s. The square sales office and diagonal three window sales office designs were cheaper to build than the streamlined version and gradually superseded it. Exxon was at the forefront of introducing the American super service station model in Europe after World War II. *Author collection*

ILLUSTRATION OF SERVICE STATION DESIGN U.K.2.

NOW HAPPY MOTORING COAST-TO-COAST

RECOGNIZE US
COAST-TO-COAST
BY THESE FINE
TRADE MARKS

HUMBLE
OIL & REFINING COMPANY

since 5 leading regional oil companies have joined to form **HUMBLE** America's Leading Energy Company

This new development in the fast advancing Age of Energy joins the skills and resources of five leading regional oil companies. To serve you better coast-to-coast, these companies have united to form a new Humble Oil & Refining Company. The name comes from an oil field and a town near Houston, which was the origin of Humble Oil Company about 50 years ago.

The new Humble Company—appropriately called "America's Leading Energy Company"—today finds, refines, distributes and markets more oil and petroleum products than any other domestic oil operation. It is backed by the nation's leading petroleum research laboratories . . . with more oil and petrochemical advances than any other U.S. research group.

Now, this great new company combines all these resources to bring you "Happy Motoring" products and services through more than 30,000 service stations coast-to-coast.

This Humble leadership promises you more of the best of new products first. Not only products for your car . . . like the remarkable new Uniflo Motor Oil . . . but many other new products for better living, made possible by Humble research.

Trademark restrictions plagued Exxon's expansion in America and forced it to run expensive split-run advertising campaigns. Exxon reorganized its American operations in November 1960 with Humble Oil as the holding company. The Esso brand was retained on the East Coast, while Enco (stood for Energy Company) gradually replaced Carter, Pate, and Oklahoma in the rest of the United States. *Author collection*

unlike Texaco, Shell, and Mobil, without expensive split-print runs.

The iconic "Put a Tiger in Your Tank" campaign in the spring of 1964 supplied an instantly recognizable trademark that transcended the Esso, Enco, and Humble brands and provided unprecedented brand unity (see Chapter 2).

Exxon introduced a new look in early 1965. It refreshed its Esso and Enco logos with a thicker, light blue oval outline, and a thicker light red typeface. Gas stations were solid white with a thick red stripe interspersed with the new Esso or Enco logos, while gas pumps were white with red or blue squares on the pump doors for grade identification with new custom-made red and grey pump island lamps. In spite of these changes, the need for a single

brand name was imperative. The cartoon tiger was a key element in the Exxon brand launch in the fall of 1972 that replaced the Esso, Enco, and Humble brands in the United States. The Esso brand is still used to this day worldwide outside America.

Exxon took a cautious but determined approach towards self-service across Europe during the late 1960s and pioneered electronic self-service gas pumps in Great Britain in 1971 (see Chapter 8).

Mobil

Mobil, like Exxon, had a legacy of many different gas station designs, inconsistent pump color schemes, and subsidiary brands within the United States and overseas. Mobil addressed this issue threefold during the late 1940s. First, Mobilgas was now the regular grade gasoline with solid red pumps, and Mobilgas Special was the premium grade gasoline with red and white pumps in the United States and overseas. Second, instantly recognizable custom-made script top pumps, known as the model 80, were developed for the American market and manufactured by Martin and Schwartz, which was jointly owned by Mobil, Conoco, Sunoco, and Standard Oil of Indiana. Third, Mobil developed a consistent white gas station design surmounted by a red cut-out Pegasus flying-horse logo. The gas station fascia had two red pinstripes above and below the Mobilgas and Mobiloil blue logos. In America, porcelain enamel panels were used exclusively that could be easily retrofitted onto existing structures, even ornate Wadhams' Chinese pagodas in Milwaukee, Wisconsin. In Europe, an identical design was introduced, but cement render was used instead of porcelain enamel panels.

Exxon launched its hugely successful "Put a Tiger in Your Tank" campaign in May 1964, which unified the Esso, Enco, and Humble brands and gave Exxon a superb branding device. The cartoon tiger put fun back into gas advertising, increased repeat purchases, and boosted dealers' morale. *Author collection*

In early 1965, Exxon introduced a modified oval logo and new color schemes for gas pumps and stations. The emphasis on white with bold red stripes gave Exxon a sharper, more brisk image. Note the wing-shaped roof on the sales office, which was retrofitted to harmonize with neighboring houses. *Author collection*

Why is this gasoline the top choice for new and late model cars?

New Golden Esso Extra is the finest gasoline ever refined — with a combination of performance qualities unequalled by any other motor fuel at any price.

You can expect quicker starting, faster warm-up, anti-stall protection . . . and will find that it keeps new engines in new-car condition longer. If you have a new, or late-model car, you can't buy better performance than you get in this gasoline created by Atomic Research. So if your car means more to you than just transportation, fill the tank with New Golden Esso Extra today.

NEW GOLDEN ESSO EXTRA

 ESSO STANDARD OIL COMPANY, *makers of three great gasolines: "Golden" — truly in a class by itself; New Formula Esso Extra; Esso — the popular "regular" gasoline.*

Check out the Golden Esso Extra 100 octane pump that was introduced in 1956 to meet the demands of the Detroit horsepower race. *Author collection*

We're changing our name, but not our stripes.

We're changing the Esso name to Exxon. But we haven't changed our stripes. The fine people and products the Tiger stands for are the same we've always known. But soon you'll find them under the Exxon name. Why the new name? Because for years we've had different brand names in different parts of the country.

Complicated for us. And confusing for our customers. So we're changing our name. Soon you'll have just one name to look for. Our Tiger is traveling across the country displaying our brand-new name. We hope you'll like it. Because while we're changing, we don't want you to change.

An old friend has a new name.

(Below) In common with its American parent company, Exxon introduced more harmonious gas station designs in Great Britain during the late 1960s, shown by this architect's model. Note the single-story design with emphasis on horizontal lines and the extensive use of brick. *Author collection*

Exxon pragmatically launched Exxon as the single brand across America in the fall of 1972. The tiger played a vital role in promoting the change in nationwide press campaigns and point of sale publicity. Esso remains in use outside America. *Author collection*

Mobil was able to easily update its gas stations, pictured here. Bolt-on porcelain enamel panels were applied to give the station a new look. The gas station was located in Milwaukee, Wisconsin, and photographed during the early 1950s. *Charles Skagg*

The launch of Mobilgas in Europe, which replaced the local CIP and Sphinx brands, was helped immeasurably by Mobiloil's long-established reputation as an excellent specialist brand. Ironically, the latter's distribution suffered when rival gasoline retailers refused to stock a competitor's product. This was particularly true in Great Britain where Mobil had not sold gasoline before World War II.

The Mobilgas/Mobil Economy run, with its emphasis on careful driving and regular vehicle maintenance, was a marketing triumph in the United States and Europe throughout the 1950s and 1960s. Mobil gained priceless publicity from extensive press coverage of the annual events and advertising by automobile and component manufacturers who won the annual event outright or came first in their category. Mobil was held in very high regard by competitors internationally for shrewd and sophisticated marketing.

The antiquated Mobilgas shield logo, a legacy from Socony, was replaced by the emphatic Mobil chevron logo in 1956. The only drawback of this new trademark was the drastic reduction in size of the much loved flying-horse symbol. During the early 1960s, a new retrofit gas station design was created for the Mobil brand. A broad light-blue fascia extended across the front of the station surmounted by a large red chevron with the flying-horse symbol. At the same time, Mobilgas became Mobil regular and Mobilgas Special became Mobil premium, although Special was retained in Europe.

Growing public concern over garish roadside billboards and unsightly gas stations in America during 1963 and 1964, combined with lobbying by Lady Bird Johnson, wife of President Lyndon Johnson, encouraged Mobil to commission the eminent industrial designer Eliot Noyes to develop a new highly distinctive but low-key gas station design. The net result was the 1966 Pegasus design, complete with unique and instantly recognizable silver and black cylindrical pumps, which is still regarded as one of the most outstanding examples of corporate identity (see Chapters 6 and 7).

Shell

Shell had the unique advantage of a long-established, instantly recognizable trademark with the scallop shell and a highly distinctive yellow and red corporate color scheme worldwide. No other oil company could match this.

During the late 1940s, Shell embarked on an intensive gas station research program in the United States and sent out detailed questionnaires to all its credit card holders to ascertain what they

Mobil, like Exxon, had a stringent corporate identity policy that was strictly enforced worldwide. The Whirlwind gas station was photographed in Birmingham, Great Britain, during 1955. *National Motor Museum/MLP*

The Mobilgas/Mobil Economy Run was the cornerstone of Mobil's marketing worldwide during the 1950s and 1960s, as seen in this 1951 advertisement. The annual competitions that ran in America, Europe, and Australia, generated priceless publicity from widespread press coverage and advertising by automobile manufacturers that won the event outright or came first in its class. The emphasis on careful driving and regular maintenance projected a responsible, frugal corporate image. *Author collection*

expected from a gas station in terms of forecourt layout, automobile servicing, valet service, and restrooms. Armed with this information and some assistance from Norman Bel Geddes, the industrial designer, Shell built a full-scale wooden mockup gas station in its Brooklyn, New York, bulk depot, which was systematically examined by Shell dealers from all over America and modified according to their suggestions. The net result was a stripped-down version of the 1935 Marysville, California, art deco design. The new design, known as the box or class A station, had a protruding lip with "SHELL" in cut-out letters immediately above the sales office window, which was now flush with the building. Customers and dealers alike essentially endorsed the practicality of the Marysville, California, layout.

The American scallop shell script logo, cream and red color scheme and ultimately the box gas station design were adopted by Shell in Europe during 1948. For a brief period of time between 1948 and 1952, American and European Shell pump color schemes were virtually identical, apart from a vertical red pinstripe on the sides of European pumps. The box gas station was widely built in Great Britain, Italy, France, and French North Africa during the mid-1950s with a white color scheme. Assured of an instantly recognizable trademark, Shell always prided itself on its flexible response to local market conditions, which inevitably led to some variation in its European gas station designs. Shell-Mex & BP Ltd (60 percent owned by Shell, 40 percent owned by BP), as previously mentioned, experimented briefly with prefabricated super service stations in Great Britain during 1955 and 1956. The same flexibility was demonstrated by Shell in the United States during the late 1950s when a local California planning board requested a more harmonious gas station design for a new housing development. The net result was the ranch gas station, which proved to be highly successful and quickly replaced the box nationwide during the 1960s (see Chapter 6).

(Top) Mobil in Great Britain cleverly used the new chevron logo to outline an inverted roof above the sales office. The stepped effect with the sales office lower than the service bays and use of brick at the side enabled the gas station to blend in with neighboring houses. The design was widely used throughout Great Britain, as seen in this 1961 Shepperton photograph. *National Motor Museum/MPL*

Les stations Mobil inaugurent de nouvelles couleurs pour la naissance du Mobil Economie-Service

Pour ceux qui roulent, une idée neuve : le Mobil Economie-Service

C'est très simple aujourd'hui d'économiser méthodiquement votre essence et de valoriser votre voiture : dans chaque station Mobil vous trouvez le premier service automobile complet spécialement conçu pour cela — le Mobil Economie-Service.

En allant régulièrement dans les stations Mobil, vous faites des économies à coup sûr, parce que vous y trouvez un bon service et de bons produits :
- le *service* entretien Mobil, service complet, vous évitera la plupart des incidents,
- les *carburants* Mobil (Mobilgas et

Mobilgas Special) vous offrent le meilleur rendement pour la consommation la plus réduite possible.
- les *lubrifiants* Mobil (Mobiloil et Mobiloil Special) vous assurent les meilleures performances avec le minimum d'usure.

Le Mobil Economie-Service est vraiment organisé pour vous faire faire des économies.

Arrêtez-vous à la station Mobil près de chez vous et demandez la brochure "15 conseils pour conduire économiquement". Elle vous sera précieuse : elle est le résultat de l'expérience acquise par des conduc-

teurs chevronnés sur plus de 3 millions de kilomètres, au cours de soixante "Mobil Economy Run" (les célèbres épreuves de consommation) !

Le Mobil Economie-Service économise l'essence, évite des réparations, valorise votre voiture.

Demandez à la station Mobil près de chez vous cette brochure gratuite : elle vous fera faire des économies

The Mobil Economy Run, with its emphasis on careful driving and regular maintenance, translated brilliantly into any language because motorists worldwide had identical requirements! This French advertisement appeared during the early 1960s and featured the new light blue fascia and red chevron station design. *Author collection*

(Below) Victor Christ-Janer created this internally lit canopy for Mobil during the early 1960s. Although it was expensive to build, it provided perfect publicity for Mobil, especially at night. Considerable thought went into providing protection from the rain and effectively draining it. This example, photographed in Dartford, Great Britain, in December 1965, was one of a number built in Great Britain and Italy. *Richard W. Marjoram*

Mobil reasserted stringent corporate identity with the introduction of the classic Pegasus design in 1966. The highly distinctive circular canopies and cylindrical pumps provided instant brand recognition almost to the exclusion of the Mobil brand or Pegasus logo. This early self service station located on the outskirts of Paris, France, was photographed in October 1971. *Alan Pond*

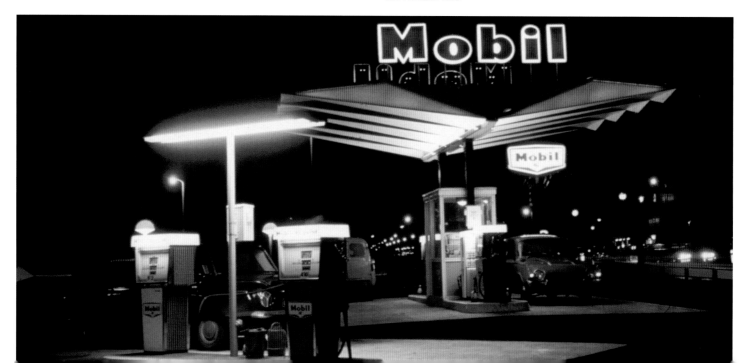

Shell introduced new grade identification and pump color schemes for the United States and Canada in the late 1950s. Shell regular was a solid yellow pump with the Shell logo on a red square, and Super Shell was a solid white pump with the Shell logo on a silver square. Overseas, the new Shell pump color scheme for all grades including diesel fuel was red side panels with yellow doors. Shell later reverted to a solid yellow color scheme in 1965. During the early 1960s, Shell introduced a new pole sign with the Shell logo on a red square in North America. A similar design was later introduced in Europe.

Raymond Loewy, the renowned industrial designer, created the Pecten, a radically new Shell logo, and a white, yellow, and red color scheme in 1970, which was introduced across Europe in 1972 and elsewhere in 1973, except America. In 1971, just before the Shell Pecten was introduced, Raymond Loewy developed the MAYA (most advanced, yet acceptable) modular gas station for use worldwide. This was created after extensive consultation with a specially assembled team of Shell marketing executives from around the world. A number of MAYA stations were built in Europe, notably in Great Britain and Italy. None were built in the United States. The subsequent 1973 OPEC Oil Crisis stopped any further development. The Shell Pecten logo was not adopted in America until 1976 and in a modified format.

Shell, in common with all its European counterparts during the 1960s, developed self-service retail. In fact, Great Britain's first self-service gas station, which opened in April 1963, sold Shell gasoline (see Chapter 8).

Texaco/Caltex

Texaco built large numbers of the streamline moderne EM stations across the United States throughout the 1950s and a few in Europe

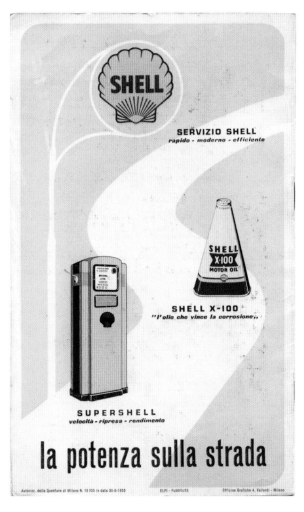

By 1953, Shell had a standardized corporate identity across Europe that consisted of an overhanging pole sign, yellow pumps with vertical red stripes and cream and red oil cans, which were proudly advertised on the back of this Italian map. *Author collection*

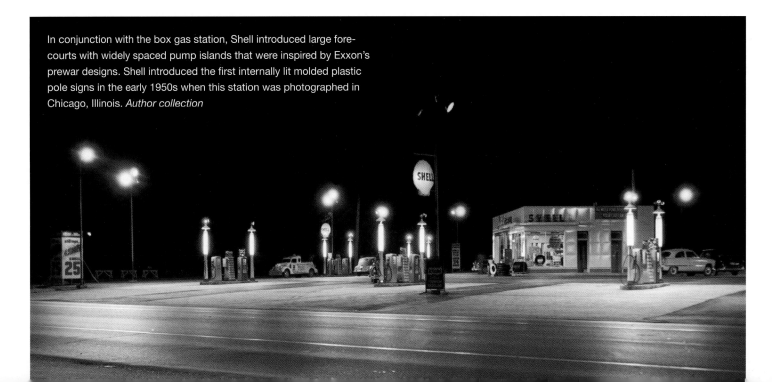

In conjunction with the box gas station, Shell introduced large forecourts with widely spaced pump islands that were inspired by Exxon's prewar designs. Shell introduced the first internally lit molded plastic pole signs in the early 1950s when this station was photographed in Chicago, Illinois. *Author collection*

under the Caltex brand. Chevron had acquired a 50 percent stake in Texaco's international operations outside North and South America and West Africa in 1936. The international network was rebranded Caltex (CAL for California and TEX for Texas) after World War II. Caltex had a strong presence in Scandinavia, Belgium, and the Netherlands, and had a small presence in Italy, Germany, France, and Ireland. Apart from the modified red star logo, Caltex corporate identification, packaging, and gas station design was very similar to that of Texaco in America. Texaco acquired Regent (owned by Trinidad Leaseholds), which had the third largest share of the British gasoline market in 1956. Both companies had a marketing and supply agreement that dated back to 1948 when Regent took over Texaco's British assets and launched Havoline and Marfak lubricants on the British market. The Texaco color scheme was introduced in July 1960, and the Regent brand was retained until early 1969. In 1959, the French Caltex operation was sold and later rebranded as Elf in 1967. Texaco acquired Deutsche Erdol in Germany during 1967. In 1968, Texaco and Chevron dissolved their joint European Caltex operation and divided it into separate Texaco and Chevron networks that included a number of British stations, as well. The Caltex brand is still used in Africa, Asia, Australia, and New Zealand.

Shell's new European corporate identity worked equally well with older prewar gas stations, shown so dramatically in this July 1954 photograph taken in Landshut, Germany. Note the use of the red wainscoting with yellow pinstripe. *Helmuth Markowski*

(Right) Shell always prided itself on its ability to adapt to local market conditions. The class E design, shown here in Frankfurt, was widely used throughout Germany, the Netherlands, and Belgium. This photograph was taken during the early 1950s. *Shell International Petroleum Company*

The box design was finally adopted in Great Britain during 1956 and 1957. Just like its European and North African counterparts, the British Shell box gas stations had sales offices that projected forward from the service bays. This example was photographed in about 1962. *BP Archive*

(Right) A variant of the class E design was specially developed for hot climates with an overhanging canopy to provide shade for the sales office. There was also an alternative design that had the service bays parallel to the sales office. The photograph was taken in Casablanca, Morocco, during the early 1950s. *Shell International Petroleum Company*

Throughout the 1950s and early 1960s, Texaco's pristine brand image was maintained by extremely effective advertising that was increasingly at odds with the by-then old-fashioned 1937 streamline moderne EM station design, which was made worse by the dowdy, dark green color scheme. Texaco introduced a more sharp-edged version called the EP in the early 1960s, which was little more than a stopgap. In 1964, Texaco launched the Matawan design, which like Shell's ranch gas station, blended in well with suburban single-story residential neighborhoods and touted a new hexagonal logo (see Chapter 6). Unfortunately, the Matawan design was virtually impossible to retrofit onto existing stations and only worked when genuine rough-hewn sandstone or rock cladding was used. There were a few disastrous attempts to install synthetic glass-fiber rock/boulder cladding, which made a mockery of the Matawan design. Strangely, many Texaco gas stations retained the obsolete round logo banjo signs, which did not help brand consistency. At the same time, Texaco clung onto nation-wide retailers as the cornerstone of its marketing, which dictated the use of smaller, less efficient oil refineries and lower profit margins. Shell, by contrast, had virtually developed logistics and found it was more cost-effective to have high-volume gas stations in key locations supplied by strategically placed high-volume, low-cost oil refineries.

No service station is an island.

Service stations aren't isolated structures in the middle of nowhere. They're put where they're needed. Near people who need them.

So most stations are in towns and cities. And the way they look affects the way the town looks.

That's why before we move into an area, we study the area. The architecture. The traffic patterns. The landscaping.

We want every station to blend in. Not stand out. And we work hard to make every Shell station an attractive addition to the local scene.

Otherwise we wouldn't feel welcome in your town. Or any town.

To make sure we get handsome stations, Shell maintains a talented staff of architects—and gives them freedom to use the finest building materials. The kind you see in expensive homes.

And once we put up a new station, we want to keep it new. Keep it clean. Free of flapping pennants, gaudy banners, and razzle-dazzle displays.

Building and maintaining beautiful stations is just part of Shell's broader commitment to improving the quality of the environment.

Our commitment goes all the way from anti-litter campaigns to a multimillion-dollar anti-pollution program.

A Shell station is not an island. And neither is the Shell Oil Company.

During the 1960s, Shell built very large numbers of the ranch gas station throughout America in response to consumer demands for more harmonious designs. The ranch design blended in very well with suburban single-story housing developments, thanks to the use of a low-pitched gable roof and brick. No ranch stations were built outside North America. *Author collection*

(Above two images) Raymond Loewy, the renowned industrial designer, created a radical new logo and corporate identity for Shell in 1970, which were even more eye-catching than their predecessors. The new Shell Pecten logo/corporate identity was introduced across Europe in the summer of 1972, as seen here at a Reading self-service station in Great Britain, and elsewhere during 1973. A modified version of the Shell Pecten logo was finally introduced in America during 1976. *Austin J. Brown*

Gulf

Gulf's postwar history was similar to that of Texaco's. Its heartland was in the South where it had blanket coverage. The New Orleans, Louisiana, market was a typical example. As late as 1976, Gulf was still the market leader in Louisiana; however, it was dependent on low-volume neighborhood dealers or lessee station operators in New Orleans who had little inclination or ability to build high-volume sales. During the early 1970s, Shell, Exxon, and Texaco had high-volume company-owned sites at key intersections in the New Orleans suburbs of Carrollton and Metairie, which catered exclusively to transit and commuter traffic, while Gulf had virtually none. This may in part explain why Gulf clung onto the streamline moderne icebox gas station design until the early 1960s. Gulf built a large number of high-volume company-owned sites in the South and New England during the 1950s, but these seem to have been built more as a reaction to Shell and Exxon's competitive activity than as the result of any strategic thinking. Gulf introduced a slablike retrofit design in the early 1960s that was uninspired in comparison with Shell and Mobil's

Throughout the 1950s, Texaco ran extremely effective advertising campaigns that spelled out its product benefits simply and dramatically and was backed up by excellent point-of-sale material. These more than compensated for Texaco's increasingly archaic gas stations. *Author collection*

Between January 1963 and August 1963, Texaco ran a superb advertising campaign series, as seen in these two examples that pledged high-quality Texaco products and helpful service across the United States. Unfortunately, this outstanding campaign was in stark contrast to Texaco's now obsolete gas station network. This must have been the decisive factor in encouraging Texaco to develop the Matawan station design in 1964. *Author collection*

Regent, a British gasoline company, was acquired by Texaco in 1956. The Texaco color scheme was introduced in the summer of 1960, and the Regent brand was phased out by early 1969. This photograph was taken during 1966 when two women were promoting the Regent "I'm a Lively One" campaign in response to Exxon's Tiger. *LAT Photographic*

designs along with a new logo with a horizontal white stripe that improved legibility. Gulf had a highly successful reciprocal marketing agreement with the Holiday Inn franchise operation. The Holiday Inn accepted the Gulf credit card for meals and rooms (see Chapter 4). Gulf, like Phillips 66 and Amoco, expanded into the West Coast when it acquired Wilshire Oil in the early 1960s. Unfortunately, these companies made little headway in the face of entrenched local competitors, particularly in Los Angeles, the world's most competitive gasoline market. Gulf had better luck with its extension into Canada when it acquired BA, the British American Oil Company, during the mid- to late 1960s, which provided a well-established gas station network across Canada. Gulf's retail network in Europe was very similar to Caltex's. It expanded into Italy during the early 1950s, followed by Great Britain and West Germany in the early 1960s. Gulf had a miniscule share of these markets, apart from in the Netherlands, Belgium, and Sweden.

Chevron

Chevron introduced a highly functional international-style gas station design with an integral canopy and very wide boulevard sign during the early 1950s that remained intact until the late 1960s. The new gas stations may have been inspired by a one-off design for a Norwalk dealer in Bakersfield, California, created by the Austrian émigré architect Richard Neutra during the 1940s.

Chevron launched a multitiered branding strategy just at the point that Mobil simplified its strategy in 1946. Company-owned

Texaco's European network was renamed Caltex after World War II as a result of Chevron acquiring a 50 percent stake in Texaco's international operations apart from Canada, South America, and West Africa in 1936. Caltex built a number of EM stations in Belgium, Sweden, France, and Italy. The color scheme and corporate identity were very similar to that of Texaco's in America. *Author collection*

CARTE ROUTIÈRE DE BELGIQUE ET DU LUXEMBOURG
WEGENKAART VAN BELGIE EN LUXEMBURG
ROAD-MAP OF BELGIUM AND GRAND DUCHY OF LUXEMBURG
Prix — Prijs — Price : B. Fr. 20.—   EDITION — UITGAVE — EDITION 1953

Gulf cares

You get the finest service where you get the finest products—
at that clean, friendly Gulf station. Stop for Gulfpride Select,
the motor oil that *works* as clean as it *looks*. It won't break
down, even under the most severe driving conditions.

CLEARLY...THE WORLD'S FINEST MOTOR OIL.

(Above) Gulf's 1958/1959 advertising campaign was unfocused and dissonant, which was in stark contrast to Texaco's. The sophisticated presentation eclipsed the product's benefits. *Author collection*

(Right) The canopied version of Gulf's icebox station was a familiar sight throughout the South during the 1950s, as seen here near Fort Worth, Texas, around 1955. Note the use of custom-made gas pumps that Gulf had pioneered during the mid-1930s. *Author collection*

sites remained Standard stations, and where permitted by trademark ownership, they maintained the familiar blue, white, and red Chevron pole sign/color scheme and solid red pumps. Pump grades were renamed Chevron for regular on a blue disc and Chevron Supreme for premium on a white disc. By contrast, dealer-owned sites were renamed Chevron with a mauve sign without the Chevron logo with a cream and pistachio green color scheme for the station and gas pumps. The only common links between the two operations were the Chevron and Chevron Supreme blue and white discs on the gas pumps. Things were further complicated by the launch of the Calso network on the Atlantic seaboard during the early 1950s, which had nothing in common with other operations. The logo was a burnt orange disc with white lettering. Pump color schemes were solid burnt orange for regular and a white top and burnt orange base for premium. During the mid- to late 1950s, Chevron quietly dropped the two-tier system and introduced new pump color schemes: solid red for regular, solid blue for premium, and solid white for super premium. The East Coast Calso network was finally rebranded as Chevron during 1959 and 1960.

Chevron's expansion eastwards concluded with the acquisition of Standard Oil of Kentucky in 1961, which automatically gave Chevron a very strong presence in Kentucky, Alabama, Mississippi, Georgia, and Florida, with rights to the Standard brand. Chevron was overly protective of its rights to the Standard brand on the West Coast and in the South, which blinded them to the benefits of the unique, instantly recognizable Chevron brand that was used on the East Coast and subsequently in Europe from 1968 on. By contrast, Exxon was already looking for a noncontentious brand that could be used anywhere in the world, which culminated with the introduction of Exxon in the fall of 1972. The Chevron brand name was finally used in all territories during the late 1970s and

A travel agency  with pumps?

If you're taking a trip in your car or boat or even your own plane, see Gulf. Our Tourgide® Service can give you map, motel, sightseeing and other travel information. And our Gulf Travel Card lets you charge Holiday Inn rooms and meals and even Avis car rentals.

Just look for the big orange disc. We have 35,000 easy-to-find dealers coast to coast.

You still haven't seen the Grand Canyon? Or Yellowstone? Or San Francisco? Or New Orleans?

It's time you discovered America.

Our Gulf Tourgide® Service can help you plan your entire trip and have more time for fun along the way. We'll send you maps and travel folders showing the scenic way to get where you're going, or the fastest way. Where to stay. And what sights to take in along the way. We'll also include the latest Holiday Inn Directory. Just ask your Gulf dealer for a Gulf Tourgide Service request card. No charge, of course.

Your Gulf dealer can also handle your application for a Gulf Travel Card. With that handy piece of plastic in your pocket, you can stay at any of the more than 900 Holiday Inns coast to coast. You can dine com-

fortably at the always-good Holiday Inn restaurants and charge everything, rooms and meals, on your Travel Card.

As for your car needs, you'll find Gulf stations in every state (plus 5,000 British-American stations in Canada). You can charge not only gasoline and oil, but those unexpected expenses like a tire, battery or repairs. For your needs we hope you'll use Gulf restrooms. You'll find them neat and clean because Gulf girls called Tourguards make "inspection tours" to make sure of it.

This year, take a vacation from vacation troubles and get more for your travel dollar.

Visit your nearest Gulf dealer's station before you go, and find out why we call it "The Travel Agency with Pumps."

Gulf Oil Corporation

Gulf had highly successful marketing agreements with Holiday Inn motels and Avis car rentals during the late 1960s, as featured in this May 1968 advertisement. Both companies accepted payment by Gulf credit card, which boosted its popularity and eliminated worries about cash or travelers checks. Bankamericard (now Visa) and Mastercard credit cards did not come into widespread use until the mid-1970s. *Author collection*

concluded with the corporate name change to the Chevron Corporation in 1984 after the acquisition of Gulf.

In 1969, Chevron introduced a modified logo with the Chevron device against a white background and "Standard" or "Chevron" in black letters. During 1970, Chevron launched the Hallmark gas station and custom-made silver and white pumps, which were clearly in response to Mobil's 1966 Pegasus design and the trend towards more harmonious designs (see Chapter 6).

BP

Similar to Shell and Exxon, BP had a well-established retail network throughout Europe during the early 1950s. Apart from Great Britain, where it jointly dominated the market with Shell, BP was a distant third behind Shell and Esso in Europe. BP used

this to its advantage with a marketing philosophy that was similar to the Avis car rental slogan: "We're Number 2. We Try Harder!" which was renowned for its trendsetting and flair that generated considerable publicity.

BP, like Exxon and Mobil, launched a strong corporate identity that consisted of a green and yellow color scheme for gas pumps, packaging, and tank trucks with a modified shield logo across Europe in 1947. This unusual but eye-catching color scheme clearly differentiated BP from Exxon and Mobil's more conventional use of white, red, and blue and provided a superb brand identity. The latter compensated for a considerable variation in gas station designs across Europe. In Germany, BP employed a highly functional service building design and an elegant free-standing canopy. In France, BP had a distinctive service building with a protruding semicircular sales

During 1963 and 1964, Gulf launched a new logo with a white stripe that provided better legibility. Shortly before, a new retrofit gas station design was introduced that gave existing stations a sharper look with an overhanging orange lip around the top of the building and, where applicable, the canopy. In most cases, new larger vertical format porcelain enamel panels replaced smaller square panels. In residential areas, as shown in this illustration, red brick replaced porcelain enamel panels for better integration. *Author collection*

office window. In Great Britain, BP relied on designs jointly developed with Shell. Around the same time Mobil introduced its new emphatic Chevron logo in 1956, BP commissioned Raymond Loewy and his French company, Compagnie pour l'Esthetique Industrielle (CEI), to develop a more contemporary corporate identity and logo. The new 1958 corporate identity and logo shrewdly retained the distinctiveness of the previous one, but in pastel shades and with a greater use of white. Ironically, the pastel yellow had been previously used by BP's German subsidiary, BP OLEX, up to 1947! It is almost certain that BP's bold use of pastel green and particularly pastel yellow inspired Mobil's later use of bright blue fascias for its stations during the early 1960s.

Within three years of Sunoco launching blender gas pumps in America during 1956, BP introduced them in Germany and

In 1969, Chevron introduced a new Chevron logo with a white background and black lettering. The following year a new more harmonious station design was introduced for residential areas that sported a greater use of brick and a white pump color scheme. *Author collection*

(Below) The major drawbacks of Chevron two-tier marketing policy were the lack of commonality and diminution of branding. Although this Chevron dealer's station was a typical company design, it is hard to find any links with the company-owned site already featured. The site was located in Porterville, California, and photographed in 1953. Chevron later reverted to a common identity and color scheme for all outlets. *Author collection*

Sweden and offered a choice of five grades. Cost-conscious German and Swedish motorists welcomed the opportunity of getting the exact grade at the right price without wasting money on a high grade. The German and Swedish success encouraged BP to introduce Super Mix blender pumps across most of Europe, Australia, and Canada during the early to mid-1960s and finally Great Britain in October 1966, where they were known as Superblend pumps. The blender pump proved to be the decisive factor in self-service ergonomics (see Chapter 8). In 1964, BP set up a network of coin-operated self-service blender pumps, known as Munztank, across Germany that enabled motorists to buy gasoline when the station was closed. These were very popular, especially among taxicab drivers. This success encouraged BP to experiment with self-service in Great Britain. BP went to extraordinary lengths to get local communities on its side by keeping them fully informed. British local licensing and fire authorities gave BP approval for self-service stations largely on the strength of its comprehensive German experience and exemplary safety record.

While the European gasoline market was growing at a very healthy rate throughout the 1950s and 1960s, BP realized that it had to have a presence in the United States, the world's largest single gasoline market, in order to achieve sustained long-term growth. BP set up a Canadian retail network in Ontario and Quebec during 1958 with an eye to expanding south into the United States. A Department of Justice decision in 1969 provided BP's entry into the United States, when Atlantic Richfield (ARCO) was forced to sell off 10,000 Sinclair gas stations on the East Coast to BP in exchange for permission to purchase Sinclair. Fortuitously, BP was on the verge of making huge oil discoveries in Alaska. Coincidently, Sohio, the leading marketer in Ohio, had a large stake in these discoveries. BP subsequently entered into a highly lucrative marketing partnership with Sohio, which helped BP become firmly established in the United States.

In June 1946, Chevron created two completely different identities for its company-owned and dealer-owned sites. The former retained the familiar Standard brand name; blue, red, and white color scheme; and solid red pumps. The latter were renamed Chevron dealers and had a cream, pistachio green, and mauve color scheme for both buildings and pumps. This was in stark contrast to Exxon and Mobil's introduction of single, stringent corporate identities. *Author collection*

(Below) During the early 1950s, BP developed a number of radical semicircular showcase gas stations in Morocco and Algeria, which were still part of French North Africa at the time. The eye-catching designs caused much comment and were featured prominently in BP's corporate press relations. The designs were, however, very expensive to build and dependent on custom-molded glass panels with highly skilled installation. A less extreme version with a semicircular bay window was subsequently used across France. *BP Archive*

(Above two images) For a brief period of time during the early 1950s, BP and Shell gasolines were sold jointly in Great Britain under the Selective Representation scheme together with an affiliate, National Benzole, and one of two secondary brands: Power or Dominion. The site was located in Willingdon and photographed around 1955. The introduction of a third 100 octane grade in July 1956 made this scheme impractical; BP and Shell were sold separately thereafter. *BP Archive, Caffyns*

(Bottom) This highly functional gas station design was introduced by BP in Germany during the early 1950s. This design, along with elegant free-standing canopy, remained in use until the late 1960s. *Author collection*

In Great Britain, BP used the same gas station designs as Shell, its joint marketing partner, until the early 1970s. The sales kiosk was photographed in Rivenhall End during 1957. *BP Archive*

BP made very good use of color advertising, as shown in this June 1952 German advertisement, to emphasize the new green and yellow color scheme. *Author collection*

(Below) BP introduced its modified green and yellow shield logo in 1947 together with an unusual but very eye-catching corporate identity that was remarkable for its consistency from gas pumps, oil cans, to tank trucks. This unified a wide variety of BP gas station designs across Europe. *BP Archive*

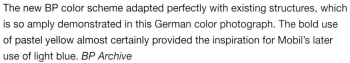

The new BP color scheme adapted perfectly with existing structures, which is so amply demonstrated in this German color photograph. The bold use of pastel yellow almost certainly provided the inspiration for Mobil's later use of light blue. *BP Archive*

BP was launched in America on April 29, 1969, in Atlanta, Georgia, thanks to a Department of Justice decision that forced Atlantic Richfield (ARCO) to dispose of 10,000 gas stations, as well as oil refineries, in exchange for acquiring Sinclair. A subsequent alliance with Sohio, a joint producer of Alaskan oil, helped BP become firmly established in the United States. *BP Archive*

(Below) Within three years of Sunoco introducing the blender pump in America during 1956, BP launched the Super Mix blender pump in Germany and Sweden. Cost-conscious European motorists were quick to appreciate the advantages of getting the exact grade required at the right price. Blender pumps were a central feature of BP's international marketing, apart from in France and America. *Author collection*

Hier erhalten Sie BP BENZIN und BP SUPER in ausgezeichneter Qualität. Und extra noch drei motorgerechte Kraftmischungen: BP SUPER MIX mit 25, 50 und 75% Superanteil.

SUPER MIX

Münztanken ist so leicht wie Telefoniere: Geld einwerfen, Kraftstoffsorte wähle dann sauber und sicher tanken. Das ist eins-zwei-drei geschehen.

münz-tank

(Above) In 1964, BP set up a network of Munztank coin-operated, self-service pumps across Germany that enabled customers to refuel when the stations were closed, as shown in this 1965 advertisement. The Munztank pumps were very popular, especially amongst taxi drivers. The success of the pumps provided invaluable experience for BP's subsequent introduction of self-service in Great Britain. *Author collection*

Epilogue

THE TWO MAJOR OIL SHOCKS of 1973 and 1979 had a catastrophic impact on the American and European economies. The 1973 oil shock had the most immediate effect in Europe, whereas the 1979 oil shock had a far greater impact in the United States.

The fourfold increase in the cost of crude oil in 1973 and 1974, combined with very high gasoline taxes, forced major oil companies in Europe to drastically reappraise all their capital expenditure programs and eliminate marginal activities. The net result was new self-service networks, relying on electronic dispensers, more efficient logistics, and termination of low-volume contracts. In the United States, the changes were more gestural than substantial, with a choice of self-service or attended service islands, the closure of low-volume sites, and withdrawal from marginal sales regions.

The second oil shock in January 1979 hastened major changes in America. This coincided with two other significant factors. Increasingly stringent federal Environmental Protection Agency (EPA) regulations for gasoline-vapor recovery and storage tanks required greater capital investment. For example, steel storage tanks had to be replaced by fiberglass tanks by 1990. Moreover, shrewd investors were increasingly aware that many American oil companies' stocks were undervalued in the face of skyrocketing crude oil prices and could realize substantial profits if the assets were broken up. Gulf fell victim to this activity and was rescued by Chevron in 1984. Sadly, the Gulf brand later disappeared. In the light of these developments, every American oil company realized that it had to overhaul all of its operations radically to minimize costs and enhance profits. Greater numbers of gas stations were shut down, and many oil companies withdrew from even larger regions because of inadequate growth potential or low

market share. By the late 1980s, ARCO had completely withdrawn east of the Mississippi River. Spiraling labor costs combined with gasoline price inflation forced the American consumer to wave goodbye to the pump attendant and serve himself or herself, just like in Europe ten years earlier.

The liberalization of planning laws in Europe, particularly Great Britain, during the early 1980s created an avalanche of out-of-town supermarkets with cut-rate gasoline. European consumers welcomed the convenience of one-stop budget shopping, ample parking, and very cheap gasoline. Supermarket chains quickly gained significant shares of national gasoline markets across Europe. It is now estimated that up to 40 percent of all gasoline sold in France is bought from a supermarket outlet. The figure for Great Britain is around 25 percent. In the face of these developments, Mobil entered into a partnership with BP. The latter acquired a controlling interest in Mobil's European refineries and retail network, which was rebranded BP during 1995. At the same time, Exxon launched the highly effective "Price Watch" campaign in Great Britain, which put all supermarkets on notice that they would match them on price no matter how low.

The sheer cost of finding and developing new oil fields encouraged a number of major oil companies to merge during the late 1990s; most notably BP with Amoco (formerly known as Standard Oil of Indiana), Exxon with Mobil, and Chevron with Texaco. In Europe, major oil companies are shutting down or selling off excess oil-refining capacity. BP in particular is now acquiring much of its European fuel requirements on the spot market and effectively matching the European supermarkets as low-cost suppliers.

Thousands of obsolete gas stations were shut down in the late 1970s. Shrewd entrepreneurs turned them into bakeries, organic food shops, or bicycle repair shops. The forecourts provided ample space for parking and open air dining. This eye-catching 1920s Spanish colonial station is located on St. Charles Avenue in New Orleans. *Author collection*

In August 1979, American motorists had to endure long gas lines just as in the previous 1973 OPEC oil crisis. This marked the beginning of a radical overhaul of the American oil industry with more stringent EPA regulations for gasoline vapor recovery and storage tanks, the widespread introduction of self-service, mergers of major oil companies, and the disappearance of iconic brands, such as Gulf. *Author collection*

The Bluebird Garage, located on Kings Road, London, was Europe's largest gas station and garage during the late 1920s. Terence Conran, the noted British designer and bon viveur, brilliantly turned a derelict site into a gastronomic delight with a choice of restaurants, open-air dining, and gourmet shops. *Conran Restaurants Ltd./Bluebird Cafe*

The golden age of cheap, full-service gas for the consumer is over, and oil companies are faced with the headache of finding increasingly scarce crude oil, often at unimagined prices, and yet making minimal profits at retail outlets. In many respects, we have traveled full circle. The out-of-town supermarket gas station of today is exactly like the country store with a curbside gas pump from almost a hundred years ago.

The country store was the most common outlet for gasoline in the early 1900s, as seen in this example from Poronyo, Iowa. The same is almost equally true today with supermarkets accounting for almost 40 percent of French and 25 percent of British gasoline sales. This Sainsbury's supermarket is located in Coventry, Great Britain. *Author collection*

Index